Muleshoe and Grulla
National Wildlife Refuges

Comprehensive Conservation Plan

July 2004

Prepared by
U.S. Fish and Wildlife Service
Region 2, Division of Planning
P.O. Box 1306
Albuquerque, New Mexico 87103

Comprehensive Conservation Plans provide long term guidance for management decisions; set forth goals, objectives, and strategies needed to accomplish refuge purposes; and identify the Fish and Wildlife Service's best estimate of future needs. These plans detail planning program levels that are sometimes substantially above current budget allocations and, as such, are primarily for Service strategic planning and program prioritization purposes. The plans do not constitute a commitment for staffing increases, operational and maintenance increases, or funding for future land acquisition.

COMPREHENSIVE CONSERVATION PLAN APPROVAL

for

Muleshoe National Wildlife Refuge, Muleshoe, Texas and
Grulla National Wildlife Refuge, Arch, New Mexico
U.S. Fish and Wildlife Service, Region 2
July 2004

The attached Comprehensive Conservation Plan for the Muleshoe and Grulla NWRs has been prepared by Regional Office and Refuge Staff. The contents and format are found to be in compliance with Service Policy on the preparation of Comprehensive Plans, and is hereby submitted for approval.

Submitted by:

_____   _7-19-04_____
Carol Torrez   Date
Biologist/Natural Resource Planner

Approved by:

_____   _7-23-04_____
Harold Beierman, Refuge Manager   Date

Concurrence by:

_____   _7/29/04_____
Aaron Archibeque, Refuge Supervisor, OK/TX   Date

_____   _8/6/04_____
Dom Ciccone, Chief, NWR System, R2   Date

_____   _8/6/04_____
H. Dale Hall   Date
Regional Director, Region 2
U.S. Fish and Wildlife Service

EXECUTIVE SUMMARY

The Comprehensive Conservation Plan (CCP) for Muleshoe National Wildlife Refuge (NWR) and Grulla NWR will serve as a management tool to be used by the refuge staff and its partners in the preservation and restoration of the ecosystem's natural resources. In that regard, the plan will guide management decisions over the next 15 years and set forth strategies for achieving refuge goals and objectives within that time frame. The results of the planning process are represented within this document. Management actions identified within this document reflect a need to achieve a number of refuge goals that are supported by measurable objectives and specific implementation strategies.

The goals of the CCP are designed to fulfill the U.S. Fish and Wildlife Service's (Service) mission for the National Wildlife Refuge System (Refuge System), as well as the established purposes of Muleshoe and Grulla NWRs. The accomplishment of the management objectives and the employment of associated activities and strategies will assist in the achievement of the following broad refuge goals:

Goal 1:   Natural Diversity: Provide habitat and manage for migrating and wintering waterfowl, sandhill cranes, other migratory birds, threatened and endangered species, and other species of concern by implementing appropriate management strategies.

Goal 2:   Cultural Resources: Identify, protect, and interpret the prehistoric and historic cultural resources on Muleshoe and Grulla NWRs for the benefit of present and future generations.

Goal 3:   Ecological Integrity: Protect the areas' resource values through land protection strategies that protect tracts of land with desirable habitats. Strategies could include agreements with private land owners, and consideration of developing boundary expansion proposals for eventual purchase of fee title and less than fee title interest in adjacent lands.

Goal 4:   Recreational Uses: Further the public's interest and involvement with Muleshoe and Grulla NWRs through wildlife interpretation, education/outreach programs, and quality wildlife-dependent recreational opportunities.

Goal 5:   Partnerships and Interagency Coordination: Maintain or strengthen existing interagency and jurisdictional relationships and establish new partnerships within the community to cooperate on mutually beneficial programs for improving wildlife and habitat resources on the refuge, within the High Plains region, and the Edwards Plateau Ecosystem.

Goal 6:   Administrative, Budgetary and Staff Resources: Develop program support sufficient to provide the necessary staffing, facilities, equipment, and operational funds to accomplish the goals of the refuge and fulfill the mission of the Refuge System.

Objectives with measurable outcomes will guide the refuge staff in a consistent direction toward the accomplishment of each goal. The major objectives of the CCP include the following:

- Document the diversity of native flora on refuge lands by developing a comprehensive vegetation map of Muleshoe and Grulla NWRs by 2006.

- Develop a comprehensive biological data base for Muleshoe and Grulla NWRs, revise and update the refuge biological program including wildlife inventory plans using the most current information, and prepare habitat management plans for Muleshoe and Grulla NWRs by 2006.

- Continue and improve protection strategies for populations of rare and declining species (including endangered and threatened species and species of concern) and maintain or improve their habitats on refuge and adjacent lands.

- Implement waterfowl management activities to provide migrating and wintering habitat for a minimum of 10,000 lesser sandhill cranes, 150 Canada geese, and 3,000 ducks. When possible, address and incorporate the goals of the North American Waterfowl Management Plan, Central Flyway, and regional plans into refuge habitat and inventory plans.

- Implement a long-term (10 year) monitoring program for priority species of neotropical migratory birds, shorebirds, and other nongame migratory birds to determine density and population response to management. Incorporate population and habitat objectives developed for priority species in refuge wildlife and habitat management programs by 2008.

- Enhance populations of lesser prairie chickens and other upland bird species on Muleshoe NWR through habitat restoration of 200 acres of native grasslands.

- Manage refuge grasslands using the most effective methods available to maintain the natural range of diversity in the native short and mid-grass prairie that occurs on the refuge. Enhance the plant species diversity on 3,725 acres of native grasslands through natural plant succession and land management programs such as prescribed fire, grazing, and removal of invasive and invader plant species; and implement vegetation monitoring to document changes as a result of management activities.

- Secure and protect existing water sources and pursue alternative water sources to support wetlands on Muleshoe and Grulla NWRs.

- By 2006, establish dialogue with area universities (Eastern, UNM, Texas Tech, Texas A&M, etc) and other institutions to develop research that will improve the biological or archaeological database of the refuge and contribute to habitat restoration and management activities.

- By 2010, survey for archaeological sites on current refuge lands and future acquisitions to obtain baseline archaeological information. Monitor known sites for disturbance or deterioration. Ensure all refuge management activities are in compliance with the Archaeological Resources Protection Act (ARPA).

- Pursue land protection strategies involving private land adjacent to the refuges (approximately 350 acres at Grulla NWR and 370 acres at Muleshoe NWR) that are necessary to improve boundary management at both refuges, increase opportunities for management and protection of wildlife habitat, and provide additional public access.

- Establish a bi-annual review process for Farm Service Agency (FSA) inventory lands to protect and enhance native biological communities by 2008.

- Maintain and/or install 32 miles of boundary fences at Muleshoe and Grulla NWRs to protect the refuge habitats from disturbance by humans (both refuges) and overgrazing by trespassing cattle (Grulla only). This includes 27 miles of fence maintenance at Muleshoe and 5 miles of new fence construction at Grulla.

- Develop a land protection proposal for review by the Regional Office to better protect area lands with important water resources by 2010.

- Provide interactive visitor services and enhance current visitor facilities, increase public contacts, and better secure public use areas on Muleshoe and Grulla NWRs.

- In cooperation with TPWD, develop and improve compatible wildlife-dependent recreational opportunities on refuge lands to increase visitation by 10 percent within three years and 20 percent within 10 years.

- Develop an outreach program that interprets the resources of the area and generates interest in the refuge. Pursue contacts with school groups, community business groups and adjacent land owners. Provide at least five community outreach programs annually by 2010 in towns of Muleshoe, Morton, Littlefield and Sudan, Texas. These products and activities might include community presentations, community involved habitat restoration projects, and/or refuge staff representation at public events that will foster the public's appreciation and understanding of fish and wildlife resources and the mission of the Refuge System.

- Participate with other government, non-governmental organizations (NGO)s, and private groups in partnerships such as the High Plains Initiative, Partners in Flight (PIF), and Playa Lakes Joint Venture that are mutually beneficial and will ultimately benefit the fish and wildlife resources of the refuge and surrounding private lands within the High Plains region and the Edwards Plateau Ecosystem.

- Provide the funding and support of Regional Office (RO) staff specialists to accomplish the goals of this plan.

- Continue to provide a safe, efficient, and productive work environment for refuge employees and a safe infrastructure for refuge visitors.

The goals and objectives of this plan are the management framework providing direction and continuity in refuge programs over a 15 year period. Strategies and management activities are suggested to progressively work toward achieving the specific objectives. The strategies may be modified in the future as a result of a broader understanding or knowledge of an issue.

Table of Contents

VISION

Muleshoe and Grulla National Wildlife Refuges (NWRs) will preserve, restore, and enhance the ecological integrity of the High Plains mixed grass prairie. These refuges will continue to provide quality habitats for a variety of native plants and wildlife, with emphasis on migratory birds and threatened and endangered species, for the benefit of present and future generations. They will provide interpretation of natural and human history of the area and a place where people can learn about wildlife and their habitats and enjoy wildlife-dependent recreation that is compatible with refuge purposes. Whenever possible, habitats and populations will be managed in partnership with local landowners, local and regional organizations, and local, State and other Federal agencies to achieve regional conservation goals. These efforts will result in greater protection of wildlife, fish and plant resources throughout the High Plains region.

Muleshoe NWR

Located in the south plains of west Texas, this refuge's unique features include three shallow playa lakes and almost 5,000 acres of native mid to shortgrass prairie. Only small areas of refuge sod have ever been broken. Much of the refuge grasslands are pristine examples of what the surrounding area was like before agricultural development. The refuge will continue to be characterized by exemplar preagriculture grassland conditions through the implementation of effective land management programs that restore native species diversity and protect the natural biological communities.

Management efforts will be focused on grassland management. Grazing and prescribed fire techniques that mimic natural ecological processes will be used, as well as biological or mechanical control of invading woody species such as mesquite and other shrubs. All management activities will be designed to enhance native plant communities and protect sensitive areas such as wetlands, prairie dog towns, and current/proposed lesser prairie chicken leks.

The Service will pursue all opportunities to protect water sources that provide wetland habitats for waterfowl, sandhill cranes, many other migratory bird species, and resident wildlife. The Service will strive to acquire adjacent lands with water wells or springs that can provide water resources for the refuge. Other sources that may supply water to refuge wetlands will also be protected through easements. The refuge's wildlife resources will be further enhanced and protected through strong partnerships with other agencies, organizations, and landowners to assist with wildfire suppression, avian disease outbreaks, crop depredation, habitat restoration, and central flyway waterfowl population issues.

A healthy refuge environment will continue to provide opportunities for visitors to enjoy wildlife viewing, photography, and camping in a natural setting. Through high quality interpretive and environmental education programs, the public will have opportunities to visit and gain appreciation of the unique ecosystem of the refuge and an understanding of its role in the National Wildlife Refuge System. Interpreting wildlife and the refuge's unique heritage, as well as improving facilities will enhance the visitor's experience while protecting the cultural integrity of the area. The office headquarters will have several interactive displays focused on the value of this refuge to the central flyway and information interpreting the archaeology of the area. Additional wildlife viewing facilities will be developed. Interpretive and environmental education programs will approach new audiences and generate more interest in the refuge through innovative community outreach programs. Local residents and visitors will view refuge lands with a sense of pride and value their relationships with the U.S. Fish and Wildlife Service.

Grulla NWR

Located on the High Plains of eastern New Mexico adjacent to the Texas state line, this refuge consists of the 2,300 acre shallow Salt Lake and 936 acres of native grasses and shrubs. Salt Lake provides habitat for migratory birds only during wet periods when the lake holds precipitation and runoff. The boundary of this refuge is very irregular and runs through the lake bed in several places. Only one access point is currently available to the public and the Service; all other access points require permission from adjacent landowners. The Service will strive to improve access to enhance management and public wildlife viewing opportunities.

The refuge provides outstanding wildlife habitat and viewing opportunities when Salt Lake holds water; however, these opportunities are limited by local precipitation. The public use facilities will continue to be minimal with a parking area, interpretive site, and overlook at the existing refuge entrance. Depending on the acquisition of other access points, the Service will provide additional lake overlooks for wildlife viewing. During periods of high bird use, the refuge staff will coordinate with other agencies, universities, volunteers, and Audubon birding groups to provide guided bird tours, and other special events advertised through the local chambers of commerce and the media. These efforts will provide an opportunity to increase the public's awareness of this refuge and its value within the mission of the larger Refuge System.

1.0 INTRODUCTION AND BACKGROUND

This Comprehensive Conservation Plan (CCP) will guide the development and management of the refuge for the next 15 years (2003 through 2018). The goals and objectives contained in this document reflect a natural management theme and focus on issues pertaining to the refuge. The refuge will manage for ecological integrity with emphasis on protection and enhancement of habitat for waterfowl and other wildlife. The purpose of the actions in this plan are to facilitate achievement of the refuge goals and the purposes for which these refuges were established.

1.1 Purpose and Need for Action

The purpose of comprehensive conservation planning is to "provide long-range guidance for the management of national wildlife refuges." As such, all lands of the Refuge System are to be managed in accordance with an approved CCP that will guide management decisions and set forth strategies for achieving refuge purposes. The National Wildlife Refuge System Improvement Act of 1997 requires all refuges to have a CCP and provides the following legislative mandates to guide refuge management and planning:

- Wildlife has first priority in the management of refuges.

- Wildlife-dependent recreation involving compatible hunting, fishing, wildlife observation and photography, environmental education and interpretation are the priority public uses of the Refuge System.

- Other uses have lower priority in the Refuge System and are only allowed if they are compatible with the mission of the Refuge System and the purpose of the individual refuge.

This CCP provides management direction to present and future Refuge Managers for the next 15 years. It describes all management activities that occur on the refuge and provides management goals, measurable objectives, and management actions or strategies designed to enhance, protect, and restore habitats for the benefit of wildlife.

The Service's goals for the Comprehensive Conservation Planning Process are to:

- provide a clear statement of desired future conditions (vision) for each refuge or planning unit;
- provide a forum for the public to comment on the type, extent, and compatibility of uses on refuges – provide refuge neighbors and visitors with a clear understanding of the reasons for management actions on and around the refuge;
- ensure that the refuge is managed to fulfill the mission of the System as well as the specific purposes for which it was established;
- ensure public involvement in refuge management decisions by providing a process for effective coordination, interaction, and cooperation with affected parties, including Federal agencies, State conservation organizations, adjacent landowners, and interested members of the public;
- encourage refuge planning that considers an ecosystem approach;

- demonstrate support for management decisions and their rationale by sound professional judgement, biological initiatives, and public involvement;
- provide long-term continuity in refuge management; and
- provide a uniform basis for budget requests for operational, maintenance, and capital improvement programs.

1.2 Legal, Policy, and Administrative Guidance

This Section outlines current legal, administrative, and policy guidelines for the management of national wildlife refuges. It begins with the more general considerations such as laws and executive orders for the Service, and moves toward those guidelines that apply specifically to the Muleshoe and Grulla NWRs.

This unit also includes sections dealing with specially designated sites such as historical landmarks and archaeological sites, all of which carry with them specific direction by law and/or policy. In addition, consideration is given to guidance prompted by other formal and informal natural resource planning and research efforts.

All the legal, administrative, policy, and planning guidelines provide the framework within which management activities are proposed and developed. This guidance also provides the framework for the enhancement of cooperation between the Muleshoe and Grulla NWRs and other surrounding jurisdictions in the ecosystem.

Administration of national wildlife refuges is governed by the designated purpose of the refuge unit as described in establishing legislation or executive orders, Service laws and policies, and international treaties. A list of most of the pertinent statutes establishing legal parameters and policy direction for the National Wildlife Refuge System is included in Appendix G, along with a summary of those laws that provide special guidance for the Service and national wildlife refuges. Many of the summaries have been taken from *The Evolution of National Wildlife Law* by Michael J. Bean. For the bulk of applicable laws and other mandates, legal summaries are available upon request.

Key concepts and guidance of the System are covered in the NWRS Administration Act of 1966, the Refuge Recreation Act of 1962, Title 50 of the Codes of Federal Regulations, Executive Order 12996 (Management and General Public Use of the National Wildlife Refuge System, the Fish and Wildlife Service Manual, and most recently, through the National Wildlife Refuge System Improvement Act of 1997.

The National Wildlife Refuge System Improvement Act of 1997 amends the Refuge System Administration Act of 1966 by including a unifying mission for the Refuge System, a new process for determining compatible uses on refuges, and a requirement that each refuge will be managed under a Comprehensive Conservation Plan (CCP or Plan). The Refuge System Improvement Act states that wildlife conservation is the priority of System lands and that the Secretary of the Interior shall ensure that the biological integrity, diversity, and environmental health of refuge lands are maintained. Each refuge must be managed to fulfill the Refuge System mission and the specific purposes for which it was established. The Act requires the Service to monitor the status and trends of fish, wildlife, and plants in each refuge. Additionally, the Act identifies and establishes the legitimacy and appropriateness of six wildlife-dependent recreational uses. These uses are hunting, fishing, wildlife observation and photography, environmental education and interpretation. As priority public uses of the Refuge System, these uses will receive enhanced consideration over other uses in planning and management. Furthermore, this Act requires that a CCP be in place for each refuge by the year 2012 and that the public have an opportunity for active involvement in plan development and revision. It is Service policy that CCPs are developed in an open public process and that the agency is committed to securing public input throughout the process. This Act amended portions of the Refuge Recreation Act and National Wildlife Refuge System Administration Act of 1966.

Lands within the National Wildlife Refuge System are different from other multiple-use public lands in that they are closed to all public uses unless specifically and legally opened. No refuge use may be allowed unless it is determined to be compatible. A compatible use is a use that, in the sound professional judgement of the refuge manager, will not materially interfere with or detract from the fulfillment of the mission of the Refuge System or the purposes of the refuge. Sound professional judgement is further defined as a decision that is consistent with the principles of fish and wildlife management and administration, available science and resources, and adherence with law. Priority public uses, and other uses, can be allowed on refuges if they are compatible with the purpose of the refuge and funding is available to support them. Uses may be allowed through a special regulation process, individual special use permits, and sometimes through State fishing and hunting regulations.

1.3 U.S. Fish and Wildlife Service Mission and Goals

Since the early 1900s, the Service mission and purpose has evolved, while holding on to a fundamental national commitment to threatened wildlife ranging from the endangered bison to migratory birds of all types. The earliest national wildlife refuges and preserves are examples of this. Pelican Island, the first refuge, was established in 1903 for the protection of colonial nesting birds such as herons and egret, which were then under threat of extinction due to the demands for their plumes for the millinery trade. The National Bison Range was instituted for the endangered bison in 1906. Malheur National Wildlife Refuge was established in Oregon in 1908 to benefit all migratory birds with emphasis on colonial nesting species on Malheur Lake. Thus began the commitment of public lands for the preservation of migratory birds and other wildlife. The Service's responsibility broadened during the 1930s. As a result of drought, drainage of wetlands for agriculture, and unregulated hunting, waterfowl populations nationwide became severely depleted. Passage of the Migratory Bird Hunting and Conservation Stamp Act in 1934 made funds available to purchase acreage for waterfowl habitat. During the next several decades, the special emphasis of the Service (then called the Bureau of Wildlife and Sport Fisheries) became restoration of critically depleted migratory waterfowl populations.

The passage of the Endangered Species Act of 1973 refocused the activities of the Service as well as other governmental agencies. This Act mandated the conservation of threatened and endangered species of fish, wildlife, and plants both through federal action and by encouraging the establishment of state programs. In 1974, the Bureau of Wildlife and Sport Fisheries was renamed the U.S. Fish and Wildlife Service to broaden its scope of wildlife conservation responsibilities to include endangered species, as well as game and nongame species. Lands continued to be added to the Refuge System for various wildlife protection purposes including endangered species conservation. Several additional environmental laws and conservation-related laws were passed throughout the 1970s. The Fish and Wildlife Conservation Act of 1980 emphasized the conservation of nongame species and broadened management responsibilities for non-game migratory birds on national wildlife refuges.

The Service has no "organic" act to focus upon for the purposes of generating an agency mission. The agency mission has always been derived in consideration of the various laws and treaties that collectively outlined public policy concerning wildlife conservation.

The Mission of the Service is:

> *"working with others to conserve, protect, and enhance fish, wildlife, and plants and their habitats for the continuing benefit of the American people."*

The goals of the Service, which are aimed at fulfilling this mission, are: 1) sustaining fish and wildlife populations including migratory birds, endangered species, anadromous fish, and marine mammals; 2) conserving a network of lands and waters including the National Wildlife Refuge System; 3) providing Americans opportunities to understand and participate in the conservation and use of fish and wildlife resources.

By law and treaty, the Service has national and international management and law enforcement responsibilities for migratory birds, threatened and endangered species, fisheries and many marine mammals. The Service assists state and tribal governments and other Federal agencies in helping to protect America's fish and wildlife resources, and the National Wildlife Refuge System plays an important role in fulfilling many of these responsibilities.

1.4 National Wildlife Refuge System Mission and Goals

The National Wildlife Refuge System (System) is the world's largest collection of lands and waters set aside specifically for the conservation of wildlife and ecosystem protection. The Mission of the National Wildlife Refuge System is:

> *"...to administer a national network of lands and waters for the conservation, management, and where appropriate, restoration of the fish, wildlife, and plant resources and their habitats within the United States for the benefit of present and future generations of American"* (National Wildlife Refuge System Improvement Act of 1997, Public Law 105-57).

Goals of the System are to 1) preserve, restore, and enhance threatened and endangered species in their natural ecosystems; 2) perpetuate the migratory bird resource; 3) preserve a natural diversity and abundance of refuge flora and fauna; provide the public an understanding and appreciation of fish and wildlife ecology; 5) provide visitors with wildlife-dependent recreation.

Over 540 National Wildlife Refuges and 38 wetland management districts covering over 94 million acres are part of the national network today. With over 77 million acres in Alaska and the remaining 17 million acres spread across the other 49 states and several island territories, over 34 million visitors annually hunt, fish, observe and photograph wildlife, or participate in environmental education and interpretative activities on refuges.

Individual national wildlife refuges are acquired under a variety of legislative acts and administrative orders and authorities. These orders and authorities usually have one or more purposes for which land can be transferred or acquired. These System units provide important habitat for many native mammals, birds, reptiles, amphibians, fish, invertebrates, and plants. Most national wildlife refuges are strategically located along major bird migration corridors ensuring that ducks, geese, and songbirds have rest stops on their annual migrations.

Individual refuges provide specific requirements for the preservation of trust resources such as migratory birds. For example, waterfowl breeding refuges in South and North Dakota provide important wetland and grassland habitat to support breeding populations of waterfowl as required by the Migratory Bird Treaty Act and North American Waterfowl Management Plan. Other refuges in Louisiana and Texas (such as Muleshoe and Grulla) provide migration and wintering habitat for these populations. The network of lands is critical to these birds' survival. A deficiency in one location can affect the species and the entire network's ability to maintain adequate populations.

Other refuges may provide habitat for threatened and endangered plant or animals. Refuges in these situations ensure that populations are protected and habitat is suitable for their use. Refuges, by providing a broad network of lands throughout the United States, help prevent species from being listed as threatened or endangered by providing secure habitat for their use and providing recovery habitats in portions or all of a species range.

Resource management programs on refuges include water, grassland, forest, natural area, and cropland management; historical/archaeological resource management; wilderness management; and wildlife law enforcement activities. National wildlife refuges are extensively used for biological research to benefit wildlife and to improve our understanding of the environment. Scientific programs of wildlife management, wetlands management, forestry, agriculture, and soil conservation are combined for the enhancement and management of wildlife populations. In addition to protecting the Nation's natural resources, national wildlife refuges offer the public a wide variety of recreational and educational opportunities through fishing, hunting, wildlife trails, wildlife observation, nature photography, visitor centers, and environmental education programs, all of which attract millions of visitors each year.

Fulfilling the Promise
This 1999 report resulted from the first-ever System Conference held in Keystone, Colorado in October 1998, and attended by every refuge manager in the country, other Service employees, and leading conservation organizations. The report contained 42 recommendations packaged with three Vision statements dealing with *Wildlife and Habitat, People, and Leadership*. The recommendations in the *Fulfilling the Promises* report

have been incorporated into the development of goals and objectives in this draft plan, to the fullest extent possible.

1.5 Refuge Purpose Statement(s)

Formal establishment of a unit of the National Wildlife Refuge System is usually based upon a specific statute or executive order specifically enumerating the purpose of the particular unit. However, refuges can also be established by the Service under the authorization offered in such laws as the Endangered Species Act of 1973 or the Fish and Wildlife Act of 1956. In these cases, lands are identified by the Service that have the right elements to contribute to the recovery of a species or the maintenance of habitat types. Often, the Service works in cooperation with private nonprofit organizations in efforts to acquire suitable lands. Each refuge in the System is managed to fulfill the mission of the Refuge System as well as the specific purposes for which the refuge was established. Purpose statements are used as the basis for determining primary management activities, and for determining allowable uses of refuges through a formal "compatibility" process.

Muleshoe NWR was established on October 24, 1935 by Executive Order No. 7214 , "...for the use of the ....as a refuge and breeding ground for migratory birds and other wildlife...". This acquisition was implemented under the authority of the:

> Migratory Bird Conservation Act (16 U.S.C. 712d) also established that the refuge is: *"for use as an inviolate sanctuary, ...for any other management purposes, ...for migratory birds."*

> Consolidated Farm & Rural Development Act... *"for conservation purposes..."*(7 U.S.C   )

Grulla NWR was established on November 6, 1969 by Public Land Order No. 4742, transferring the land from the BLM. It was established under the authority of the:

> Migratory Bird Conservation Act (45 Stat. 1222, as amended; U.S.C. 715), implementing the Migratory Bird Treaties... *"for a migratory bird refuge primarily for the benefit and use of the lesser sandhill crane."*

> The Refuge Recreation Act (16 U.S.C. 460-1) states that the refuge is... *"suitable for incidental fish and wildlife oriented recreational development, the protection of natural resources, and the conservation of endangered or threatened species."*

1.6 Refuge Overview: History of Establishment, Acquisition, and Management

With the alarming depletion of the migratory bird populations during the late 1920s and early 1930s, efforts were made by the Service (formerly Bureau of Biological Survey) to protect, through acquisition, those areas where numbers of migratory waterfowl naturally concentrated (USFWS, 1935). The plains of west Texas and eastern New Mexico have historically been the favored wintering grounds for the bulk of the North American lesser sandhill crane population as well as large concentrations of ducks and geese.

Figure 1. Central Flyway route.

The management activities of these refuges contribute to the objectives of the Central Flyway Management Program. The refuge serves the objectives of its establishment by providing a protected roost site for cranes and quality winter habitat to sustain the condition of migratory waterfowl for spring migration and reproductive success. The Cental Flyway (Figure 1) is an extensive geographical area that reaches from Alaska and Central Arctic Canada to South America. Many factors within the lands of the Cental Flyway can affect the migratory bird resource. Conversely, management activities that occur on these refuges can have wide ranging effects on the bird populations of the entire Central Flyway. Maintaining the health and condition of the birds wintering at Muleshoe and Grulla NWRs affects their spring migration and reproductive success each year. Factors influencing the bird use of this area include the activities of other countries, local farming practices on neighboring farms, the activities of federal and state agencies, private organizations, local governments, the influence of treaties affecting wildlife and wildlands, and finally, natural factors such as climate.

1.6.1 Muleshoe NWR

Muleshoe NWR, established in 1935, is the oldest national wildlife refuge in Texas (Map 1). Located in the High Plains of west Texas at an elevation of 3,750 feet above MSL, it is one of a vital chain of refuges providing significant habitat for birds migrating within the Central Flyway. The refuge consists of 5,809 acres broken by two caliche rimrock outcrops. Nearly 4,800 acres are covered with native grasses and scattered mesquite. Three saline lakes on the refuge provide nearly 1,000 acres of wetlands when full.

Early refuge documents indicate that considerable complaint had come from this region because of damage by waterfowl to the grain and other crops. It was believed that the acquisition of refuge lands and the subsequent planting of grain crops would furnish a feeding ground for waterfowl and eliminate to some extent at least the cause of the complaint (USFWS 1935).

Paul's Lake (photo by Don Clapp)

*Lower Goose Lake in December
(photo by Don Clapp)*

White Lake (photo by Don Clapp)

Over 20 areas in the Texas Panhandle were considered by refuge site examiners; the Muleshoe Lakes area ranked as one of the best for acquisition and development by the Bureau. It lies directly in the heart of the country that reported the most damage from feeding activities of migratory birds, and was highly desirable for the purpose of establishing feeding fields for the birds. It also had the most permanent water supply and developmental possibilities of any of the areas considered in this particular region. Establishment of a refuge in this region of reported crop damage by birds was especially desirable from the standpoint of increasing the respect for game laws and reducing the number of birds killed (USFWS 1935).

One of the primary purposes of the establishment of the refuge was to provide lands that could be put to feed crops for the waterfowl and thus reduce the amount of crop injury that resulted from having them depend entirely on feeding in fields that were grown for commercial purposes. In this respect, it was thought that there would be a much better attitude among the farmers and local sportsmen toward respect for game laws and enforcement (USFWS 1935).

Justification for the project (acquisition of the refuge) included: providing a necessary link in Migratory Waterfowl Conservation Program; providing winter refuge area for resting and feeding; providing crop areas that would be used expressly for feed for wild fowl thus reducing crop damage to crops grown for commercial purposes; and providing increased employment in the development of the area.

The U.S. Fish and Wildlife Service (then called the Bureau of Biological Survey) selected the Muleshoe Lakes as a desirable site for a migratory bird refuge due to the three permanent lakes (White Lake, Goose Lake, and Paul's Lake) that seldom froze and provided a natural concentration area for large numbers of migratory waterfowl, particularly during the winter months.

The acquisition of land progressed quickly after President Roosevelt signed the Executive Order establishing the refuge in 1935. The first tract purchased was 738 acres from George and Mattie Robison and Annie Robison on August 17, 1936. This is now the northwest part of the refuge, including where the refuge headquarters is located. The second purchase, which comprised all of the refuge land located east of highway 214 including Paul's Lake, was completed on December 23, 1936, when 1,417 acres was purchased from F.A. and Mattie Paul and J.H. Paul. The third tract was purchased on February 6, 1937, from Henry and Vivian Wilson and consisted of 2,214 acres of land that is located at the southeast part of the refuge including White Lake. The fourth and final land acquisition occurred on 1938, when 1,440 acres was acquired from Isaac and Crawford Enochs. This area is the southwest part of the refuge. These land acquisitions resulted in a refuge that now encompasses a total of 5,809 acres.

Refuge lands were first placed under the protection of a caretaker in May of 1937. The refuge's first manager, James Walton, took charge on August 24, 1937. The original plan of development and management for the Muleshoe Migratory Waterfowl Refuge (USFWS 1938) included provisions for water developments, including a system of dikes, dams and diversions to assure that there would be a permanent source of water on the refuge even in times of extreme drought; raising crops to provide feed for wintering

Muleshoe National Wildlife Refuge

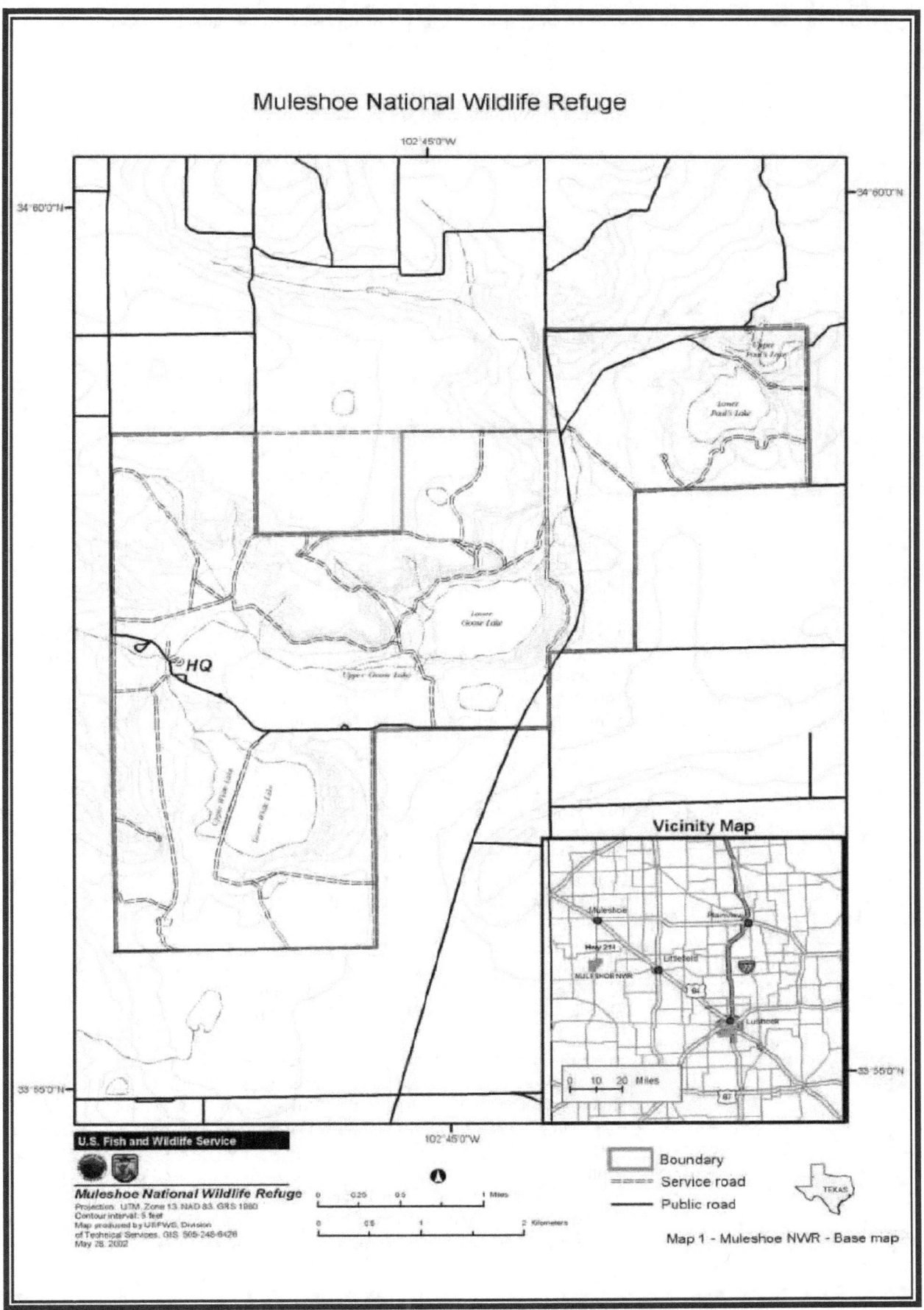

Map 1 - Muleshoe NWR - Base map

waterfowl on the refuge; planting trees and shrubs in uplands; and managing for upland game birds.

A Work Progress Administration (WPA) project was established February 1, 1938, and work started on the headquarters buildings and other refuge facilities. By June of 1938, there were 112 WPA laborers working at the refuge. Work was frequently hampered by problems getting WPA workers to the refuge from the towns of Muleshoe and Morton due to wet, slippery road conditions. Between May 1, 1938 and May 24, 1942, all of the buildings (managers quarters, vehicle storage building, and refuge office), which still exist today; along with major road improvements; and dikes across each of the three refuge lakes, were all completed by WPA labor. Refuge records indicate that WPA workers also planted approximately 80,000 tree and shrub seedlings on refuge lands during the spring of 1938. All seedlings were obtained from the U.S. Department of Agriculture's Soil Conservation Service. Nearly 50,000 were desert willow; the remainder were wild choke cherry, wild plum, mulberry, Russian Olive, and sumac. Laborer numbers had dropped drastically by 1939 and only about 10-15 individuals worked in 1942, when the WPA project was terminated due to lack of manpower.

WPA workers planting trees (courtesy of Muleshoe NWR)

The dikes, which divided the refuge's three lakes into six impoundments in the late 1930s, were constructed to hold more water for the large wintering waterfowl numbers. Water is very much the limiting factor in the Service's ability to provide wetland habitat in appropriate quality and quantities for wintering and migrating birds. Attempts to locate a reliable water source for these lakes during the past 60 years have been unsuccessful.

In the early years (1930s and early 1940s), refuge lakes held water throughout much of the year and wintering waterfowl numbers often ranged from 300,000 to 700,000. Geese were never present in large numbers like ducks, but several thousand usually used the lakes. Sandhill crane numbers on the refuge were sporadic (between 1,500 and 3,500 birds) at that time due to water depths that did not offer optimum roosting conditions.

Refuge personnel spent many hours during the refuge's early years conducting depredation control activities by using depredation techniques to haze wintering waterfowl from adjacent landowner's crops.

In January 1945, the refuge was documented as being the site of the first know case of avian cholera in wild free flying waterfowl. It was believed this first outbreak was the result of infected domestic chickens being disposed of in roadside ditches near the refuge. The first major cholera outbreak recorded on the refuge was in 1948 when 9,000 ducks died of cholera. Other reports regarding large cholera outbreaks on or near the refuge occurred in 1949, 1951, 1953, 1955, 1956, 1957, 1960, 1980, and 1981. Outbreaks still occur on the refuge and cholera outbreaks occur nearly every year somewhere in the Panhandle killing thousands of birds.

Through the 1940s, crane use increased, and by 1949 the species had become an abundant winter resident as lake depths had decreased. The expansion of irrigated agriculture in the High Plains has continued to lower the Ogallala Aquifer, which has caused many of the playa lakes to dry up. The loss of the playa lake habitat initially led to a decrease in waterfowl use of the refuge. However, lower lake levels provided ideal roosting sites for wintering sandhill cranes. In addition, agricultural operations in the surrounding areas converted to growing winter wheat and grain sorghum (milo) which is utilized as a food base for wintering cranes, and has resulted in population increases. The surrounding grain fields usually had an abundance of food. The peak was reached in 1981 when 250,000 cranes were recorded on the refuge.

Since the early 1980s, crane numbers on the refuge and in the surrounding area have declined. The major reasons are the lowering of the water table and past drought conditions affecting lake levels, as well as the loss of grain fields that the crane depended upon for winter forage. Many acres of the surrounding area are being converted back into grassland and dryland agriculture due to less available irrigation water. As this transition occurs, the crane use in the area will continue to decrease. The Conservation Reserve Program (CRP) was established by the federal government during the late 1980s. This program paid farmers to plant grass instead of grain in wind-eroded farm lands. Recent annual peak populations have remained around 10,000 cranes.

Muleshoe NWR and the surrounding area supported native shortgrass prairie before the area was settled in the late 1800s. The grass was used by native wildlife, especially the American bison and black-tailed prairie dogs. Prior to settlement, a large prairie dog town supposedly stretched from Lubbock, Texas to Amarillo, Texas. Cattle grazing provided the first economic use of the this land and the entire area was grazed. In many areas, overgrazing had allowed wind and water to erode the lands so drastically that much of the native grasses had disappeared. By the late 1800s, farming was beginning to displace large portions of the original High Plains natural prairie. Areas not suitable for farming were used as range for domestic livestock. Ranches were primarily cattle operations, usually in large holdings. Species such as mesquite, prickly pear, redberry juniper, and cholla were quick to invade and become established on the disturbed rangeland. Limited agriculture developed as more people moved into the area. The rich soil encouraged agriculture, but the dry climate and strong winds held back development. With the onset of irrigation capabilities in the late 1940s, most of the lands were plowed under for row crop production.

Sorgum planted in East Farming Unit in 1966 (courtesy of Muleshoe NWR)

Farming on the lands acquired by the Service was minimal. Only two tracts (225 acres) had been farmed; one field directly northeast of the refuge headquarters and a smaller acreage just west of Lower Paul's Lake. It was thought that by producing forage crops on refuge lands, crop depredation on adjacent commercial farm lands would decrease (USFWS, 1935). A small farming program continued on the refuge until 1969. Without the ability to irrigate crops, farming attempts were not very productive.

The refuge has historically had some form of a grazing program since its early years. Refuge records show that in the late 1930's when the refuge was established, refuge grasslands were severely over-grazed by previous landowners. During the early refuge years Managers rested the over-grazed refuge grasses for a few years before establishing a refuge grazing program in 1942. A local livestock owner that had previously grazed the refuge lands when they were privately owned was selected as the grazing permittee and allowed to graze cattle on the refuge year round.

In the early 1980's, the refuge initiated a rest rotation grazing program that was used until the year 2000. Light to moderate grazing was allowed by cattle on these grasslands during May through October. Livestock were rotated among several pastures to provide the best utilization of available grasses.

The refuge also began a burning program in the early 1980's; from two to five hundred acres of alkali sacaton were burned per year. The purpose of the burning was to burn mature sacaton growing in clumps and creating bare areas in order to create a more diverse plant community. Controlled burning was last conducted on the refuge in 2000.

This refuge maintains one of the last shortgrass prairie environments on the southern High Plains of Texas with over 5,000 acres of shortgrass rangelands scattered with mesquite (McMahan et al., 1984). Muleshoe NWR is part of the High Plains Natural Area, designated as a National Natural Landmark of the Great Plains Natural Region (designated August 11, 1980) and serves as a cornerstone to efforts promoting good land stewardship for the protection and restoration of the natural resources of the area.

The refuge has changed very little since the "early" days. Wildlife is still abundant during winter months, only now it is sandhill cranes instead of ducks that attract visitors to this winter haven. Only three new buildings, an office and shop in 1982 and a storage building in 1979, have been added in the years since the WPA days.

The refuge's management goals and objectives have evolved over the years to include: providing migration and wintering habitat for naturally occurring wildlife species threatened with extinction; provide habitat for sandhill crane and other marsh and water birds, shore birds, raptors, and other wildlife; provide environmental education and enhance the public's awareness of wildlife and the environment.

The refuge allows bird watching, photography, and camping. Hunting and boating on the lakes is prohibited. During the past few years, public use has averaged about 12,000 visitors a year. Virtually all of these visits are for wildlife observation.

1.6.2 Grulla NWR

Grulla NWR is located in Roosevelt County, New Mexico near the small village of Arch, approximately 25 miles west northwest of Muleshoe NWR (Map 2). The refuge contains 3,236 acres, of which 906 are grassland and 2,330 are saline lake bed. Grulla was officially established as a national wildlife refuge on November 6, 1969 by Public Land Order No. 4742 transferring the land from the Bureau of Land Management (BLM). Since Grulla NWR is located three miles south and east of the community of Arch, New Mexico (USFWS, 1966), it was recommended that Salt Lake be renamed Arch NWR to eliminate confusion with the multitude of other Salt Lakes occurring in the same vicinity. However, it was named Grulla, a Spanish word for crane.

Grulla National Wildlife Refuge

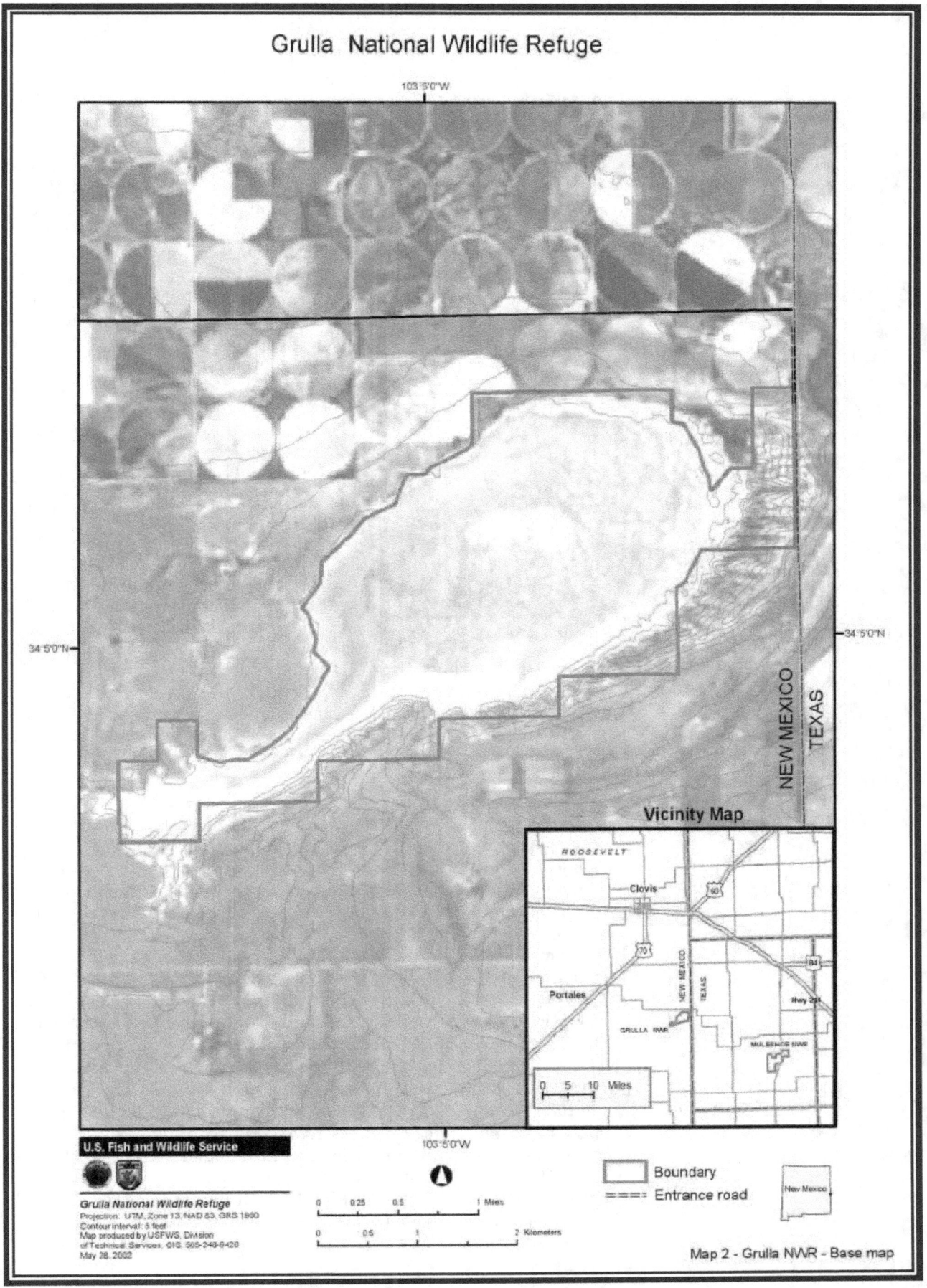

103°5'0"W

34°5'0"N

34°5'0"N

NEW MEXICO
TEXAS

Vicinity Map

U.S. Fish and Wildlife Service

Grulla National Wildlife Refuge
Projection: UTM, Zone 13, NAD 83, GRS 1980
Contour interval: 5 feet
Map produced by USFWS, Division
of Technical Services, GIS 505-248-6428
May 28, 2002

103°5'0"W

☐ Boundary
=== Entrance road

New Mexico

Map 2 - Grulla NWR - Base map

0   0.25   0.5   1 Miles
0   0.5   1   2 Kilometers

ROOSEVELT
Clovis
60
70
Portales
NEW MEXICO
TEXAS
84
Hwy 214
GRULLA NWR
MULESHOE NWR
0   5   10 Miles

Previous to Service ownership, these Public Domain lands had been scheduled for disposal under the terms of the Classification and Multiple Use Act (88-607) by the BLM. Vegetation on the site is typical of the grasslands of eastern New Mexico and west Texas. Dominant vegetative types in the area included alkali sacaton, seasonal grama grasses, saltbush, and yucca. The lands surrounding the refuge were mixture of pasture and irrigated farmland. At the time of acquisition, cultivated crops included sorghums, corn, barley, and alfalfa; the major cash crop was stripper cotton. Grazing and cattle production was a significant economic base, although the stocking rate recommended by the BLM was from three to five head per section. Seasonal stocking of the grassland areas was determined primarily by the amount of precipitation received. No BLM gazing permits were in effect on these lands at the time of refuge acquisition. There were no buildings, water impoundments, control structures, or diversion structures on acquired lands. Roads and trails existed on the southern perimeter of the area, but all were unimproved. There were fences along the east and portions of the south boundaries, but it was recognized that new fencing would be required to exclude livestock and control vehicle access.

Salt Lake after summer rains (photo by Don Clapp)

This area was recommended for acquisition because it provided a unique, specialized and strategically located habitat type necessary to accomplish the distributive management of lesser sandhill cranes on their wintering grounds. Salt Lake is normally a dry playa that contains shallow water only after locally heavy rains. Ducks utilized this area as a migration resting site after feeding in adjacent grainfields when water was present in the lake. The lake bed was also used as a roosting ground for large numbers of wintering lesser sandhill cranes, especially during periods of severe weather when freshwater or less brackish areas are frozen over.

This area was classified by the BLM as available for disposal, but disposal could have jeopardized the continued use of the lakebed as a crane wintering ground. A May 23, 1967 Memo concerning the Service's Application for Withdrawal, documented that the requested withdrawal would insure the lands remain in public ownership and minimal management and development activities would be permitted.

The wintering population of the North American lesser sandhill crane is normally volatile and shifts according to the availability of feed and the presence of hunting pressure. Patterns in the sandhill crane wintering and migration movements tend to shift eastward into central Texas and Oklahoma where crop depredation has historically been a serious problem. The eastward movement of the birds has been, in part, attributed to harassment and hunting pressure, particularly on roost areas which are unprotected from human disturbance. Salt Lake provides a uniquely specialized and strategically located habitat component, which is necessary to distribute these birds on their wintering grounds. The availability of this type of land is limited at present to a few smaller tracts in private ownership, scattered from Portales, New Mexico, to Lubbock, Texas. By protecting this roosting habitat, the cranes concentrate in close proximity to large feeding areas and disperse over both grasslands and croplands, lessening serious depredation problems. Another factor influencing the retention of these lands in public ownership was the ability to sustain a huntable crane population in eastern New Mexico consistent with the objectives of the Central Flyway Management Plan. This plan allows harvest of cranes in those Texas and eastern New Mexico counties which are between the migration route of the whooping crane and wintering grounds of the greater sandhill crane (USFWS, 1966). For these reasons, these lands were retained in public ownership through a land transfer from the BLM and established as a national wildlife refuge to serve as a migratory bird resource.

Wetlands on Grulla NWR consist of 2,330 acres of the lake bed of Salt Lake. This lake intermittently catches runoff from rainfall and is dry much of the time. No other management is possible due to the limited availability of water and the fact the refuge does not own all of the lake bottom. Part of the bed of Salt Lake on Grulla NWR is classified as "Saline Lands" which means that they must be retained in public ownership as long as they are classified as such.

Grasslands cover the remaining 906 acres of Grulla NWR. Most of this habitat is composed primarily of pure stands of native grass species; however, there are areas with only a sparse covering of grassland plants and areas with bushy overstory. Blue grama and buffalo grass dominate except on the high lime soil adjacent to Salt Lake where alkali sacaton is dominant. Cattle from adjacent private lands graze most of the refuge grasslands. Fencing is not possible due to the irregular nature of the present boundary which extends into the lake bed in some areas and runs on the shoreline in other areas. Approximately 200 acres on the east side of the refuge was fenced in 1985 and trespass grazing is restricted from this area.

Any fence along Salt Lake is nearly impossible to maintain (photo by Don Clapp)

Wildlife use at Grulla NWR depends heavily on the amount of water in Salt Lake. Although the flat lake bed is often dry or nearly dry for several consecutive years, large concentrations of sandhill crane, waterfowl, and shorebirds use the lake when water is available, or when surrounding playa lakes are frozen. The record peak of 85,000 cranes occurred on the refuge in December of 1975. Numbers of these species are very small during the summer or when the lake is dry. The number of raptors and other birds that are not directly dependent on water in the lake is more stable.

The boundary of this refuge is very irregular and runs through the lake bed in several places. Only one access point is currently available to the public and the Service; all other access points require permission with adjacent landowners. Since the boundary is not adequately fenced, trespass cattle overgraze part of the refuge. Due to its remote location and lack of resident staff, some vandalism and ORV trespass also occur. The refuge provides outstanding wildlife habitat and viewing opportunities when Salt Lake holds water; however, these opportunities are limited by local precipitation. The public use facilities are minimal with a parking area, interpretive site, and overlook at the existing refuge entrance.

The operation of Grulla NWR has little impact on the surrounding area, except for the farming areas within 30 miles. With no employees stationed at the refuge and limited public access, impacts are limited to include depredation by sandhill cranes on agricultural crops, primarily milo, trespass grazing by cattle from adjacent private lands, destruction of soil quality on private lands adjacent to the refuge by alkali dust blown from the lake bed, and sandhill crane hunting around the refuge boundary.

Both Refuges

In the 1980s and 1990s, conservation efforts began to focus outside refuge boundaries to a larger area of concern encompassing the surrounding lands of a region. In the High Plains, these surrounding lands were primarily in private ownership and had been converted to irrigated and dry land agriculture. The once contiguous short and mixed grass prairie habitats had become increasingly fragmented. The condition of the range varied tremendously depending on grazing pressure, the water resources had become depleted and unpredictable, and fish and wildlife populations began declining. Numerous playas and saline lakes have been lost through agricultural practices involving pumping water out of them, farming, or overgrazing.

Conservation efforts also began focusing on species other than migratory waterfowl. While Muleshoe and Grulla NWRs were established as habitat for migrating waterfowl, these areas were providing habitats for sandhill cranes and other migratory, resident, and threatened or endangered species that in many cases have now become management priorities. Private land stewardship initiatives like the High Plains Partnership (HPP) and Playa Lakes Joint Venture have recently become the focus of agencies like the Service as the key to protecting and possibly restoring water resources and habitat values of the native short and mixed grass prairies and preventing fish and wildlife declines in the High Plains region.

2.0 PLANNING PERSPECTIVES, CONSIDERATIONS, AND ISSUES

The refuge represents one segment of a multifaceted system of lands dedicated to the conservation and management of wildlife resources. The development of this CCP has incorporated the directives, policies, and regulations of the Service, the Refuge System, and the purpose for which the refuge was established to assist in providing guidance to the refuge for long-range management decisions.

2.1 Planning Process and Public Involvement

This CCP establishes the goals, objectives, and management strategies for both Muleshoe and Grulla NWRs. It is guided by the established purposes of each refuge, the goals of the System, Service compatibility standards, and other Service policies, legal mandates, and laws directly related to refuge management. The plan is in compliance with the requirements of the National Environmental Policy Act (NEPA). It addresses several bird conservation initiatives (such as the North American Waterfowl Management Plan and Partners in Flight), private land initiatives, and the Service's ecosystem management plans (as discussed below, in sections 2.2 through 2.4).

The plan is developed with specific activities to be implemented during a short time-frame. Activities proposed for implementation over the longer term, 10 to 15 years, are sometimes stated broadly with the intent that detailed step-down plan will be developed. Step-down plans for particular management programs such as grazing, public use, and prescribed fire will include implementation, monitoring and evaluation criteria. This CCP will direct the preparation or revision of step-down plans and justify budget approval for specific programs over the next 15 years.

The CCP and step-down plans provide the Refuge Manager a rationale and justification to guide management decisions affecting the refuges' natural resources. It is the intent of the planning process that management actions developed in both the CCP and the step-down plans be documented, reviewed, and evaluated within a reasonable time-frame. To optimize the effectiveness of the plans, amendments will be incorporated based on management outcomes and current Service policy.

To begin the CCP process, a comment period notification was published in the Federal Register in June, 1998. In an effort to involve the local community and officials, the Service distributed a fact sheet at the refuge headquaters to interested parties in June 1999. The fact sheets described the CCP process and goals, objectives, and long-range plans of the refuge. The fact sheets, draft documents, and other relevant information have been available for public review at the refuge headquarters. The Service did not receive any comments as a result of the fact sheet distribution and it was determined that a scoping open house for Muleshoe and Grulla NWRs was not necessary. These actions satisfied the scoping requirements under the National Environmental Policy Act of 1969 (NEPA). Issues identified during the planning process are outlined in section 2.7.

The *Draft Comprehensive Conservation Plan and Environmental Assessment* (Draft CCP/EA) was released in October 2003. The Service published a formal notice in the Federal Register requesting comments and advice from the public. The Draft CCP/EA was sent to more than 70 individuals, private businesses, consulting companies, non-governmental organizations, State and Federal agencies, and City, County, State, and Federal officials, as wells as local public libraries and media outlets (see Appendix I). A 45-day public review period was provided, with an open house held at the refuge headquarters on November 5, 2003. Comments received during the public review period were considered, and to the degree possible, incorporated into the final document (see Appendix H).

The CCP must be formally revised within 15 years (or earlier, if it is determined that conditions affecting the refuge have changed significantly). Implementation of the Plan will be monitored to ensure that the strategies and decisions noted within are accomplished. Data collected in association with routine inspections or programmatic evaluations will be used to continually update and adjust management activities.

Adaptive Management
The Service acknowledges that much remains to be learned about species, habitats, and physical processes that occur on the refuge, and about the ecological interactions between species. When faced with uncertainty resulting from complex ecological interactions or gaps in available data the most effective approach to resource management over the long term is an adaptive one. *Adaptive management* refers to a management style in which the effectiveness of management actions is monitored and evaluated, and future management is modified as needed, based on the results of this evaluation or other relevant information that becomes available. The Service has been practicing adaptive management on the refuges since their establishment and plans to continue this practice. Accordingly, the management scenario proposed in this CCP provides for ongoing adaptive management of the refuges is described more fully in Chapter 6, *Plan Implementation*.

NEPA and This Document
As the basic national charter for the protection of the environment, NEPA requires Federal agencies to consider the environmental effects of all actions they undertake. Under NEPA and implementing regulations, *action* refers to a policy, plan, program, or project that is implemented, funded, permitted, or controlled by a Federal agency or agencies. Agencies must also consider the environmental effects of all reasonable and feasible alternatives to a proposed action and possible alternatives. If adverse environmental effects cannot be entirely avoided, NEPA requires an agency to show evidence of its efforts to reduce these adverse effects and to restore and enhance environmental quality as much as possible. The EA that addresses the environmental effects of implementing this CCP is attached.

2.2 The Ecosystem Approach to Management

In 1994, the Service adopted an ecosystem approach to more effectively achieve its mission of fish and wildlife conservation for future generations. The ecosystem approach is defined as "protecting or restoring the natural function, structure, and species composition of an ecosystem while recognizing that all components are interrelated".

Ecosystem management includes preservation of the natural ecological integrity, ecosystem health, and sustainable levels of economic and recreational activity. This approach emphasizes the identification of goals that represent resource priorities on which all parts of the Service will collectively focus their efforts. These cross program partnerships within the Service and partnerships with outside entities assist in the identification of common resource goals and contribute to the accomplishment of those goals in an effective and timely manner.

The Service has defined 53 ecosystems within the United States and U.S. Carribean Islands, based US Geological Survey watershed boundaries. All of the Service's field units (National Wildlife Refuges, National Fish Hatcheries, Law Enforcement, Ecological Services Offices, Fishery Resources Offices) within an Ecosystem Unit are involved in preparing a resource management plan for the Unit. The Ecosystem Approach also mandates cooperation between the Service and the various entities that control land or make decisions about land management within the Ecosystem Unit, including other federal agencies, state agencies, municipalities, private interests, organizations and individual landowners. In order to implement the ecosystem approach, the Service has established ecosystem teams consisting of members representing the various field stations and programs within the Service in any given area. These teams are helping the Service present a more unified approach and will work closely with traditional partners, as well as expanding partnerships with others. The refuge plays an integral role in the coordination of, and is an active participant in, projects identified by the ecosystem team as priority projects in order to accomplish the overall goals of the team. Management decisions incorporate pertinent biological and socioeconomic parameters within the ecosystem. Each team developed an ecosystem plan with input from its partners. This plan is used to implement collaborative projects across Service programs and with partners. The ecosystem that the Muleshoe and Grulla NWRs fall within is known as the Edwards Plateau Ecosystem (Figure 2).

2.3 The Edwards Plateau Ecosystem

The Edwards Plateau Ecosystem includes the plateau of central and west-central Texas, extending into New Mexico, and the playa lakes region of the southern High Plains. This dynamic and varied ecosystem contains geologic and hydrologic systems that support highly diverse floral and faunal communities. The playa lakes and Gulf of Mexico estuaries provide habitat for a significant portion of the Central Flyway waterfowl and sandhill crane populations, as well as migratory songbirds. The ecosystem also provides freshwater to the Gulf of Mexico estuaries areas.

The proposed management priorities for the Edwards Plateau Ecosystem focus on trust resources, including traditional recreational opportunities and more recent directions involving ecological integrity, water conservation issues, and private lands initiatives. The refuge staff and the Service are integral to the implementation of this Ecosystem Plan. Many of the goals and objectives of the Ecosystem Plan have been specifically incorporated into this CCP, where appropriate. The Edwards Plateau Ecosystem Plan (USFWS, 1994) has identified the following goals:

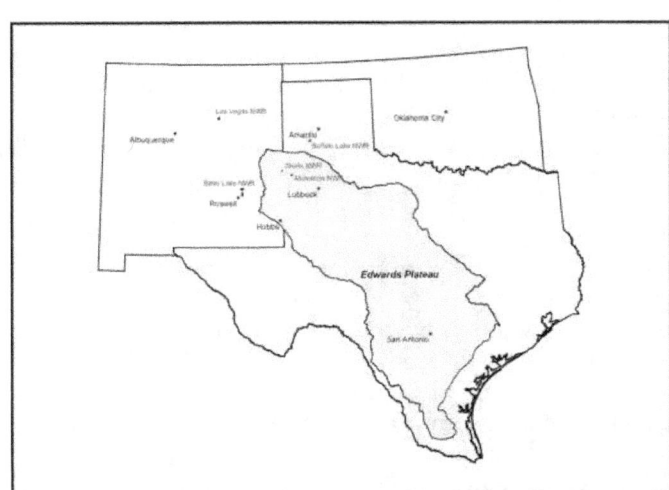

Figure 2. Edwards Plateau Ecosystem boundary

Goal 1: Conserve the full range of natural biological variations, including landscapes, communities, populations, and species.

Goal 2: Promote conservation of water quality and quantity for human and natural resources benefits.

Goal 3: Provide high quality recreational experiences to the extent these activities support the resources and priorities identified by the team.

Goal 4: Promote an awareness, understanding, and appreciation of natural resources and the human role in the environment.

In developing goals and objectives for the refuges in this CCP, each of these ecosystem goals was considered and addressed to the greatest extent feasible within the purposes of the refuges. While management activities on the refuges can potentially play an important role in achieving each of these goals, specific objectives to some of these goals mention refuge programs directly supporting the goals. Refuge activities or programs sited in the Ecosystem Plan include the following:

Ecosystem Goal 1, Objective#2: Provide technical assistance to landowners that support reliable wildlife management practices that are economical, legal, and biologically sound; includes reference to development of a fire management program at the refuge. This type of assistance is addressed in strategies identified under CCP Goal 1, Objectives 5 and 7.

Ecosystem Goal 1, Objective #3: Conserve and monitor significant and unique natural resources in the Edwards Ecosystem; calls for initiating plant and animal community/population surveys on the refuge. Such surveys are mandated under CCP Goal 1, Objectives 1, 2, 3, and 6.

Ecosystem Goal 3, Objective #2: Assist private landowners in developing additional and non-traditional economic wildlife opportunities from recreational activities on their land; discusses the Refuge hosting workshops and demonstration areas on wildlife management techniques in cooperation with TPWD and others. Strategies described under CCP Goal 4, Objective 3 and CCP Goal 5, Objective 5 work toward meeting this ecosystem goal.

Ecosystem Goal 4, Objective #1: Promote an awareness, understanding, and appreciation of natural resources and the human role in the environment; mentions developing and disseminating education and outreach materials to various audiences. This need is addressed in strategies identified under CCP Goal 1, Objective 3; CCP Goal 4, Objective 3; and CCP Goal 5, Objective 5.

The ecosystem is primarily influenced by human development, which affects the preservation of natural resources. Human habitat modifications have resulted in the reduction, and in some areas, extirpation of native plants and animals. The introduction of a nonnative plant, salt cedar (*Tamarisk* spp.) used for bank stabilization in the 1940s, has significantly altered both the stream channel morphology and the structure of riparian plant communities. Alteration of natural river flow regimes through the construction of dams for consumptive uses, flood control, and controlled releases have further altered habitats and impacted native aquatic communities. Land use practices over the past century, primarily farming and ranching, have significantly altered surface soils and the vegetation of the area. Continued development of groundwater resources threatens wildlife habitats throughout the Ecosystem.

There are complex resource management issues associated with this ecosystem. A diversity of human cultures competing for limited access to water rights and growing resource demands have depleted, and at times, contaminated ground and surface water. Impacts from previous water and land management practices for agricultural needs have seriously altered the Edwards Plateau Ecosystem by reducing native habitats and species diversity. Impacts from oil and gas development, mining, and urbanization further increased the need for more responsible utilization of land and water resources that support the remaining native communities.

2.4 Area of Ecological Concern

While there is a larger defined area known as the Edwards Plateau Ecosystem, this CCP will focus primarily on Service lands within an Area of Ecological Concern known as the Pecos and Staked Plains region (or the Llano Estacado) or the Texas High Plains. Of particular interest is the area where portions of the Pecos and Staked Plains physiographic region, Short Grass Prairie BCR, Playa Lakes Region, and the Edwards Plateau Ecosystem overlap (Figure 3). An area of ecological concern can be defined as "an essentially complete ecosystem (or set of interrelated ecosystems) of which one part cannot be discussed without considering the remainder" (USFWS, 1985).

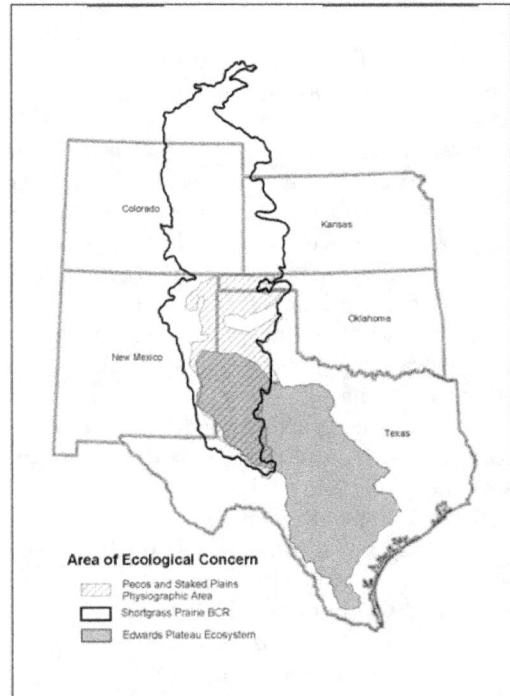

Area of Ecological Concern
- Pecos and Staked Plains Physiographic Area
- Shortgrass Prairie BCR
- Edwards Plateau Ecosystem

Figure 3

The High Plains, a native short and mixed grass prairie ecosystem, once encompassed over 350,000 square miles in 10 states, and stretched along the eastern slope of the Rocky Mountains from Canada to southwestern Texas. It is drained by three major river systems: the Missouri, the Arkansas, and the Red Rivers. The Pecos and Staked Plains (or Llano Estacado), is the largest nonmountainous geological region in North America (Rose and Strandtmann, 1986). It is a physiographic region that marks the southern end of the High Plains and covers the western Panhandle of Texas, the west end of the Panhandle of Oklahoma, and extensive areas in eastern New Mexico. It is comprised of about 20,000,000 acres and is characterized by a flat, featureless, relatively high plateau devoid of trees. This plain is one of the largest flat areas of its size in the world. It is predominantly shortgrass prairie dominated by grama and buffalo grasses, but there are also extensive areas of shinnery, a midgrass prairie with low shrubs. The elevation is 3,000 to 4,500 feet above mean sea level (MSL), sloping gently toward the southeast. The surface is interrupted at various locations by thousands of small ephemeral lakes or playas, dune fields, draws, and drainages which are tributaries to the Canadian, Red, Brazos, and Colorado Rivers. There are over 20,000 playa lakes scattered throughout the region that collect rainwater. Some are very large, and almost permanently filled with water.

This shortgrass prairie is bisected by the Canadian River breaks in the northern Panhandle and gradually blends into the Edwards Plateau and Trans-Pecos subregions in the south. The eastern edge is sharply delineated by the cap rock escarpments which form a natural boundary between the upper shortgrass plains and the taller mixed grass rolling plains found in lower elevations toward the east. Trans-Pecos shrub savannah becomes more dominant towards the south and, chaparral and pinyon-juniper occur in the mesas and Plains toward the west.

The North American grassland began to develop approximately five million years ago under the conditions dictated by a cool, wet climate. However, for the past 12,000 years, these conditions have steadily and progressively shifted to the warmer, drier climate of today. As the mid continental grasslands developed under these more modern mesic conditions, two significant factors contributed to the successful stage of the prairie ecosystem. First, the expanse of grassland sustained large herds of grazing animals with some estimates as high as 50 million bison, 50 million pronghorn, and one billion or more prairie dogs. The prairie community became adapted to periodic grazing, and in some cases, dependent on this type of disturbance. Secondly, grasslands were subjected to periodic burning either by man or by natural causes such as lightning. The High Plains was a shortgrass prairie that had developed under an influence of factors such as grazing by native herbivores, periodic fire, and climate conditions that were characterized by a small amount of effective precipitation.

The vegetation on the High Plains is variously classified as mixed prairie, shortgrass prairie, and in some locations as tallgrass prairie. There are distinct differences among the plant communities found on the hard lands, mixed lands, sandy lands, draws, and caliche breaks. On most upland sites throughout the High Plains, the blue grama and buffalo grass series was the dominant shortgrass community type. However, a variety of other mid and shortgrasses such as sideoats grama, sand dropseed and threeawn were also present. Western wheatgrass, vine-mesquite grass, and silver bluestem often occurred on more favorable sites. The cottonwood-tallgrass series which contained big bluestem, switchgrass, eastern grama grass, and Indian grass was present but was restricted to moist creek bottoms and swales in the central and eastern Panhandle. Mesic canyons within the Canadian breaks and the eastern caprock escarpment provided a localized habitat for the Rocky Mountain, oneseed, and redberry juniper-midgrass communities. Junipers have spread out of some of the breaks onto the plains proper. Forbs, legumes, and shrub species were also present in the shortgrass prairie, but were generally not as plentiful as in the higher rainfall areas to the east. Moderate amounts of mesquite and yucca have invaded some of the area. Sand sage and shinnery oak are common on the sandy lands. The few drainages and stream areas are lined with cottonwoods, soapberry, and hackberries as the dominant woody plants (TPWD, 2000).

By the late 1800s, farming was beginning to displace large portions of the original High Plains natural prairie. By the early 1900s, much of the original shortgrass prairie had been converted to farming which increased with the onset of deep well irrigation. The Ogallala Aquifer is a primary source of water for many of the region's municipal and agricultural endeavors. Areas not suitable for farming were used as range for domestic livestock. Ranches were primarily cattle operations, usually in large holdings. Species such as mesquite, prickly pear, redberry juniper, and cholla were quick to invade and become established on the disturbed rangeland.

The principal large wildlife species such as pronghorn (antelope), bison, prairie gray wolf, Plains grizzly bear, and Plains elk have been extirpated. There have been few listed species and few Endangered Species Act (ESA) conflicts in the region. However, habitat fragmentation and poor range conditions of remaining native grasslands can be a factor in declining fish and wildlife species. Several species are being considered for listing. To prevent further declines in at risk species, efforts are being made to protect the remaining native habitats, particularly through efforts with private landowners. This region has traditionally contained over 90 percent in private ownership.

Today, prairie restoration through practical stewardship practices is being carried out on some public and private lands. Although the shortgrass prairie of the High Plains is lacking in its original diversity and complexity, remnant populations of both flora and fauna are being gradually revived in some areas (TPWD, 1999).

Limited water supply and potentially increasing demands in the Texas High Plains make water resource management a high priority for the area of concern. The future availability of water remains the number one concern for the region. The efficiency of use has increased, but the amounts utilized is greater than the supply is recharged. The High Plains Ogallala Area Regional Water Management Plan was initiated in 1994 by regional water users. This plan has been instrumental in shaping statewide regional water planning as required by recently enacted legislation (Senate Bill 1), outlining water planning guidelines that each region was required to develop to be assure that future state water needs are met (Texas Tech, 2000).

2.5 Relationship to Migratory Bird Conservation Initiatives

There are several ongoing migratory bird conservation initiatives that all refuges should participate in to the extent applicable and practical. The following documents influence the future management of Muleshoe and Grulla NWRs, as well as the Area of Ecological Concern. The goals and objectives identified in this document for both refuges contribute to the implementation of following initiatives (see strategies under CCP Goal 1, Objectives 2, 5, 4, 6, and 7; Goal 3, Objective 4; and Goal 5, Objective 1). Muleshoe and Grulla NWRs are located in the Central Flyway, a route traveled annually by numerous species of waterfowl and migratory birds. Three hundred and twenty bird species have been documented on these refuges (see Appendix A for a complete list). Thirty two of these are waterfowl. These refuges provide wintering habitat and a stopover point for waterfowl species within the Cental Flyway. More information on the Central Flyway Council, which predates many of the following Conservation Initiatives, can be found at http://centralflyway.org/.

North American Waterfowl Management Plan

Waterfowl populations in North America had plummeted to record lows by 1985. Recognizing the importance of waterfowl and wetlands to North Americans and the need for international cooperation to help in the recovery of shared resources, the Canadian and United States governments developed a strategy to restore waterfowl populations to levels seen in the 1970s through habitat protection, restoration, and enhancement. The strategy was documented in the *North American Waterfowl Management Plan* (NAWMP or Plan) and was signed in 1986.

The plan was originally signed by the United States Secretary of the Interior and the Canadian Minister of the Environment with an initial goal of restoring waterfowl population numbers to levels observed in the 1970s. The North American Waterfowl Management Plan Committee realized that to make the plan effective it would have to be updated regularly to consider changes in the environment, society, and political policy. In 1994, the NAWMP was updated and became truly continental in scope when the Secretario de Desarrollo Social Mexico joined the United States Secretary of the Interior and the Canadian Minister of the Environment as a signatory of the plan.

The most recent update of the plan was in 1998. The updated goals seek the protection of 12.2 million acres of wetland ecosystem habitat and the restoration and enhancement of 15.2 million acres of wetland habitat. Waterfowl population goals continue to be the restoration of population numbers as seen in the 1970s.

The plan's success depends upon partnerships involving federal, state provincial, and local governments, businesses, conservation organizations, and individual citizens. These partnerships are called joint ventures. Through these joint ventures, NAWMP is able to achieve its objectives with the assistance of its partners to collectively accomplish what is often difficult or impossible to do individually.

Implementation of the plan is at the regional level, through 12 regional habitat "Joint Ventures" in the United States. The Muleshoe and Grulla NWRs are within the Playa Lake Joint Venture area. The playa lakes on the refuge provide vital habitat for migratory birds and resident wildlife. They are important for resting, breeding, nesting and/or winter residency for many species. The Playa Lakes of Texas are the second most important winter region for waterfowl in the Central Flyway. Additional information on NAWMP and joint ventures can be found at http://northamerican.fws.gov/NAWMP/jv.htm.

Partners in Flight

Partners in Flight (PIF)/*Companeros en Vuelo / Partenaires d'Envol* was launched in 1990 in response to the growing concerns about declines in the populations of numerous neotropical migrant landbird species, and to emphasize the conservation of birds not covered by existing conservation initiatives. The initial focus was on species that breed in the Nearctic (North America) and winter in the Neotropics (Central and South America), but the focus has since expanded to include all land birds of the continental United States.

PIF is a cooperative effort involving partnerships among federal, state, and local government agencies, philanthropic organizations, professional organizations, conservation groups, industry, the academic community, and private individuals.

The goal of PIF is to focus the combined resources of agencies, academia, and private organizations on the improvement of monitoring and inventory, research, management, and education programs relating to landbirds and their habitats. Implicit in the plan is the need to identify, protect, manage and restore essential habitat for declining species.

Muleshoe and Grulla NWRs are within PIF Physiographic Area #55, the Pecos and Staked Plains, which covers the western panhandle of Texas, the west end of the panhandle of Oklahoma, and extensive areas of eastern New Mexico (shown in Figure 3). These high dry plains are covered with a shortgrass prairie dominated by grama and buffalo grasses. There are also extensive areas of shinnery, a midgrass prairie with low shrubs. The area grades into taller grass to the east, to Trans-Pecos shrub savannah to the south, and more chaparral and pinyon-juniper in the Mesas and Plain to the west. Priority bird populations and habitats in this physiographic area include: for *Grassland/Shrub* - Lesser prairie chicken, mountain plover, long-billed curlew, Ferruginous hawk, scaled quail, burrowing owl, and Cassin's sparrow; and for *Wetland/River Systems* - snowy plover and interior least tern. Most of these species occur or have potential habitat on Muleshoe/Grulla NWRs and are further discussed in sections 3.4 and 3.5 of this document. Additional information on PIF and species priorities for the area can also be found at http://www.partnersinflight.org and http://cbobirds.org/pif/physios/index.html.

U. S. Shorebird Conservation Plan

The U.S. Shorebird Conservation Plan is a partnership involving organizations throughout the United States committed to the conservation of shorebirds. The organizations and individuals working on the Plan have developed conservation goals for each region of the country, identified critical habitat conservation needs and key research needs, and proposed education and outreach programs to increase awareness of shorebirds and the threats they face. The Plan has three major goals at different scales. At a regional scale, the goal of the Plan is to ensure that adequate quantity and quality of habitat is identified and maintained to support the different shorebirds that breed in, winter in, and migrate through each region. At a national scale, the goal is to stabilize populations of all shorebird species known or suspected of being in decline due to limiting factors occurring within the U.S., while ensuring that common species are also protected from future threats. At a hemispheric scale, the goal is to restore and maintain the populations of all shorebird species in the Western Hemisphere through cooperative international efforts.

The Plan is designed to complement the existing landscape-scale conservation efforts of the North American Waterfowl Management Plan, PIF, and the North American Colonial Waterbird Conservation Plan. Each of these initiatives addresses different groups of birds, but all share many common conservation challenges. One major task is to integrate these efforts to ensure coordinated delivery of bird conservation on the ground in the form of specific habitat management, restoration, and protection programs. Additional information on this plan can be found at http://www.manomet.org/USSCP.html.

North American Waterbird Conservation Plan

In July of 1998, the North American Colonial Waterbird Conservation Plan was initiated to advance the conservation of colonial-nesting waterbirds and their habitats in North America. A partnership of non-governmental agencies, researchers, private individuals, academics, and federal and state government agencies was assembled to gather information and developing the plan. The mission was to create a cohesive multinational partnership for conserving and managing colonial nesting waterbirds (seabirds, wading birds, terns, and gulls) and their habitats throughout North America. The goal was to produce a plan whose implementation results in maintaining healthy populations, distributions, and habitats of colonial nesting waterbirds in North America throughout their breeding, migratory, and wintering ranges. In 2000, the focus of this conservation planning effort expanded beyond colonial waterbirds to include non-colonial waterbirds and secretive marshbirds not covered by other conservation plans, such as rails, bitterns, grebes, etc. The name of the plan changed accordingly to the North American Waterbird Conservation Plan. The plan is still under development, but when completed the plan will be used in future refuge planning.

North American Bird Conservation Initiative

The primary role of the North American Bird Conservation Initiative (NABCI) is to coordinate, not duplicate, the efforts of the four major land bird plans: North American Waterfowl Management Plan, Partners In Flight, U.S. Shorebird Conservation Plan, and North America Waterbird Conservation Plan. Many of the birds targeted by these plans share the same habitats. By leveraging the plans limited resources, both human and financial, we will improve the outlook for bird conservation across all of North America. The NABCI, a coalition of U.S., Canadian, and Mexican governmental agencies and private organizations, is the most inclusive framework for bird conservation ever assembled on this or any other continent.

The purpose of the NABCI is to ensure the long-term health of North America's native bird populations by increasing the effectiveness of existing and new bird conservation initiatives, enhancing coordination among the initiatives, and fostering greater cooperation among the continent's three national governments and their people. All of this will be done with appreciation of the cultural and biological differences that make each country unique.

This conservation approach is expressed through NABCI's goal of delivering the full spectrum of bird conservation through regionally based, biologically driven, landscape-oriented partnerships. "Regionally based" partnerships involve all stakeholders across ecoregions and are the proven means of effectively delivering bird conservation. "Biologically driven" means that there must be explicit linkages among population objectives, habitat goals, and conservation actions. It also means that evaluation and adaptability are critical components of successful conservation efforts. "Landscape-oriented" recognizes the response of bird populations to habitat conditions across broad ecoregions and the need for conservation to operate at multiple geographic scales.

The NABCI vision is one of habitat partnerships, based upon the North American Waterfowl Management Plan's joint venture model, covering the continent coast-to-coast. It is hoped that each existing and new partnership will consider delivering conservation to all birds in all habitats and that these partnerships eventually move toward conservation of biological diversity using Bird Conservation Regions (BCRs) as the ecological unit in which to achieve their goals

The refuges are within the Shortgrass Prairie BCR (shown in Figure 3). The Shortgrass Prairie lies in the rainshadow of the Rocky Mountains, where arid conditions greatly limit the stature and diversity of vegetation. Some of the continent's highest priority birds breed in this area, including the mountain plover, McCown's longspur, long-billed curlew, ferruginous hawk, burrowing owl, and lesser prairie-chicken. Reasons for the precarious status of these birds are poorly understood but could involve a reduction in the diversity of grazing pressure as bison and prairie dogs have largely been replaced by cattle. For migrants, its is possible that conditions of wintering grounds could also be having a negative impact. The Playa Lakes area in the southern portion of this region consists of numerous shallow wetlands that support many wintering ducks, migrant shorebirds, and some important breeding species, such as the snowy plover. Additional information on the BCRs can be found at http://www.nabci-us.org/.

2.6 Planning Perspectives

This CCP identifies goals and objectives for the management of the refuge and strategies to achieve those goals and objectives. The CCP establishes a practical foundation for preparing realistic and justifiable budgetary request. Its implementation will ensure consistency of management over time while providing the flexibility needed to address particular issues as they arise.

This comprehensive planning effort will integrate the following perspectives so that management direction over the next 15 years will produce holistic management approaches for Muleshoe and Grulla NWRs:

1. A broad perspective for overall environmental contextual issues including endangered species, ecological integrity, water issues, interjurisdictional cooperation, and socioeconomic considerations.

2. A focused perspective for the Refuge System related to policy issues that affect the Muleshoe and Grulla NWRs programs (compatibility, endangered species management, etc.).

3. A local perspective for refuge related activities and programs affecting land and species management (habitat management, land protection, endangered species management, research, contaminants, recreational use, etc.).

4. Concurrent development, approval and implementation of the station's FMP. The prescribed fire objectives in the FMP will be supportive of refuge goals and objectives and serve to further endangered species and ecological integrity perspectives.

An understanding of these perspectives and the relationship between them lead to the formulation of an integral set of refuge goals, objectives, and management actions for the next 15 years.

2.7 Issues and Challenges

The following is a list of major issues and challenges related to the management of Muleshoe and Grulla NWRs, many of which were derived from ongoing management concerns since the refuge's establishment. The sources of these concerns and issues include internal scoping, responses to a questionnaire prepared for the process, and input from refuge neighbors and partners including TPWD. Goals and objectives have been designed to effect habitat restoration and protection of existing habitat for the benefit of a diversity of wildlife and plants. The questions under the issues that follow are addressed in the text of the CCP and/or within the goals and objectives section.

Muleshoe NWR:

Issue 1.   Private Land Initiatives

Much of the High Plains grasslands are in private ownership. To provide contiguous quality habitats that can support diverse native biological communities, the Service needs to encourage landowners to evaluate their existing range practices and experiment with management options that would enhance habitats for wildlife while still serving the purposes of private ownership. Although lands in private ownership are managed primarily for economic benefit, including grazing and agricultural operations, the use of prescribed fire will be explored as opportunities arise to promote diversity and return native biological communities toward more natural conditions.

There are many opportunities to enhance the ecological integrity of the High Plains ecosystems by providing viable recommendations from proven rangeland management practices for grazing and grassland management to local landowners.

* Should the refuge coordinate with the NRCS to be included in the partnership efforts with private landowners to improve grassland management for the restoration of the native prairie habitats?
* How should the refuge encourage participation in private land initiatives with the local landowners?
* How can the refuge maintain and improve its relationship with adjacent landowners?
* Should the refuge establish areas demonstrating rangeland practices, including prescribed fire, that enhance grassland diversity and benefit wildlife?

Issue 2.   Water Management

Local and regional water use has, over time, lowered the groundwater aquifer which has affected the groundwater resources throughout the area. The State of Texas ruled that the water flowing into the refuge is dispersed groundwater and not subject to a claim of water rights. Two of the three lakes at the Muleshoe NWR depend entirely upon rainfall for surface water runoff. The third lake, Paul's Lake, normally holds water year round as it is fed by a spring on adjacent private land. It is not likely that this land could ever be acquired, although the possibility of acquiring an easement to maintain this water source should be pursued. Nearly all wells drilled on the refuge since its establishment in 1935 have been non-productive and no productive wells have been found on adjacent private land for a radius of several miles. Even if water was available to pump into refuge lakes, the lake beds are not conducive to holding water for any length of time. It is unlikely that any additional water sources could be developed for the refuge.

Key issue questions include:
- Should the refuge request technical advice from the water resources branch of the Service on the appropriate locations of developing wells and assist with procedures for obtaining permits to develop new wells and acquire rights to pump groundwater?
- Should the refuge staff pursue the development of appropriate easements for protecting springs on private lands that supply the refuge wetlands?
- Should the refuge investigate other water sources (wells and springs) that may be used to supply water to refuge wetlands.

Issue 3.   Environmental Education and Community Outreach

The National Wildlife Refuge System Improvement Act of 1997 encourages managers to consider incorporating compatible environmental education and interpretation opportunities for the public into refuge programs. The refuge has many opportunities to increase community involvement and assistance in natural resource programs, enhance compatible wildlife-dependent recreation opportunities, and expand wildlife education and community outreach. There are several areas where, through the enhancement of wildlife compatible recreational opportunities and expanded wildlife education programs, the refuge could increase the public's appreciation of wildlife and thereby increase community involvement in natural resource programs. Community outreach and environmental education would be instrumental in building a supportive constituency and improving the public's understanding, appreciation, and stewardship of our natural resources. This would potentially increase visitation and increase revenue through visitor spending in the nearby towns.

- How should the refuge pursue funding resources necessary to support the primary components of the National Wildlife Improvement Act of 1997?
- How can the Service improve the recognition of the refuge?
- How can the Service increase the public involvement in natural resource programs?
- Should grazing continue to be implemented as a management tool?
- How can the refuge demonstrate the benefits of prescribed burning to the economic and personal goals of the private community?
- How should the refuge expand its current outreach to the larger nearby towns in New Mexico (Clovis and Portales) and Texas (Plainview and Lubbock)?
- What environmental education, interpretation and outreach programs should be implemented?
- What new, creative, and innovative literature can be developed for the refuge?
- What interpretive signage can be provided for the public by the Service?

- What educational services or programs should the refuge offer to the communities?
- What universally accessible facilities are needed on the refuge?

Issue 4.   Resource Information

There are several resource areas where information and/or management direction are needed. These areas include the management of black-tailed prairie dogs and archaeological resources.

Currently, the black-tailed prairie dog populations have declined from historic levels. This species is considered a key indicator of the health of the prairie grassland habitats. It is a candidate species, which means that the Service has sufficient information to propose listing as a threatened or endangered species, but the listing action has been precluded by other higher priority listing activities. There is an opportunity to develop a grassland management plan as part of the High Plains Partnership (HPP) addressing specific management strategies to enhance grassland habitat components, protect species that are currently threatened or endangered, and prevent further declines in species being considered for listing status.

- What should the refuge do to protect and manage black-tailed prairie dogs?
- How can grazing continue to be implemented as a management tool to restore grassland diversity while still protecting species diversity?
- How can prescribed fire be integrated with other management activities to improve habitat for the black-tailed prairie dog?
- What are the fire effects specific to the refuge, including impacts of timing, location, and duration; and how do those factors impact plant succession?

During the 1970s, an exposed mammoth tusk was discovered in one of the refuge's dry lakes. The area has a unique geology and analysis of pollen samples taken from lake sediments indicates new evidence regarding the age of the glacier lake basin sediments. There is an opportunity to pursue cooperative agreements with Eastern New Mexico University to complete analysis and publication of existing sites.

- What Service priority is placed on the archeological resources of the area?
- What baseline surveys are needed to identify archaeological sites?
- What level of protection should these sites be given from degradation or disturbance?
- Should the Service pursue funding to assist with further archaeological and geologic investigations?
- How should the refuge acquire funding to encourage and partially support research on the geology and archaeology of the area?

Issue 5.   Wildlife Depredation

Sandhill cranes will forage on grain crops grown on surrounding private lands. During most years, the cranes arrive when the milo has already been harvested so the birds forage on waste grain. Damage primarily occurs when wheat crop growth is retarded due to lack of moisture during early fall; then as a result of late moisture, the shoots are young and tender when the cranes arrive. During most years, there is enough moisture to plant the wheat early in the fall so the plants are large enough that the cranes do less damage to the crop. In the past, farmers have received assistance in the form of scare devices from Muleshoe NWR. Through coordination with local landowners, an opportunity exists to be prepared for the times when the cranes foraging on the late planted crops can damage the production.

- How can the refuge improve communication with local landowners and neighbors regarding crop depredation by birds?
- What strategies can be developed to decrease depredation on surrounding croplands when crops are planted late in the season?
- What role should the refuge play in the issue of crop depredation on private lands?
- Can prescribed fire be used to attract cranes and still meet other fire management objectives?

Issue 6.   Grassland Management

Native short and mixed grass prairie ecosystem of the High Plains developed under an influence of factors such as grazing by native herbivores, periodic fire, and climate conditions which were characterized by a small amount of effective precipitation. Throughout the last century, improper grazing and inadequate burning activities have resulted in declines in grassland quality for native wildlife and migratory birds. Properly managed grazing and prescribed fire serve to maintain and encourage native grasses and forbs, and to cycle nutrients through the ecosystem. Key issue questions include:

- Should habitat plans be developed to address conservation needs for restoring native grassland?
- What strategies should the refuge implement to restore, maintain, and protect grasslands to benefit native plant and animal communities?
- Should grazing continue to be used as a management tool?
- What are the minimum, appropriate tools necessary to better inventory, monitor and evaluate resources?
- Should a permanent monitoring program be established to evaluate the transition from a degraded grassland habitat to a restored grassland habitat?

Issue 7.   Funding and Staffing

Current base funding provides for minimal refuge operations that focus on a few maintenance projects and is inadequate to upgrade heavy equipment. The refuge is responsible for protecting the resources and maintaining fee title transfer inventory lands and conservation easements.

There are many opportunities for the refuge to conduct more biological surveys, improve the refuge infrastructure, restore habitats, and provide programs that encourage visitation. The refuge needs to conduct weed control and other minimal management activities to maintain fee title and easement lands. Implementation of any of these programs beyond those of minimal management activities is dependent on additional funds and staff. The Muleshoe NWR will host a comprehensive fire management program in conjunction with a restrictive grazing program. Grulla NWR and inventory lands will be managed less extensively due to limiting factors such as size, small staff, limited habitat, and distance. Since the operational involvement of regular on site field station employees at the Muleshoe NWR is presently limited due to staff size, most operational aspects of the fire management program will be charged primarily to the District Fire Management Officer (DFMO) and staff located at Witchita Mountains NWR in southwestern Oklahoma.

- What funding is required in order to achieve the goals and objectives of this plan?
- What specific positions should be identified for the near term that will assist in plan implementation?
- What staff positions will be required to meet the long-term goals of the refuge?
- Are current refuge facilities and equipment adequate?
- What avenues should the Service pursue to enhance existing management and public use programs?

Grulla NWR:

Issue 1.   Water Management

Salt Lake on Grulla NWR holds water only occasionally. Normal rainfall provides insufficient runoff for this large basin to maintain water on a regular basis. Water that does find its way to the lake is lost through evaporation and seepage through the sand bottom. There is limited potential for cost efficient water developments. Although a couple of wells adjacent to Grulla NWR on private lands are capable of pumping large amounts of water it is unlikely that a productive well could be developed on the refuge. Like Muleshoe NWR lakes, the Salt Lake bed at Grulla NWR would not hold water for any length of time nor would its light soils be suitable for dike construction. Some adjacent land may be available for acquisition or trade.

- Should the Service pursue acquisition of adjacent parcels and investigate management options to pump the well and maximize the ponding of this water to create wetland habitat in a small impoundment?
- Where should the refuge develop wells for supplemental water sources?
- Can the Service get water rights to pump groundwater from newly developed wells?
- Can the refuge get assistance from the water resources branch of the Service to provide technical advice on the appropriate locations of developing wells and process the permits with the New Mexico State Engineers Office to develop new wells?

Issue 2.   Boundary Management and Access

The refuge boundary of Grulla NWR is irregular and runs through the Salt Lake bed making fencing difficult and providing only one access point for the public or Service personnel to enter refuge lands. Trespass of cattle and people is an ongoing problem resulting from the partially unfenced boundary. Cattle from adjacent private lands roam onto the refuge; resulting in many areas being overgrazed. Many of the boundary signs are also knocked down since the cattle use the signs as scratching posts. Trespass also occurs by people riding off-road vehicles on the dry lake bed and hunters unaware of the boundary. Logistically, fencing is not currently possible because the refuge is surrounded by private land with limited access points and parts of the refuge boundary run through the lake bed.

Adjacent landowners have been contacted and are willing to participate in agreements that would provide sufficient solid ground along the lake bed to install fencing. While purchase of interest in land (i.e. fee simple or less than fee simple) would most easily facilitate solutions to the access problem, there are other approaches such as agreements with adjacent land owners that should be explored. Better access is needed to the lake area for wildlife surveys, boundary posting, and fencing. Fencing and posting the refuge boundary would protect native grassland communities from overgrazing, restoring some of the native ecological integrity, and protect wildlife populations from disturbance. Land acquisition from willing sellers should continue to be discussed, however, additional policy and NEPA compliance would be necessary beyond this CCP in order to authorize expansion of the refuge boundary.

- What are the best strategies to assist improving staff access to the lake area? What kinds of agreements would be possible between the Service and private land owners?
- Should the Playa Lakes Joint Venture be used to facilitate private land agreements and/or possible purchase of interest in lands from willing sellers using North American Waterfowl Conservation Act (NAWCA) funds?
- How can the refuge acquire funding to purchase private land to provide access points to refuge lands?
- What funding sources are available for the refuge to fence and post boundary segments most conducive to trespass?
- How can the refuge improve communication and encourage opportunities to work with adjacent landowners for a land exchange?

Issue 3.   Resource Information

Available resource data for Grulla NWR consists of wildlife observations conducted infrequently. Only occasional visits are made to observe range conditions and wildlife use. More information is needed to make informed management decisions. Resource data would provide baseline information and rationale for decisions affecting biological resources. Appropriate data would augment planned management programs to protect, maintain, and restore native habitats particular wintering waterfowl habitats

- How can the refuge acquire additional manpower (direct hire or contracting) to develop a complete data base of biological information?
- What funding sources are available to contract or hire seasonal positions to obtain the resource data needed?
- In what areas could access be improved to allow better logistics to implement surveys?
- What fire effects data are required to enhance long-term management of the refuge?

In recent years, an archaeological site involving 500 year old bison bones was discovered in Salt Lake on the Grulla NWR and evidence of ancient culture sites have been found on its lake shores. The refuge may also have additional prehistoric and historic cultural sites that are currently undocumented. There is an opportunity to pursue cooperative agreements with Eastern New Mexico University to complete analysis and publication of existing sites.

- What Service priority is placed on the archeological resources of the area?
- What baseline surveys are needed to identify archaeological sites?
- What level of protection should these sites be given from degradation or disturbance?
- Should the Service pursue funding to assist with further archaeological and geologic investigations?
- How should the refuge acquire funding to encourage and partially support research on the geology and archaeology of the area?

Issue 4.   Public Involvement

Grulla NWR is a very low profile refuge. Few people are aware of the wildlife viewing opportunities available when sufficient water provides habitat to attract large numbers of migratory birds on Salt Lake. The primitive status of Grulla NWR and minimal access points extremely limit the potential for wildlife viewing at this refuge.

- Should the Service pursue eventual discussions leading to an expansion of the refuge boundary in order to improve access points?
- What funding mechanisms are available to improve the existing interpretive area and replace interpretive signs?
- What is the best way to facilitate the development of overlook sites around the lake for wildlife viewing if additional access points are provided through either future land acquisition or through agreements with private lands owners?
- How can the refuge develop a communication network to inform the public of viewing opportunities when habitat conditions prevail?
- What type of outreach activities and interpretive programs should be developed to encourage visitation and local support of the refuge?

Issue 5.   Private Land Initiatives

Most of the grasslands in the High Plains are privately owned. To provide contiguous quality habitats and encourage diverse native biological communities, the Service should encourage wildlife habitat enhancement on these lands. Presently, a U.S. Fish and Wildlife Service biologist with the Service's Ecological Service's Office, located at Tulsa, Oklahoma, is responsible for working with High Plains Partnership (HPP). In addition, the Arlington Ecological Service's West Texas Sub-Office, located in Canadian, Texas, has a biologist that is responsible for working on private land activities in the panhandle and west Texas. The HPP is focusing initially on the lesser prairie chicken and other species sharing the same habitat. An integral partner in this effort is the Lesser Prairie-chicken Interstate Working Group which is composed of representatives from the five State wildlife agencies. States involved include Oklahoma, Kansas, Colorado, New Mexico, and Texas. Other partners include the FWS, Western Governor's Association, American Farm Bureau Federation, U.S. Forest Service, three Natural Resources Conservation Service (NRCS) regions, and innumerable private groups and private landowners.

Although NRCS District Conservationists work primarily with private land owners and are primarily responsible for wildlife habitat programs in conjunction with farm subsidies, conservation reserve programs (CRP), and other agriculture programs associated with wind breaks and soil erosion control, the refuge could become more actively involved with wildlife oriented issues and activities. Input from refuge personnel and other Service employees may be required to enhance wildlife habitat in areas adjacent the Grulla NWR. Refuge personnel could become more involved in the High Plains Partnership for Species at Risk by supporting and implementing habitat improvement initiatives regarding lesser prairie chickens.

Typical lesser prairie chicken habitat is comprised of large acreages of mixtures of short - to mid - warm season bunch grasses which includes a brush species such as sand sage, shinnery oak, skunkbush sumac, sand plum and other woody species. Although these habitat conditions are not found on the Grulla NWR, they do exist on area private lands, especially to the northeast across the State line in Texas. Prairie chicken leks are annually found here by Texas Parks and Wildlife Department (TPWD) biologists.

If funding was made available, some of the FWS private land initiatives associated with the Grulla NWR could include evaluating wildlife habitat, research, and coordinating management techniques such as controlled burning, grazing management, and invasive plant species control.

- Should the refuge coordinate with the NRCS to be included in the partnership efforts with private landowners to improve grassland management for the restoration of the native prairie habitats?
- How should the refuge encourage participation in private land initiatives with the local landowners?
- How can the refuge maintain and improve its relationship with adjacent landowners?
- What strategies can the refuge employ to resolve cattle trespass problems at Grulla NWR?
- Should the refuge pursue the purchase of private lands around Salt Lake to acquire a uniform boundary line that would allow fencing?

2.8 Expected Planning Outcomes for Both Refuges

The following components specific to comprehensive conservation planning should evolve from this planning effort:

1. Ensure that management of Muleshoe and Grulla NWRs reflect the policies and goals of the Refuge System and the purposes for which the refuges were established.
2. Ensure that Muleshoe and Grulla NWRs contribute to the conservation of ecological integrity and to the structure and function of the ecosystem in which they are located.
3. Provide a clear statement of desired future conditions for Muleshoe and Grulla NWRs as a result of the successful accomplishment of the refuges' stated goals and objectives.
4. Provide a systematic process to aid decision making by identifying opportunities, issues, and concerns; collecting, organizing, and analyzing information; and developing and considering a range of management alternatives.
5. Provide a forum for determining the compatibility of uses on each refuge.

6. Ensure other Service programs, other agencies, and the public have opportunities to participate in management decisions for Muleshoe and Grulla NWRs.
7. Provide a consistent approach for budget requests for operational, maintenance, and capital development programs that accomplish the purposes of each refuge and the Service mission.
8. Provide a basis for monitoring progress and evaluating plan implementation on each refuge.
9. Provide long-term continuity in the management of each refuge.
10. Integrate the goals and objectives of the FMP into the goals and objectives of the CCP to ensure coherent management directed toward meeting the refuges' purpose.

U.S. Fish and Wildlife Service

Grulla NWR, Muleshoe NWR, and Vicinity

Projection: UTM Zone 13, DAC 83, GRS 1980
Imagery: Landsat TM scene acquired September 1995
Reproduced by USFWS Denver
of Terminal Geonomic, 1334, 303-748-6459
May 30, 2002

MULESHOE NWR

GRULLA NWR

NEW MEXICO
TEXAS

NEW MEXICO   TEXAS

Map 3. Muleshoe NWR and Grulla NWR - Vicinity Map

0   2.5   5   10 Miles

0   10   20 Kilometers

3.0 REFUGE AND RESOURCE DESCRIPTIONS

This chapter describes the refuge and the natural and cultural resources associated with it. The primary purpose of Muleshoe and Grulla NWRs is to provide protection and habitat for migratory and resident wildlife species. Refuge habitats are managed to provide food, water, and cover for migratory and resident wildlife.

3.1 Geographic / Ecosystem Setting

Biographers have divided North America into provinces; natural regions that share similar climate, soils, topography, and vegetation. The Muleshoe and Grulla NWRs are within the region classified as High Plains within the Southwest Plateau and Plains Dry Steppe and Shrub Ecosystem, and fall within the Great Plains geomorphic province.

Muleshoe
The refuge consists of 5,809 acres located in Bailey County, Texas, in the northern part of the state in an area designated as the Panhandle Country. It straddles State Highway 214 approximately 20 miles south of the town of Muleshoe (population 4,842). It is approximately 22 miles east of the New Mexico state border; 50 miles southeast of Clovis, New Mexico (population 36,000), 120 miles southwest of Amarillo, Texas (population 172,289), and 80 miles northwest of Lubbock, Texas (population 192,732).

Grulla
Grulla NWR consists of 3,236 acres located in Roosevelt County, New Mexico, approximately 20 miles east of Portales, New Mexico (population 12,280), and 40 miles south of Clovis, New Mexico. It is approximately 25 miles west, northwest of Muleshoe NWR. The other refuges in the area are Bitter Lake NWR, 120 miles to the southwest (near Roswell, New Mexico), and Buffalo Lake NWR (near Canyon, Texas), 95 miles to the north.

Both of these refuges are situated in the heart of agricultural areas. Gradually, land use changes in the surrounding areas, reduced runoff, and the decline of the Ogallala aquifer resulted in less available habitat and subsequently less waterfowl use. With declining waterfowl numbers nationally, and more food supplies in other areas of the Texas Panhandle, the waterfowl numbers at Muleshoe and Grulla NWRs have declined in recent years to less than 10,000 ducks, a few hundred geese, and between 8,000 to 10,000 sandhill cranes. Map 3 shows the vicinity of Muleshoe NWR and Grulla NWR Texas and New Mexico, including the extent of agricultural development in the area.

3.2 Physical Environment

3.2.1 Climate
The climate at Muleshoe and Grulla NWRs is considered cool temperate. Temperatures may range from subzero in the winter to 100+ degrees F in the summer. The average low temperature is approximately 43 degrees F and the average high is approximately 74 degrees F. The normal annual precipitation for Muleshoe NWR is 16.50 inches and 16.0 inches for Grulla NWR. Rainfall in the area occurs most frequently in thunderstorms. This kind of rainfall is spotty and partly accounts for the extreme variability in precipitation. Rainfall is greatest during May, June, and July, and three-fourths of the average annual rain fall during the six-month period of May through October. Dry spells of several weeks or more are common and there are monthly periods without measurable rain. The driest period is normally November through April. The following graph summarizes annual

precipitation over an eleven year period. During the winter, snowfalls are generally light, and snow remains on the ground for only a short time. Because the wind drives much of the snow into high drifts, distribution of moisture is uneven.

Amarillo, approximately 120 miles to the northeast, is listed as the windiest spot in the nation. Strong continuous winds during March and April cause

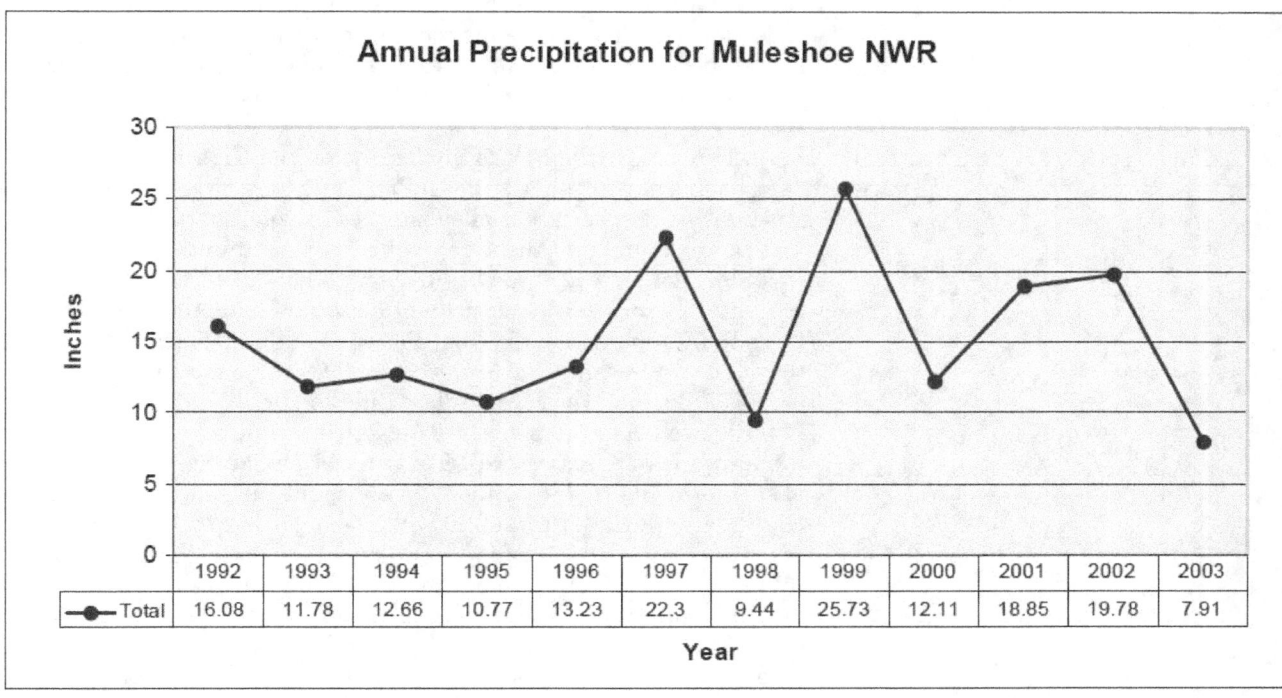

Annual Precipitation for Muleshoe NWR

	1992	1993	1994	1995	1996	1997	1998	1999	2000	2001	2002	2003
Total	16.08	11.78	12.66	10.77	13.23	22.3	9.44	25.73	12.11	18.85	19.78	7.91

Year

blowing soil and dust storms. Area winds up to 70 miles per hour have been recorded and 20 mile per hour winds are common. The prevailing winds are southerly from May through September and southwesterly during the rest of the year. There have been infrequent tornado warnings in the area. More often, tornados develop in the area and move northeast.

3.2.2 Physiography and Geology

The primary physiographic feature of Bailey County is the gently sloping, level surface of the High Plains. The High Plains surface is formed on the Ogallala formation which consists of gravels and sand deposited more than two million years ago by rivers and wind. Weathering of the Ogallala resulted in the development of caliche which today occurs only a few feet below the soils on the High Plains surface and, where eroded, forms the Caprock Escarpment on the eastern margin of the High Plains. The Ogallala formation is the main source of irrigation water in the county today.

About 250 million years ago, a shallow sea covered the area that is now West Texas. Marine muds and gypsum deposited at that time formed the Permian red beds. As sea level dropped, the Permian red beds were exposed and eroded. The climate was dry, and over time a series of rivers eroded the uplands and deposited extensive gravels and sands, forming the Triassic red beds on top of the Permian rocks. Erosion continued in the region until about 120 million years ago during the Cretaceous period, when sea levels rose and formed a seaway stretching south to north, flooding the continent from the Gulf of Mexico to the Arctic Ocean. Limestone forming marine muds accumulated on the floor of the shallow seaway, and dinosaurs lived along its shoreline. At the end of the Cretaceous period, the shallow seaway retreated and the region again was dry land. The Rocky Mountains began to be folded and pushed up at the end of the Cretaceous period, and rivers originating from the mountains and adjacent uplands eroded away many of the Cretaceous rocks that had formed on top of the Permian and Triassic red beds. Most of the Cretaceous rocks were washed away from the area that is now Bailey County; only a few remnants of Cretaceous rocks occur as outcrops along the edges of some of the large playa lakes.

Muleshoe and Grulla NWRs are located on the High Plains surface. The deep basins at Muleshoe and Grulla NWRs may have formed by collapse and subsidence over areas of subsurface dissolution of Permian evaporates. The Ogallala and its caliche caprock are exposed in the collapse basins. The early Ice Age history of the basins is not known, but 20,000 years ago during the Late Wisconsin when continental glaciers had pushed south from Canada into the northern Great Plains and alpine glaciers were present in the southern Rockies, the Muleshoe and Grulla basins were filled with water. Lake mud that accumulated in the High Plains lakes during the Late Wisconsin are named the Tahoka formation and are mapped in numerous lake basins in west Texas and New Mexico. Overflow from the basins formed a river drainage system connecting the various basins on the High Plains surface and spilling out of canyons at the eastern edge of the caprock escarpment. The present day draws on the High Plains follow the route of the old river system. About 14,000 years ago, the lakes began to dry, and since then winds that sweep across the High Plains have deflated the old lake beds, forming lee dunes on the east margins of the playa lakes. Two sets of the lee dunes occur east of Goose and White Lakes; their ages are not known, although a Folsom point was found on the outer dune and bones of the modern species of bison have been found on the inner dunes. In other areas of Bailey County, sand dunes cover the plains and form low sandy hills. Horse, camel, and proboscidian bones were recovered from sediments at the north end of Goose Lake. At White Lake, pollen analysis of the glacial age Tahoka lake deposits show that the vegetation of the High Plains during the late Ice Age was a sagebrush grassland.

The Ogallala Aquifer - The water saturated sand and gravel of the Ogallala formation is a major regional aquifer that is the source of almost all of the irrigation water in Bailey County. Several millions of years ago, strata of the Ogallala formation stretched from Texas to the Rocky Mountains. Subsequently, stream erosion removed large portions of the rock formation, resulting in the isolation of the High Plains Plateau. Today, the water that replenishes the Ogallala aquifer originates entirely from rainfall and melting drifted snow. The water table slopes gently to the southeast, following the topography of the High Plains surface, and the natural rate of water movement in the aquifer is very slow, no more than one or two feet per day. Before irrigation, the water discharged at natural springs and seeps in the playa lakes and along the caprock escarpments. Today, water is being pumped for irrigation faster than it is being restored by recharge from rainfall. Some springs have dried up and playa lake levels are depressed due to depletion of the groundwater and lowering of the water table.

3.2.3 Soils

Muleshoe

The materials from which the soils of Bailey County developed were deposited during the Pleistocene epoch from winds during the Illinoisan age. During this time, Bailey County was probably a prairie with little rainfall, and wind shifting the surface materials. When the glaciers moved south, the climate of Texas became wetter. At that time, Bailey County probably consisted of humid prairies and wooded areas along the streams. When the glaciers receded, the climate became more arid and the soils and vegetation developed as they are now.

Muleshoe NWR is divided into two areas based on vegetative cover type. Area 1 is covered with a mixture of grasses dominated by blue grama and buffalo grass. Mesquite forms an overstory in some areas. This type covers the land on top of the bluffs and along the north and west sides of the refuge. Soils in this area are primarily from the Berthoud-Mansker association which are sloping, shallow to deep, medium textured, moderately permeable soils. Several small areas along the north refuge boundary fall into the Amarillo-Arvana association; level to gently sloping, moderately deep, moderately course textured, moderately permeable soils. The vegetation in this soil varies and in optimum conditions, can have considerable diversity. The lowland areas of the refuge are strongly influenced by the saline lakes. The Arch-Drake association of soils in these areas are level to sloping, moderately deep, medium textured, high lime soils. Alkali sacaton is highly adapted to these soils and out competes most other grasses, consequently developing into dense, monotypic stands with an increasing amount of dead vegetation over time.

Grulla

The majority of the refuge (2,330 acres) is encompassed by Salt Lake, which has no soil classification according to the information for Soil Survey Area 41 in Roosevelt County, New Mexico. The remaining 906 acres of the refuge consists of several different soil types. Much of the area adjacent to the north side of the lake is classified as Church clay loam, which is a deep poorly drained soil with a surface layer of clay loam about 7 inches thick. Soft caliche is generally found at a depth of about 7 inches, and the subsurface soil layer is clay and silt clay loam about 53 inches thick. The soil is highly erodible and potentially hydric. The uplands to the east and south of the lake are classified as Drake soils, which are deep well drained soils that have an 8 inch surface composed of fine sandy loam and a subsurface of loam or silty clay loam that is about 52 inches thick. This soil is highly erodible. There are also small inclusions of Arch loam, Olton loam and Portales loam on the refuge. The lands surrounding the refuge consist of Portales loam, Arch loam, Olton loam, and Mansker and Portales loams, all of which are deep well drained soils that are highly erodible.

3.3 Biological Environment

3.3.1 Vegetation

Both Muleshoe and Grulla NWRs are part of the short and mid grass prairie complex characteristic of the High Plains. The primary grass species are native grama grasses, buffalo grass, and alkali sacaton. There are no croplands on either refuge; however, land use in the surrounding area is primarily dry land farming. The common and scientific names of the plant species that are typical of this area are listed in Appendix A.

A generalized vegetation map for Muleshoe NWR is provided in Map #4. This map represents a visual approximation of vegetation in the area, as discussed below. It is based primarily on the refuge manager's and planner's knowledge of the area (including field experience, aerial photography, available GIS data) and is not intended to be used for management-related purposes such as acreage calculation, pasture delineation, and prescribed burn boundaries. Attempts to quantify vegetation on the Muleshoe NWR into 4 different categories (grama grass, alkali sacaton, mixed grama grass/mesquite, and woodland using remote sensing techniques were unsuccessful. Three different remote sensing techniques were used in an effort to spectrally differentiate between the various vegetative types contained on the refuge. Bands 1-6 of a Landsat TM satellite image were stacked with a Normalized Difference Vegetation Index band and a 1m black and white DOQQ. Two processes utilizing ERDAS Imagine 8.5 were performed on the imagery: an unsupervised classification and a supervised classification. The unsupervised classification broke the image into 20 different classes. The 20 classes were than combined into 4 classes. The results indicated an inability of the software to spectrally distinguish between grassland types. Other errors in distinguishing grass/mesquite and woodland communities from topographic features (drainages) were also apparent. Next, a supervised classification was performed. This involved selecting polygons of known vegetative types and using them to classify the entire image. This method, however, proved no more accurate than the previous method, in that it introduced additional spectral confusion in differentiating between grassland types. SEGMENTATION, a program developed by the USFS, was then used in a third attempt to create statistically valid training sites to classify a resampled 4m black and white DOQQ. This method, again, proved no more accurate than the previous 2 methods.

Due to a limitation of time and staff, a formal accuracy assessment was not conducted. A formal accuracy assessment would involve ground-truthing a statistically valid number of samples in the field in order to calculate an error matrix and evaluate map accuracy vs. user accuracy. An informal assessment was completed. It was based on 50+ points (horizontal GPS error of plus or minus 2m) collected throughout the refuge combined with current knowledge of areas of known vegetation types. Accuracy in distinguishing between grassland types (grama grass species vs. sacaton) was 50% at best. Accuracy requirements for the NPS/NBS Vegetation Mapping Project require an accuracy of 80% for each vegetation class that is mapped (DOI/NPS 1994). At a minimum, USFWS maps vegetation to the alliance level using the National Vegetation Classification Standard. Although our objective was not to map to the alliance level, attempts to classify the refuge into 4 generalized classes proved as difficult as trying to differentiate between several alliances.

Remote sensing has been successful in classifying various geologic and hydrologic features; however, there is still confusion in trying to differentiate between grassland vegetative types. Remotely sensed data must be combined with extensive field work, taking into consideration the soils, geology, slope, elevation, and aspect of the area to accurately

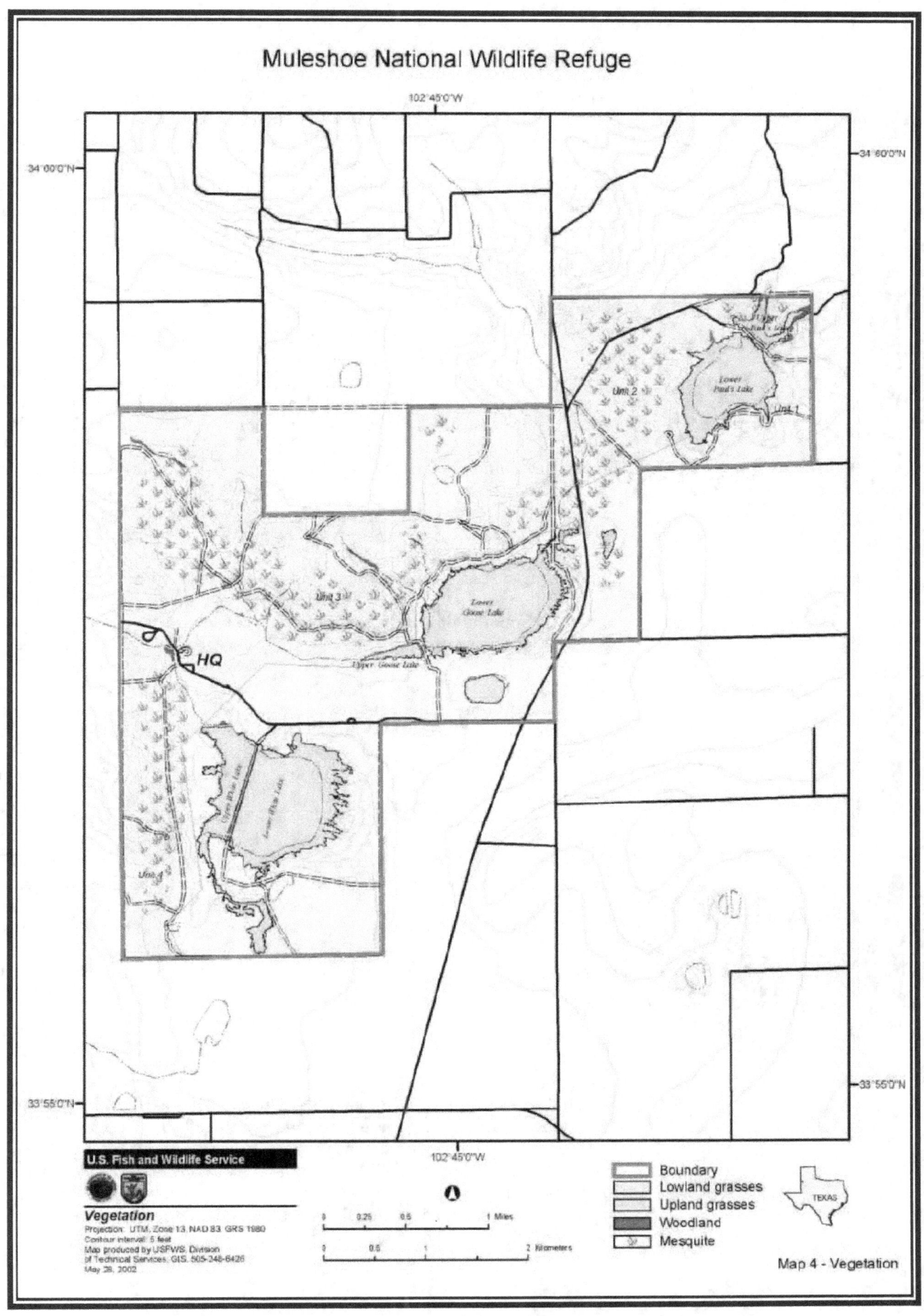

Map 4 - Vegetation

determine the associated vegetative boundaries. Rather than attempting to classify the entire refuge into specific vegetative types, it might be more practical based on time and manpower to focus on individual management units. Establishing point/line intersect transects or some other sample plots within each management unit (fire or grazing) may be a more practical, realistic means of monitoring and understanding the various vegetative trends/changes over time. The Habitat Management Step-Down Plan with further address the most efficient and practical methods of inventorying and quantifying refuge habitats.

Grasslands

Cholla in native grassland (photo by Jim McElroy, refuge volunteer)

Muleshoe

This refuge maintains one of the last shortgrass prairie environment on the Southern High Plains of Texas (McMahan et al., 1984). Common perennial grasses include buffalograss, blue grama, sideoats grama, and alkali sacaton. Other dominant vegetation includes mesquite, broomweed, and yucca. Approximately 4,649 acres of grassland occur on Muleshoe NWR, including 150 acres of restored farmlands. Upland areas are dominated by buffalo grass and blue grama. Grassland areas on top of the bluffs and along the north and west sides of Muleshoe NWR are intermixed with shrub overstory such as mesquite, cholla cactus, and salt bush. Approximately 240 acres of rimrock outcrops occur within the grasslands.

Lowland areas are influenced by high lime soils and saline lakes. The vegetation is primarily thick, monotypic stands of alkali sacaton with an increasing amount of dead vegetation occurring over time. These dense stands of alkali sacaton are rated low in preference for both wildlife and domestic cattle. However, these grasses protect the sandy soils around refuge lakes from wind erosion. Areas of alkali sacaton are burned periodically to rejuvenate rank/over-mature stands of this grass. Dry lake beds have minimal vegetation due the alkaline surface soils. Major plant species include: alkali sacaton, sideoates grama, white tridens, slim tridens, feathery bluestem, bristlegrass, blue grama, tobosagrass, buffalo grass, and sand dropseed.

Grassland habitat at Grulla NWR (photo by Don Clapp)

Grulla

The dominant vegetative cover on approximately 906 acres of Grulla NWR include alkali sacaton, mixed stands of blue grama and buffalo grass, salt bush, and yucca. Refuge grasses remain dormant many years due to below average rainfall. Major grass species in the area include: blue grama, black grama, hairy grama, feathery bluestems, little bluestems, sand bluestem, buffalo grass, sideoates grama, tobosa grass, bristlegrass, cottontop, sand dropseed, and three awn.

Wetlands

Muleshoe

Wetlands at Muleshoe NWR, when filled to capacity, can provide as much as 1,000 surface acres. The three lakes on the refuge (Paul's Lake, White Lake and Goose Lake) were divided into six lakes by dikes built by the Works Progress Administration (WPA) in the late 1930s. These lakes lie in a pronounced depression in the general prairie and form a sump for the surrounding watershed. Since there are no outlets or established watercourses providing a permanent water supply, water in the lakes comes entirely from precipitation, run-off from rain and snow, and irrigation drain water. The Texas Water Commission ruled that the lakes on Muleshoe NWR are true playa basins and the waters impounded periodically therein are not State waters. Attempts to locate a reliable water source for these lakes during the past 60 years has been unsuccessful. Of these six lakes only Upper Paul's Lake holds water year-round due to the influence of an underground spring located on adjacent private land. The refuge lake beds soak up much precipitation before holding any standing water due to the low water table of the Ogallala aquifer and the high evaporation rates during the summer months. All lakes, except Upper Goose Lake and Upper Paul's Lake, are heavily alkaline.

Water is also available at times in several other playas and impoundments on the refuge. Several of these are kept at least partially filled with water from windmills.

Consistent water levels and aquatic vegetation at Upper Paul's Lake are maintained by a fresh water spring on private land adjacent to the refuge (photo by Don Clapp)

Grulla

Wetlands at Grulla NWR consist of the saline bed of Salt Lake. The primary water source for this lake is runoff from rainfall. Normal rainfall provides insufficient runoff for this large basin to hold water on a regular basis. During recent years Salt Lake has only held water occasionally. What water does find its way to this shallow 2,330 acre lake is lost quite rapidly through evaporation and seepage into the sandy lake bottom. Management options are minimal due to the limited availability of water and the fact that the refuge does not own the entire lake bottom.

Woodland

Muleshoe

Scattered stands of trees grow in the draws and include bodarc, hackberry, Siberian elm (known locally as Chinese elm), Plains cottonwood, and sycamore-maple. Mesquite and wild plum, as well as other shrubs, are scattered throughout the grasslands. Ten acres of windbreak surround the refuge headquarters. Invasive woody species include: Russian olive, mulberry, and Siberian elm.

No management is practiced in these areas other than the removal of dead trees in the windbreak around the refuge headquarters.

Grulla
There is no woodland habitat (natural or planted) on this refuge.

Invasive Plant Species

Muleshoe
The following non-native invasive weed species are found on the refuge: salt cedar, Canada thistle, cheatgrass, Johnsongrass, blue weed, jointed goatgrass, goat's beard, Russian olive, Siberian elm, field bindweed, and common horehound. Other invasive species that are of lesser significance since they are primarily invasive in disturbed areas include common kochia, Russian thistle, white sweet clover, and yellow sweet clover, purple nightshade, and morning glory. Most of these species invade and spread quickly after some form of soil disturbance or certain environmental conditions (e.g. drought, followed by wet periods, or wet winter and early spring) that permits them to out-compete the native plant species and become monocultures. On Muleshoe NWR such conditions usually result in establishment of small areas of species such as blueweed, kochia, and Russian thistle that can be easily controlled on an annual basis through mechanical and chemical means. However, it is recognized that invasive plant species pose a threat to the native grass and riparian communities by out-competing native plant species. While it is possible for some invasive species found on the refuge to spread to nearby private lands, resulting in economic damage to their owners, it is more likely that invasive species on private lands would move into the refuge, given that the refuge is surrounded by a highly disturbed landscape. Wind borne seeds from area farm fields are considered a factor in the establishment of a number of the invasive species.

The Refuge has a small quantity of scattered Siberian elms. Siberian elms were established at old home sites and along drainages. However, they are not surviving well. Ground moisture does not appear to be sufficient for seedling establishment and survival, or even for maintenance of larger trees in some locations. The Refuge's current policy will be to take no measures against Siberian elm unless populations expand. Dead trees are preserved as wildlife perches.

Salt cedar has been mechanically removed from Paul's Lake Dike (photo Don Clapp)

At least 10 acres of salt cedar and other exotic plant species occur throughout the Refuge, primarily along Upper Paul's Lake. Salt cedar does not appear to be spreading on the refuge; however, if future moisture conditions are just right, there is potential for it to spread very rapidly in a single year. Salt cedar has a short seed viability and must receive moisture within a very narrow window of opportunity after seeding in order to become established. Since each plant has a potential of producing up to one million seeds, the population could grow logarithmically in a year or two. It would be preferable to remove salt cedar and replace it with native species, however, non-invasive native plants such as cottonwood and willow will not survive the salt lake environment that exists on the refuge. In the past, the refuge mechanically removed small amounts of salt cedar. Currently, the refuge is taking a more aggressive approach to treatment. In 2003, the refuge, with the help of the Regional Invasive Species Biologist, sprayed herbicide on 5 acres (about 50%) of the salt cedar on the refuge. Total removal of salt cedar is the planned objective on the refuge for the future.

In addition, there are several native plants which have become invasive due to changes in historical fire frequency, past grazing practices, and drought conditions. These include broom snakeweed, catclaw, yucca, cholla cactus and mesquite. Mesquite has been invading the refuge slowly in adaptable soils for years. Although complete removal of mesquite on the refuge is not a planned objective, the refuge will continue to remove mesquite for grasslands enhancement. Selected areas will be allowed to remain for habitat for grassland birds and other wildlife. Other areas will be controlled by fire, mechanical methods, and herbicide applications to restore refuge grasslands to a more natural grassland. To date, 125 acres of honey mesquite have been removed to provide migratory resting sites for sandhill cranes adjacent to Paul's Lake.

Overall, it is believed that the refuge currently has a relatively minor problem with invasive species that requires monitoring and site-specific control. In the past, management of invasive species on the refuge has included mowing thistles, spraying mesquite, and rooting out and spraying salt cedar. Through development of the Integrated Pest Management Plan, the refuge will map the location and distribution of invasive species, monitor populations, and develop plans to eradicate those species whose populations are such that eradication is a feasible goal, and control and contain those which are widespread.

Grulla

Invasive species may occur on refuge lands, but there have been no inventories and none have been identified as problems. Inventory and mapping of invasive species should be completed on this refuge, and appropriate control actions taken to eradicate and/or control those species using low impact methods whenever feasible.

Both Refuges

In addition to control and eradication of invasive species currently found on the refuges, steps will be taken to prevent the inadvertent spread of those species to other parts of the refuge, and the introduction of additional species or infestations brought in from outside the refuge. Steps to be taken include the following:

- Biological and maintenance staff will be trained to identify known invasive species of western Texas rangelands, so that control actions can be taken promptly. Hand removal of new infestations will be used where it is an effective technique for eradication.

- Vehicles and equipment used in infested areas on the Refuge will be checked as needed prior to leaving to ensure they are not transporting seeds to uninfested areas.

- Vehicles or equipment borrowed from other refuges or agencies, or loaned to other refuges or agencies, will be required to be cleaned prior to transport to or from the refuge if they have been used in areas where invasive weeds are known to occur.

- When any ground-disturbing actions are to be taken, the site will be checked for the presence of invasive species, and actions taken to ensure activities do not spread infestations both on site and to other parts of the Refuge.

3.3.2   Fish and Wildlife

Many of the birds, mammals, and reptiles that occur within Muleshoe and Grulla NWRs are found only in the shortgrass prairie habitat type or depend heavily on the type and include species such as the burrowing owl, grasshopper sparrow, Cassin's sparrow, lark sparrow, lark bunting, bald eagle, golden eagle, peregrine falcon, and mountain plover. Other species also depend heavily on the shortgrass prairie seasonally or during migrations.

Birds

Muleshoe and Grulla NWRs are located in the Central Flyway, a route traveled annually by numerous species of waterfowl and migratory birds. Three hundred and twenty bird species have been documented on these refuges (see Appendix A for a complete list). Thirty two of these are waterfowl.

Great-blue heron (photo courtesy of USFWS)

<u>Muleshoe</u>
A majority of the songbird species observed on the refuge are present during the months of October and November. Mourning doves, bobwhite quail, pheasant, mockingbirds, and lark sparrows are common nesting birds. Many of the songbird species frequently use the vegetation planted around the refuge headquarters. Neotropical migrants such as warblers, flycatchers, tanagers, orioles, sparrows, and others pass through the refuge each spring and fall with many grassland species remaining to nest. The grassland habitats on the refuge are some of the best remaining shortgrass prairie left in the High Plains grasslands. Many declining species either occasionally or commonly occur on the refuge, including the burrowing owl, longspurs, grasshopper sparrow, Cassin's sparrow, lark sparrow, and lark bunting (refer to section 3.3 Rare and Declining Species).

The ferruginous hawk, northern harrier, and burrowing owl are species commonly associated with the shortgrass prairie habitats of Muleshoe NWR. The occurrence of ferruginous hawks in many cases is related to the concentration of prairie dog towns, a primary prey base for this raptor species. Golden eagles are occasional winter residents around the refuge based on the availability of prey.

Song and nesting bird species such as mourning dove, scaled quail, common nighthawk, curve-billed thrasher, lark sparrow, loggerhead shrike, and northern mockingbird seasonally use the refuge environments. Lesser prairie chickens are rarely seen on Muleshoe NWR. Most of these species are protected by federal law and it is a fundamental refuge objective at both Muleshoe and Grulla NWRs to manage for all species that would naturally occur within the available habitat.

Populations of migratory birds are totally dependent on available habitat provided by rainfall, runoff, and to some degree agricultural drain water. The Llano Estacado Audubon Society of Lubbock frequently conducts bird counts on the refuge. In the past, this group has recorded 75 species in the spring and 52 species during a Christmas bird count.

Shorebird habitat varies with water availability. The following species have been observed on refuge lakes: Wilson's phalarope, red-necked phalarope (accidental), long-billed dowitcher, black-necked stilt, American avocet, greater yellowlegs, black tern, ring-billed gull, Franklin's gull, long-billed curlew, Baird's sandpiper, stilt sandpiper, and killdeer. Snowy plovers, avocets, and black-crowned night herons occasionally nest around Paul's lake on Muleshoe NWR. Other marsh birds observed include American coot, white pelican, eared grebe, white-faced ibis, snowy egret, and great blue heron.

Other birds rarely seen on the refuge include the mountain plover, eastern bluebird, Carolina wren, Townsend's warbler, sage sparrow, and gray flycatcher.

A few golden eagles are generally observed on the refuge during the fall and winter. The great horned owl and burrowing owl nest on the refuge. Other raptors infrequently observed on the refuge include: sharp-shinned hawk, Cooper's hawk, prairie falcon, and merlin. A complete listing of all birds found on the refuge can be found in Appendix A.

Grulla

The main attraction for migratory birds at Grulla NWR is the lake habitat which is dependent on local rainfall and runoff. During most years, with the exception of high rainfall years, the lake remains nearly dry. Wildlife surveys are difficult to conduct on this refuge because there are few access roads around the lake to allow for close observation and species identification. A few thousand lesser sandhill cranes as well as waterfowl, primarily blue-winged teal, gadwall, and mallard will use the lake in October through December when it has water. Salt Lake, with shallow water levels, can provide some excellent shorebird habitat. The following species have been observed: long-billed curlew, Baird's sandpiper, semi-palmated sandpiper, American avocet, killdeer, black tern, and Wilson's phalarope. Other notable species that have been observed on the refuge include: white-faced ibis, eastern and mountain bluebirds, cliff swallow, turkey vulture, northern harrier, American kestrel, ferruginous hawk, red-tailed hawk, and Swainson's hawk. Lesser prairie chickens have been observed in the past, but are rare. A complete listing of all birds that have been recorded on the refuge can be found in Appendix B.

Killdeer (photo courtesy of USFWS)

Migrating and Wintering Waterfowl and Cranes
The Flyway System was initiated in 1948 to allow for differing regulations relating to individual waterfowl populations migrating through each "flyway". The term "flyway" has long been used to designate the migration routes of birds. For management purposes, four waterfowl flyways - Pacific, Central, Mississippi, and Atlantic, were established in the United States. This was the beginning of large-scale species management. Further efforts toward species management came into effect when bag limits were reduced or seasons were closed on specific species that were in danger of being over hunted. Flock management within flyways was put into effect to allow more refinement in regulations for specific groups of birds (USGS 2000). To

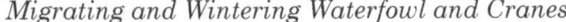

varying degrees the waterfowl populations using each of these flyways differ in abundance, species composition, migration pathways, and breeding ground origin. There are differences also in levels of shooting pressure and harvest. The refuge is located within the Central Flyway, which is an extensive geographical area that reaches from Alaska and Central Arctic Canada to South America. The portion of this flyway within the United States is comprised of Kansas, Nebraska, North Dakota, South Dakota, Oklahoma, Texas, and portions of Colorado, Montana, New Mexico, and Wyoming.

The management activities of Muleshoe and Grulla NWRs contribute to the objectives of the Central Flyway Management Program. The refuge serves the objectives of its establishment by providing a protected roost site for cranes and quality winter habitat to sustain the condition of migratory waterfowl for spring migration and reproductive success. Many factors within the lands of the Cental Flyway can affect the migratory bird resource. Conversely, management activities that occur on these refuges can have wide ranging effects on the bird populations of the entire Central Flyway. Maintaining the health and condition of the birds wintering at Muleshoe and Grulla NWRs affects their spring migrational and reproductive success each year. Factors influencing the bird use of this area include the activities of other countries, local farming practices on neighboring farms, the activities of federal and state agencies, private organizations, local governments, the influence of treaties affecting wildlife and wildlands, and finally, natural factors such as climate.

Blue-winged teal (photo courtesy of USFWS)

During the 1930s and early 1940s, water was present in nearly all lakes every year and the number of ducks using Muleshoe NWR in the winter months exceeded 300,000. Waterfowl numbers vary and have generally been greater in the past due to more available habitat. Continental duck populations have recently rebounded from low levels in the late 1980s and early 1990s. This is due to improved habitat conditions in northern breeding areas and wetland conservation efforts in wintering areas. Waterfowl numbers on the refuge, however, have steadily decreased during recent years.

Migrating waterfowl begin to arrive on the refuge during August, reach their peak by the end of December, and typically stay through March or April. Waterfowl numbers on the refuge normally peak during late winter and often include 70 to 150 Canada geese, 75 to 100 snow geese and 3,000 to 5,000 ducks. Waterfowl use of Paul's Lake includes pintail, mallard, wigeon, blue-winged teal, green-winged teal, cinnamon teal, shoveler, redhead, lesser scaup, and ruddy ducks. A few tundra swans are infrequently recorded on the refuge. A few Canada geese winter on the refuge. Small flocks of snow geese frequently visit the refuge for short periods during spring and fall migrations. Pintails and blue-winged teals are the first of the fall migrants, and are followed later by American widgeons. Mallards, the predominant species during the winter, are the last ducks to arrive. Shovelers, scaups, buffleheads, and ruddy ducks are also common during migration periods. Currently, there are very few ducks due to decreasing water levels and a shifting of area waterfowl wintering and migration patterns. Typically there is no waterfowl nesting on the refuge, but occasionally a few mallards or shovelers will nest.

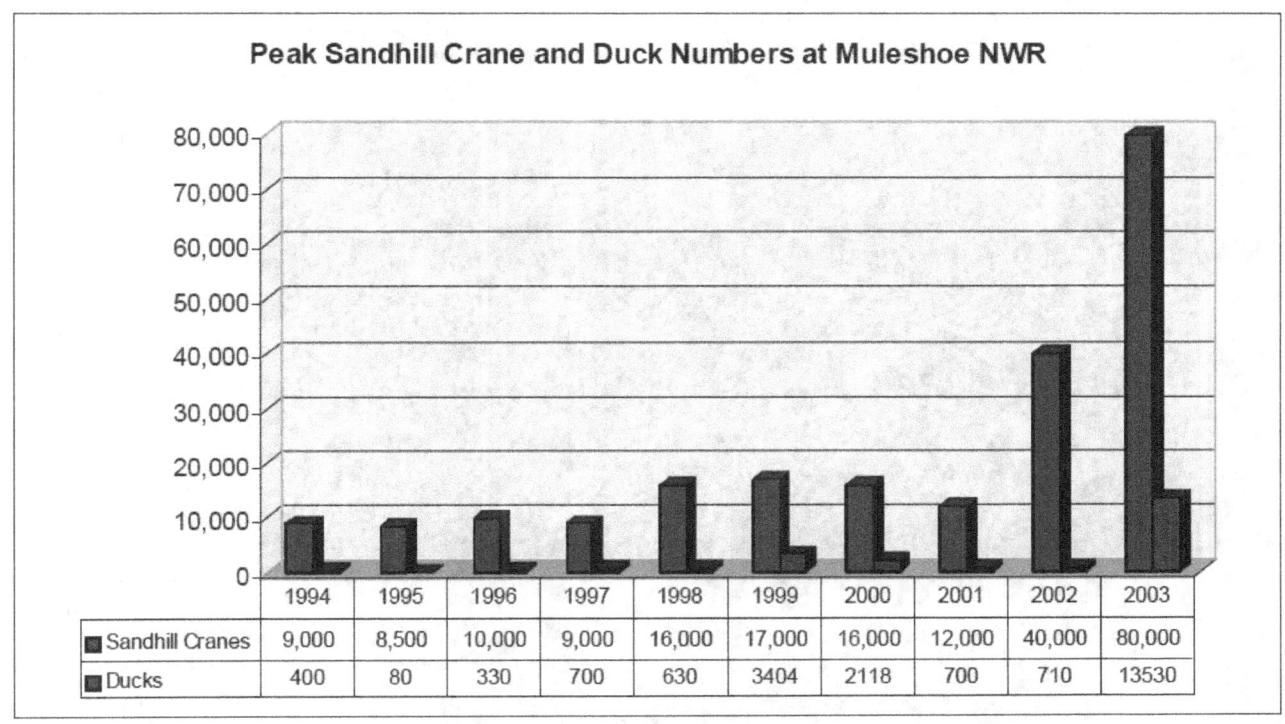

	1994	1995	1996	1997	1998	1999	2000	2001	2002	2003
Sandhill Cranes	9,000	8,500	10,000	9,000	16,000	17,000	16,000	12,000	40,000	80,000
Ducks	400	80	330	700	630	3404	2118	700	710	13530

Another outstanding feature of Muleshoe NWR is the winter population of lesser sandhill cranes. The first cranes sighted normally arrive at the refuge during the last of September or first part of October. In the six month period that the cranes are away from their arctic breeding grounds, the Muleshoe NWR population represents one of the largest concentration of lesser sandhill cranes in the South Plains; from October through February feeding flocks can be seen on winter wheat or in milo and corn stubble. The overall population of lesser sandhill cranes has steadily increased in recent years due to the remoteness of their nesting habitat and their ability to adapt to agriculturally developed wintering areas, primarily the South Plains of West Texas. The availability of waste milo grain in surrounding farmlands is equally as important as roosting lakes for sandhill cranes. As many as 400,000 cranes annually winter in the south High Plains of west Texas; however, these birds can be dispersed over a broad area depending on the availability of food and desirable roosting sites. Water is another major factor affecting local sandhill crane use. Loss of surface water in saline lakes is the greatest single threat to long-term lesser sandhill crane use of the High Plains. Iverson etal. (1985) found that 90 percent of the mid-continent population roosted in winter on only nine saline lakes in west Texas. Disease and extremes of weather on these crane concentrations could pose a threat to long-term population viability.

When Muleshoe NWR was established in 1935, crane use was minimal (between 1,500 to 3,500 birds) because the saline lakes were usually too deep to provide roosting habitat. Through the 1940s, crane use increased, and by 1949 the species had become an abundant winter resident as lake depths had decreased due to draw-down of the Ogallala aquifer, providing ideal roosting sites from October through mid-March. The cranes roost on saline or large playa lakes at night and fly out to surrounding agricultural fields at dawn to feed on waste grain. With an abundance of food available in the surrounding grain fields, crane numbers peaked in 1981 when 250,000 cranes were recorded on the refuge. In the 1990s, as many as 50,000 up to 100,000 of these birds were present. In recent years, however, wintering populations have declined. Numbers typically fluctuate based on availability of food and water. The major reasons for the decline were the lowering of the water table and past drought conditions affecting lake levels, as well as the loss of croplands (milo and other grain fields) that the crane depended upon for winter forage. The Conservation Reserve Program (CRP) was established by the federal government during the late 1980s. Under this program, farmers are paid to plant fields to grass instead of grain in wind-eroded farm lands; therefore, there is less food available to the cranes. Recent annual peak populations have remained around 10,000 cranes.

Sandhill cranes at Paul's Lake (photo by David Sams)

Since refuge acquisition, changes in land use practices in the surrounding area and an extended period of reduced runoff has resulted in a decrease in waterfowl habitat. The number of cranes and waterfowl utilizing the area in recent years has been drastically reduced from historical records. This is in response to nationwide population declines related to large scale habitat loss, but also local changes in water availability, and alternate areas of abundant food supplies in other Panhandle lakes due to increased farming and irrigation. Although less than 30,000 ducks and a few thousand geese use the area in winter, a significant number of the Central Flyway cranes (nearly 100,000) still roost and feed in areas located between Muleshoe, Texas and Portales, New Mexico from October to March.

Other Species of Special Management Concern
Nine species of birds have been identified as priorities in Grassland/Shrubland and Wetland habitats by the PIF bird conservation plan for the Pecos and Staked Plains physiographic area. These species are indicators of the condition of the grassland and wetland systems within this region (USGS, 2000). Their populations have been emphasized as a priority for monitoring. These include the interior least tern, lesser prairie chicken, mountain plover, ferruginous hawk, long-billed curlew, scaled quail, burrowing owl, snowy plover, and cassin's sparrow.

In addition to those species identified specifically for the Pecos and Staked Plains physiographic region, there are several nongame bird species that have been prioritized for the larger central shortgrass prairie region. Through the PIF prioritization process, scores designed to reflect degrees of population vulnerability were determined for relative abundance, breeding and nonbreeding distribution, threats to breeding and nonbreeding areas, population trends, and area importance using various criteria established for these categories. Depending on the scores, each species was ranked and placed in tier groups from Tier I having the highest priority for the region, and Tier II being the next group for prioritization. Species in subsequent tiers appear on other lists. Tier III consists of species of 'concern' that appear on the PIF/Audubon Watch List that for one reason or another did not factor out as Tier I or Tier II birds. Tier IV species are those species protected as federally listed threatened and endangered species (Carter et al., 2000). The bird species identified for the central shortgrass prairie region that are known to occur on Muleshoe and Grulla NWRs are listed in Table 4. A complete listing of threatened and endangered species can be found in Appendix C.

Table 1- Priority species known to occur or those that could occur in the Muleshoe and Grulla NWRs include the following: (Species highlighted in bold are further discussed as species of concern in section 3.3.3)

Tier I	Tier II
Swainson's hawk*	northern harrier*
ferruginous hawk	common nighthawk*
lesser prairie chicken	grasshopper sparrow
scaled quail*	**burrowing owl***
snowy plover*	ringed-necked pheasant*
mountain plover	black-crowned night heron*
long-billed curlew	barn owl
Cassin's sparrow*	western kingbird*
black-chinned hummingbird	Bullock's oriole*
Say's phoebe*	prairie falcon
Bell's vireo	American avocet*
Chihuahuan raven*	upland sandpiper
lark sparrow*	Wilson's phalarope
lark bunting*	chestnut-collared longspur
crissal thrasher	yellow-headed blackbird
McCown's longspur	

* known to nest locally on the refuges

Mammals

<u>Muleshoe</u>
The refuge provides habitat for some 30 species of mammals including prairie dogs, mule deer, raccoon, porcupine, woodrat, coyote, bobcat, red fox, badger, eastern cottontail, and jackrabbit. The refuge management objectives for managing these species is to maintain representative populations of each.

Mule deer are becoming more common on the refuge since the recently opened State deer hunting season has driven deer populations from the shinnery oak covered sand hills to the north.

A listing of mammals seen on the refuge can be found in Appendix A.

Coyote (photo courtesy of USFWS)

<u>Grulla</u>
Although mule deer have wandered onto the refuge at times, sightings are rare. Surveys have not been completed and a species occurrence list is not available for this refuge. However, many of the same species that occur on Muleshoe are expected to occur on Grulla.

Reptiles and Amphibians

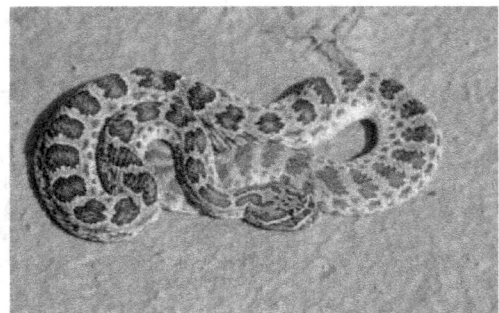

Bullsnake (photo courtesy of USFWS)

<u>Muleshoe</u>
Reptiles and amphibians often seen on the refuge include: tiger salamander, collared lizard, horned lizard, prairie rattlesnake, bull snake, hog-nosed snake, and racers. A listing of amphibians and reptiles seen on the refuge can be found in Appendix A.

<u>Grulla</u>
Surveys have not been completed and a species occurrence list is not available for this refuge. However, many of the same species that occur on Muleshoe are expected to occur on Grulla.

Prairie rattlesnake (photo courtesy of USFWS)

Fish and Invertebrates

There is no species list for fish or aquatic invertebrates that may occur in the refuge impoundments. No fish currently occur on either refuge due to the unpredictable water supply and frequent drought.

At Muleshoe, during the 1940's through the 1960's, fish stocking was conducted on the refuge, all with little success. Records indicate: a few bullheads in Upper Goose Lake in 1943 and in 1946 nearly 10,000 fish received from Dexter National Fish Hatchery were stocked in Upper Goose Lakes. Species stocked included large mouth bass, blue gill, black crappie, and channel cat. Fish were again stocked in Upper Goose Lake in 1949 but were reported to be dying due to lack of water in 1952. Records show that 18,000 fish were again put in Upper Goose Lake in 1957. The last refuge records regarding fish indicate that by 1961, over the previous nine years, 13,600 bass, 2,000 catfish, and 6,200 bluegill were stocked in Upper Goose Lake with no success. In 1962 Upper Goose Lake was reported again dry with all fish dead.

3.3.3 Species of Special Interest

The refuge provides potential habitat for a variety of rare or declining species, including several federally proposed, listed (threatened or endangered) and candidate species and other species of concern. Declines may be related to loss and fragmentation of suitable habitat, increasingly large areas being cultivated for crops, drought, loss of playa lakes, lack of natural fire regime, and the replacement of native grasses with exotic grasses. Some species inhabit the refuges on a regular or seasonal basis while others are migrants or accidental visitors that are infrequently sighted on the refuges. There are no known state or federally listed or sensitive plants on either refuge.

Management actions taken on the refuge will adhere to compatibility standards, National Environmental Policy Act (NEPA), Endangered Species Act (ESA) compliance and Service regulations to ensure that endangered species are not adversely impacted. The refuge will provide technical assistance on endangered species management to neighbors and individuals from the private sector whenever it is requested. A list of threatened and endangered species and species of concern that may be found in Roosevelt County, New Mexico, and Bailey County, Texas is provided in Appendix C.

Federally Endangered, Threatened, and Proposed Species

The purpose of the Endangered Species Act is to conserve "the ecosystems upon which endangered and threatened species depend" and to conserve and recover listed species. Under the law, species may be listed as either "endangered" or "threatened". Endangered means a species is in danger of extinction throughout all or a significant portion of its range. Threatened means a species is likely to become endangered within the foreseeable future. All species of plants and animals, except pest insects, are eligible for listing as endangered or threatened. Proposed species means any species of fish, wildlife, or plant that is proposed in the *Federal Register* to be listed under section 4 of the ESA.

Black-footed Ferret (*Mustela nigripes*)- The black-footed ferret was listed as endangered in 1967 because much of the shortgrass prairie habitat on which the ferrets depend had been plowed for crops. They rely on prairie dogs for food and shelter, living in burrows made by prairie dogs. Almost 90 percent of their diet consists of prairie dogs. Scientists estimate that over 100 million acres of western rangelands were occupied by prairie dogs in the early 1900s. Much of this area was also occupied by black-footed ferrets. It takes about 100 acres of a prairie dog colony to support one ferret family (a female and her young). Prairie dogs have been reduced in number due to habitat loss, disease, and eradication efforts. The black-footed ferret historically occurred in the High Plains, Rolling Plains, and Tran-Pecos regions. Wild populations currently exist only in Wyoming, South Dakota, and Montana.

Muleshoe - The refuge's *Annual Narrative for 1963* reports that a member of the staff observed a black-footed ferret on July 5, 1963. This was the last recorded evidence of the black-footed ferret on the refuge. They have not been observed in Texas since then (TPWD, 2000).

Grulla - There is no potential habitat on the refuge and no recorded sightings in the area.

Bald Eagle (*Haliaeetus leucocephalus*) - The bald eagle was listed as endangered on March 11, 1967, as a result of population declines due to pesticide-induced reproductive failure, loss of riparian habitat, and human disturbances, such as shooting, poisoning, and trapping. On August 11, 1995, the bald eagle was down-listed from endangered to threatened status in the majority of the contiguous U.S., including New Mexico, due to nationwide recovery efforts (USFWS 1995). In 1999, the bald eagle was proposed for delisting (USFWS 1999). The main population of bald eagles inhabiting the Southwest consists of wintering bald eagles that nest in

Bald eagle (photo courtesy of USFWS)

northern localities and a few nesting pairs. Most wintering and nesting bald eagles in New Mexico are associated with major rivers, lakes, or reservoirs. In Texas, the bald eagle is a rare to uncommon migrant, winter visitor, and local breeder (Texas Ornithological Society 1995). Their numbers appear to be increasing in winter and during migration, probably in response an increase in number of reservoirs throughout these states (Hubbard, 1978; NMDGF, 1988; Texas Ornithological Society, 1995). Bald eagles are opportunistic and will forage on prairie dogs, sick or dead waterfowl, and crippled or unretrieved cranes.

<u>Muleshoe</u> -Bald eagle occurrences in the area are generally at Muleshoe NWR. Generally between one to three bald eagles spend the winter months (November through February) on the refuge and take advantage of the varied food sources in the area. Their spring migration coincides closely with the spring departure of waterfowl and cranes (Littlefield, 2000).

<u>Grulla</u> - Bald eagles probably occurred at Grulla NWR in the past when Salt Lake held water for extended periods to attract large numbers of waterfowl.

Whooping Crane (*Grus americana*) - The whooping crane was listed as endangered on March 11, 1967 (NMDGF 1988, USFWS 1990). Once widespread in North America, by 1941 the species had declined to about 16 individuals in a single wild flock that migrated between Canada and coastal Texas (Lewis 1995). Several factors contributed to the historic decline of the species, including habitat loss and alteration, coastal and marine pollution, illegal hunting, disease, predation, collision with utility lines, loss of genetic diversity within the population, and vulnerability to natural and human caused disturbances (Lewis 1995).

Whooping Crane (photo courtesy of USFWS)

The whooping crane has begun a slow but seemingly steady recovery, and as of March 12, 2003, the wild population of crane has increased to 292 (259 adults, 33 young). Of this, the Aransas/ Wood Buffalo population accounts for 185 birds (169 adults and 16 young). The historic wintering grounds included southwestern Louisiana, the Gulf Coast of Texas, interior west Texas, the highlands of northern Mexico, and Atlantic coastal areas of New Jersey, Delaware, South Carolina, and Georgia (DeHoyo et al., 2000). During migration, they feed and roost in a wide variety of habitats, including croplands, large and small freshwater marshes, the margins of lakes and reservoirs, and submerged sandbars in rivers.

Whooping cranes are a common winter resident in Aransas and Matagorda Counties where the largest wild population of this endangered species seems to be slowly increasing (Texas Ornithological Society, 1995). Otherwise, whooping cranes are very rare in Texas, other than during migration where they utilize a narrow corridor north of their primary wintering areas. Rare sightings have been reported in the Muleshoe and Grulla areas, but no documentation exists of this species on either refuge.

Interior Least Tern (*Sterna antillarum*) - The interior least tern was listed as endangered on May 28, 1985 and is the only subspecies recognized in New Mexico (NMDGF 1990a). All subspecies of the least tern apparently were abundant through the late 1880s, but were nearly extirpated for their delicate plumage used for fashionable hats at that time. After the signing of the 1918 Migratory Bird Treaty Act, commercial harvesting became illegal and the species began to increase through the 1940s. However, human development and use of tern nesting beaches for housing and recreation subsequently led to another rapid population decline. In the interior United States, river channelization, irrigation diversions, and the construction of

dams contributed to the destruction of much of tern's sandbar nesting habitat. By the mid 1970s, least tern populations had decreased by more than 80 percent from the 1940s. This colonially-nesting waterbird is a species that seldom swims, spending much of its time on the wing (Hubbard 1985). The flight is light, swift, and graceful, and it is developed to the point that it is the major means of foraging, allowing the birds to snatch fish, crustaceans and insect food from the surface, almost without missing a beat. They nest on the ground, on sandbars in rivers or lakes or pond edges, typically on sites that are sandy and relatively free of vegetation. Interior least terns

Interior least tern (photo courtesy of USFWS)

are migratory and breed along the Red, Mississippi, Arkansas, Missouri, Ohio, and Rio Grande river systems. The nearest known nesting localities are along the Canadian River in the northeastern Texas Panhandle (Seyffert, 1985), the Cimarron River in southwestern Kansas (Thompson and Ely, 1989), and Bitter Lake NWR, New Mexico.

The only site where least terns have been reported locally is Muleshoe NWR; however, the species has not been observed since 1981. One pair may have nested in 1967. Currently, most of the large saline lakes are almost dry which would preclude additional least tern use on these refuges (Littlefield, 2000).

Candidate Species

Candidate species are those species for which the Service has enough information to warrant proposing them for listing as threatened or endangered, but these species have not yet been proposed for listing due to other higher priority listing activities. The Service works with States and private partners to carry out conservation actions for candidate species to prevent their further decline and possibly eliminate the need to list them as endangered or threatened. The following species are candidates for federal listing that have either been documented in the area or the refuge falls within their historic range, but they have not been documented in the area.

Prairie dog (photo by Jim McElroy, refuge volunteer)

Black-tailed Prairie Dog (*Cynomys ludovicianus*) - Prairie dogs live in shortgrass and mid-grass prairies and grass-shrub habitats (Finch, 1992). The historic range of black-tailed prairie dogs covered approximately 100 million acres and extended over 12 states, throughout the Great Plains from southern Canada throughout most of western United States to New Mexico. Prairie dogs have been reduced to less than one percent of their original range due to poisoning by private landowners, plague, and shooting. What remains is fragmented into remnants of various sizes. This species is considered a critical link or keystone species, one that significantly influences the distribution, abundance, and or diversity of other species

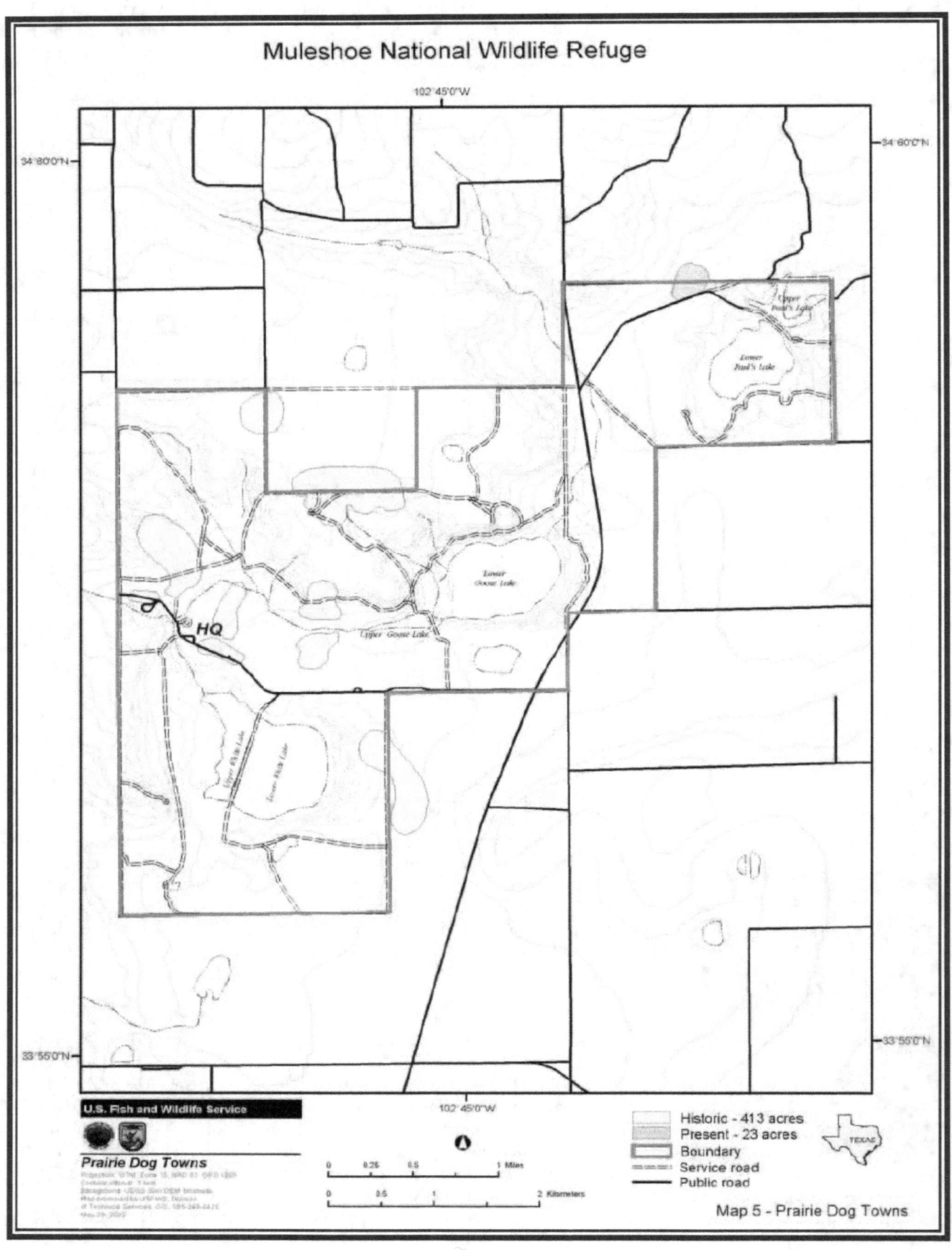

Muleshoe National Wildlife Refuge

Map 5 - Prairie Dog Towns

U.S. Fish and Wildlife Service

Prairie Dog Towns

Legend:
- Historic - 413 acres
- Present - 23 acres
- Boundary
- Service road
- Public road

(Kotliar et al., 1999; Finch, 1992). Prairie dogs are also considered an ecosystem regulator as their natural behavior patterns lead to manipulation of soils as well as increases in plant and animal densities. They are helpful to other species that benefit from holes, unvegetated areas, short vegetation, as well as to prairie dog predators (Clark et al., 1982).

One of three subspecies of prairie dogs, black-tailed prairie dogs occupy most of the eastern half of New Mexico and are cited in northwestern Texas and straddle the Texas/New Mexico border (Jones et al., 1987).

<u>Muleshoe</u> - Black-tailed prairie dog populations on the refuge have fluctuated dramatically throughout the years (see Map 5). The refuge's prairie dog towns comprised 500 acres in 1938. Bubonic plague outbreaks occurred in the refuge's prairie dog populations over the years causing the prairie dog numbers to decline sharply only to gradually increase to large numbers until the plague would again reduce their numbers. Outbreaks of bubonic plague almost completely eliminated refuge prairie dog populations in the 1950s, the 1970s, and as recently as the year 2000. In the mid 1960s, prairie dog towns covered a large amount of the refuge's grasslands, and were particularly evident around refuge headquarters. In 2002, the only prairie dogs on the refuge consisted of a small town located northwest of Paul's Lake (23 acres as shown on Map 5). However, the refuge's prairie dog population is expanding. By 2004, the colony near Paul's Lake had expanded to the south side of the road and now occupies about 30 acres. In addition, a small number of prairie dogs now reside in several areas near the headquarters.

<u>Grulla</u> - Prairie dogs are not known to exist at this refuge; however, there is a prairie dog town on private land east of the refuge entrance road.

Lesser Prairie Chicken (*Tympanuchus pallidicinctus*) - The lesser prairie chicken is an occupant of arid shortgrass prairies interspersed with shinnery oak and sand sagebrush brushlands (Oberholser, 1974; Sutton, 1967). This species was formerly abundant within this range, but has dramatically declined during the twentieth century. They are presently found in isolated regions of southwestern Kansas, southeastern Colorado, eastern New Mexico, western Oklahoma, and northwestern Texas. Their changing status in Texas reflects their historic trends throughout their range. In 1900, the Texas population was estimated at 2,000,000 birds (Oberholser, 1974). It was reduced to 12,000 by 1937, and to 3,000 in 1963. Loss of habitat is responsible for these declines, especially the conversion of native prairie to cultivated fields. Brush removal within remaining prairies is also a factor, since the oak and sagebrush provide important food and cover throughout the year (Sutton, 1967). Recent increases in this species may be the result of conversion of grassland to Conservation Reserve Program (CRP) grasslands. The preferred west Texas habitat appears to be native rangeland in association with 5 to 37 percent small grain crops (Littlefield, 2000). In an effort to protect remnants of lesser prairie chicken habitats in nearby New Mexico, the state purchased 23,000 acres (Sand, 1968). In New Mexico, its main area of occurrence is on the

Lesser Prairie Chicken (photo courtesy of NRCS)

Pecos and Staked Plains including Roosevelt County, especially in the vicinity of Portales (Hubbard, 1978).

<u>Muleshoe</u>
Prairie chicken observations on the refuge over the years have always been reported as rare. The first documented prairie chicken sighting on the refuge was in 1938. Other sighting dates on the refuge include: 1943, 1944, 1945, and 1949. Although not seen on the refuge between 1949 and 1981, there were reported sightings on surrounding private lands in 1954 and 1964. In 1981 prairie chickens were again seen on the refuge. Then in 1988, there were several observations. In February 1988, a large flock (110 birds) was observed south of the Lower White Lake near the southern Refuge boundary. Prairie chicken sightings occurred throughout the remainder of the year and included a female with seven young. In 1989 prairie chickens were seen throughout the year, most frequently seen at the northwest corner of the refuge, as there were apparently leks on private land just southwest and northwest of the refuge. From 1990 through 1991 sightings were fewer throughout the spring and early summer, but there continued to be an active lek adjacent to the refuge south of White Lake. In 1992 and 1993 prairie chickens continued to be seen adjacent to the refuge south of White Lake and another active site was found on private land about a mile west of the refuge's northwest corner. From 1994 through 2002, no prairie chickens have been seen on the refuge or on the site south of White Lake, but an active site is consistently seen one mile north of the refuge's northwest corner (USFWS narratives).

<u>Grulla</u> - Limited habitat may occur on the refuge, but no prairie chickens have been documented. The nearest known occupied habitat is on private land a few miles northeast of the refuge.

Other Species of Concern

Species of concern are species for which further biological research and field study are needed to resolve their conservation status or are considered sensitive, rare, or declining on lists maintained by Natural Heritage Programs, State wildlife agencies, other Federal agencies, or professional scientific societies. The following species of concern are known to occur or have potential habitat on the refuge:

Baird's Sparrow (photo courtesy of USFWS)

Baird's sparrow (*Ammodramus bairdii*)- The Baird's sparrow winters primarily in northern Mexico, although some may be found in southern Texas, New Mexico and Arizona. Baird's sparrow is a summer endemic species to the prairie where pairs select tall or mixed grasses, wet meadows, and occasionally fallow, stubble, or hay fields for nest placement. Nests are on the ground on ungrazed or lightly grazed sites. As with many endemic prairie species, reasons for the decline of breeding populations are probably related to the effects of drought, agriculture, and overgrazing on the shrubby shortgrass habitats favored by the species (Lane 1968). Similar impacts on migrational and winter habitat areas have no doubt also occurred, with the loss of cover and seed crops likely the most deleterious of the effects (NMDGF 1988).

<u>Muleshoe</u> - This species is very elusive, with more than 100 undocumented reports in Texas (Texas Ornithological Society, 1995). The following fall, winter, and spring records of this species occur for Muleshoe NWR: one in November of 1976, one in December of 1997, and one in April of 1981

(Littlefield, 2000). It is considered an accidental visitor to the refuge, but it may migrate through undetected in small numbers each year.

Grulla - In the past, it was relatively numerous and widespread in New Mexico (Hubbard, 1978), but in recent years has rarely been reported. Grulla is within the range of this species and may provide suitable habitat, but no Baird's sparrows have been recorded on the refuge to date.

Ferruginous hawk (*Buteo regalis*) - The ferruginous hawk is primarily found on grassy prairies, dry mesas, irrigated agricultural lands, and other habitats that support many rodents and rabbits. Ferruginous hawks range over much of the western half of the United States. It prefers forest edge or mature, isolated, flat-topped junipers, with thick support branches for nesting. It is highly sensitive to human disturbance. The ferruginous hawk preys mainly on small to medium-sized mammals (Stravers and Garber 1998). Historically, ferruginous hawks experienced declines in the southwestern states, although recent trends appear to be stable (Hall et al. 1988).

Conversion of grassland to intensive cultivation has reduced the amount of preferred habitat that is available to the ferruginous hawk and has been implicated in the population decline of the species in some areas (Schmutz, 1984; Olendorff, 1993). Agricultural development has restricted the species to areas of greater topographic relief or other areas unsuitable for agriculture (Stewart, 1975). Nest disturbance, shooting while perched along roadsides, and widespread control of prairie dogs, a vital source of food, are other factors that may have led to the current decline of this species.

These hawks migrate and winter statewide in New Mexico and are considered a regular summer resident in the eastern plains of New Mexico (Hubbard, 1978). Positive correlations occur between the location of ferruginous hawk nests and large prairie dog towns in some grassland areas of central and west central New Mexico, indicating a reliance of some breeding pairs on the availability of prairie dogs as a primary prey item (Hawks Aloft, Inc., 2000). The fall migration of ferruginous hawks is also tied to prairie dog colony locations, as the hawks eat young dogs as well as other rodents associated with the towns (Dechant et al., 1999).

Ferruginous hawks usually winter on the Pecos and Staked Plains in fairly large numbers, and in some winters, this species has been more abundant than anywhere else within its range (Littlefield, 2000). The greatest concentrations occur around the prairie dog colonies and at flooded playas with waterfowl disease outbreaks. There is a possibility that at least one pair has bred recently in southwest Cochran County (just south of Muleshoe NWR), and a few others were reported during breeding bird surveys in 1972 and 1983 (Littlefield, 2000).

Peregrine falcon (*Falco peregrinus*) - The peregrine falcon was originally listed as endangered on June 2, 1970. Their shrinking numbers were the result of decreased nesting success attributed to accumulation of chlorinated pesticides such as DDT and its metabolite DDE. The population has shown a tremendous comeback from the bird's most critical low level of 30 pairs in the mid 1960's. By captive breeding and release programs, the population of these birds has rebounded remarkably and has exceeded the recovery goals for this species. Recovery efforts resulted in delisting of the peregrine falcon on August 25, 1999 (64 <u>Federal Register</u> 46543); however, this species is still listed as State threatened in New Mexico and endangered in Texas.

Peregrines take virtually all of their prey on the wing, typically after a stoop or dive from above. Prey consists almost entirely of other birds, such as shorebirds, waterfowl, pigeons, doves, robins, flickers, jays, swifts, swallows, and other passerine birds that opportunity presents (Craig 1986). During the breeding season, a hunting range of 10 miles may be considered typical (Craig 1986); however, they may forage as far as 17 miles from the nest site (Porter and White 1973). Peregrines use a wide variety of habitats for foraging, including riparian woodlands, coniferous and deciduous forests, shrublands and prairies (Finch 1992).

Regionally, continental peregrines breed in Colorado, New Mexico, far western Texas, and in the mountains of northern Mexico. Nests are primarily on high, vertical cliffs. In New Mexico, peregrine falcon breeding territories center on cliffs in wooded/forested habitats, with large "gulfs" of air nearby in which they can forage (Hubbard 1985). Adequate nesting places are unavailable on the western Texas plains. There is no known nesting habitat on or near either refuge. However, there is migration habitat, particularly in autumn. Single birds are usually encountered near playas where waterfowl and/or shorebirds are concentrated.

<u>Muleshoe</u> - There are, on occasion, winter occurrences of peregrine falcons, particularly at times when playas have ample water, with associated masses of wintering ducks. Few peregrines have been seen in spring, but a number of Arctic bound birds apparently overfly (Littlefield, 2000).

<u>Grulla</u> - Peregrine falcons could forage in the area during migration, but they have not been documented.

Long-billed Curlew (*Numenius americus*) - Breeding long-billed curlews disappeared from large portions of their range during the late nineteenth and early twentieth centuries (Andrews and Righter, 1992; Stewart, 1975) when populations of many shorebirds were decimated by uncontrolled hunting. With protection, the populations of most shorebirds breeding in the arctic recovered. However, the long-billed curlews nest in grasslands of central and western North America, where habitat destruction and other factors have not allowed for a sustained population recovery of this species. Long-billed curlews prefer native shortgrass prairie for nesting, but also occupy grazed mixed grass communities and scrub prairie (Stewart, 1975). In general, breeding long-billed curlews are most numerous on the western Great Plains from eastern New Mexico and the Texas Panhandle north to portions of Montana and Alberta, and from Utah into eastern Oregon. Breeding bird survey data indicate that long-billed curlew populations are declining in the High Plains and the western Great Plains. During migration and winter, flocks of long-billed curlews are often found in coastal habitats, but also occur in inland grasslands and agricultural habitat such as those found in west Texas and is considered a locally common winter resident on the South Plains (Texas Ornithological Society, 1995; Sauer et al, 1995). In northwestern Texas, the species has recently been found breeding in several counties (Seyffert, 1985).

<u>Muleshoe</u> - No known breeding has recently occurred within the area, but birds have been seen in June and breeding is suspected approximately 15 miles south of the refuge in southwestern Cochran County. The species

attains its greatest annual abundance in autumn with roosting and loafing long-billed curlews observed near shallow, flooded playas, and flocks dispersing to feeding sites in surrounding croplands. As many as 3,000 to 5,000 long-billed curlews have been observed near recently harvested fields in the fall (Littlefield, 2000). They are typically seen on the refuge during spring and fall migration; however, the large numbers mentioned above (3000-5000) are exceptional and not to be expected on a regular basis.

Grulla - This species summers regularly in various parts of New Mexico, including the Portales area mainly in July and August (Hubbard, 1978). Flocks of as many as 300 birds have been seen in June on the refuge.

Scaled Quail (*Callipepla squamata*) - Scaled quail are a Chihuahuan desert grassland species found in the U.S. and Mexico generally between 3,500 to 4,600 feet above MSL. Native populations can be found in Arizona, New Mexico, Texas, Colorado, Kansas, and Oklahoma. Populations have also been introduced to Nevada and Washington. Because of their reliance upon native grasslands, these birds are susceptible to habitat disturbances by domestic livestock grazing. Much of their range has been over grazed. Livestock removes desirable cover species, thereby reducing an area's carrying capacity for the birds (Dixon and Knight, 1993). According to Brown (1989), scrub invasion is a persistent enemy of scaled quail in Arizona. "Overgrazing, summer drought, and fire suppression all favor the proliferation of woody plants over perennial grasses and the replacement of scaled quail by Gambel's quail" (Brown, 1989). This effect is evident in Arizona and much of the West, as large portions of the bird's historical range is now devoid of scaled quail populations. According to the scientific literature on scaled quail, hunting pressure has little effect on populations over the long term.

Muleshoe - It is an uncommon to locally common resident from the Trans-Pecos and the Panhandle east and south. Their summer numbers vary depending on habitat and rainfall. Spring and summer rainfall apparently influences numbers, with more birds present in the fall after abundant precipitation (Campbell, 1968). In winter, on the mesquite-prairie grasslands of Muleshoe NWR, scaled quail were recorded on 22 of 28 recent Christmas counts in numbers ranging from six to 278 (in the 1950s). In recent years, their numbers have typically ranged from 20 to 50 annually.

Grulla - This bird is a resident almost statewide in New Mexico. It is considered rare to common in grasslands and open shrublands at low and mid elevations (Hubbard, 1978). However, to date, it has not been observed on the refuge.

Burrowing Owl (*Athene cunicularis*) - Burrowing owls are found throughout grasslands and deserts in western portions of North America in drier regions of central and South America. Burrowing owls prefer open areas within deserts, grasslands, and shrub-steppe. They use well drained, level to gently sloping areas characterized by sparse vegetation and bare ground such as moderately or heavily grazed pasture. Populations in the northern part of this range are migratory. Burrowing owls prey primarily on arthropods and small mammals and are believed to be opportunistic feeders. Burrowing owls do excavate their own homes; however, they prefer to take use of other burrowing animals dens. They typically nest in vacated prairie dog burrows.

Photo by Greg Lasley

Urban development, conversion of pasture to cropland, and cultivation of grasslands limit burrowing owl populations through the destruction of nesting habitat. Elimination of burrowing rodents through control programs has been identified as the primary factor in the recent and historical decline of burrowing owl populations. The campaign to eradicate prairie dogs in the west has indirectly affected many nontarget species, the burrowing owl in particular. Prairie dogs have been reduced by 50 percent or more in many areas of the southern High Plains. Currently, the center of abundance of burrowing owls is on the shortgrass prairies where remnant prairie dog colonies continue to persist (Littlefield, 2000).

Muleshoe NWR - Burrowing owls are common on the refuge in spring, summer, and autumn, but only a few typically winter in the area. This is most likely due to the reduction in prairie dog towns on the refuge as a result of recent control and disease outbreaks. Nesting, however, does occur on the refuge, but populations fluctuate with the prairie dog population. In the past there were typically 6 to 12 pairs, but in recent years, there have only been two pairs nesting on the refuge.

Grulla - Burrowing owls summer and winter statewide in New Mexico. The Portales area is part of the northern limits of their winter range (Hubbard, 1978). To date, burrowing owls have not been recorded on the refuge, but they are likely to occur in the area.

Cassin's Sparrow (*Aimophila assinii*) - During the breeding season, Cassin's sparrows inhabit shortgrass prairies mixed with scattered shrubs. Their populations are known to experience considerable annual fluctuations in abundance, primarily in response to changes in precipitation levels. In the southwestern deserts, they are generally most numerous during wetter years, but become scarce during droughts. As a result of considerable annual fluctuations in abundance, the historic changes in Cassin's sparrow populations are poorly understood in most of their range.

Cassin's sparrows are common spring and fall migrants, and summer breeders and can be observed in the Texas Panhandle from late March through late September (Littlefield, 2000). The physiographic region of the Pecos and Staked Plains contain the highest percent of the population of this species than any other physiographic area in the region (USGS, 2000). Along Breeding Bird Survey (BBS) routes, Cassin's sparrows are most numerous from southeastern Colorado south through eastern New Mexico and adjacent portions of Texas. According to BBS survey data collected during annual surveys, the distribution of Cassin's sparrows along the New Mexico-Texas border (in the vicinity of the Muleshoe and Grulla NWRs) is between 10 and 30 birds during the month of June. Data indicates that this species exhibited a peak in its range during 1974, followed by a decline through 1981 and then fairly stable numbers despite annual fluctuations in abundance. Because of their inconspicuousness in winter, limited data exists to indicate trend estimates.

Muleshoe - Cassin's sparrows are commonly seen on the refuge in the spring and summer, but uncommon in the fall.

Grulla - This species has not been documented on the refuge, but is expected to occur in the area.

Mountain plover (*Charadrius montanus*) - The Mountain plover is endemic to shortgrass prairies. It breeds in the Plains of western North America and gathers in flocks to migrate to their wintering ground; occupying a range extending from Montana to New Mexico and Texas (Graul and Webster, 1976). It has fairly specific habitat requirements, preferring level areas with very short grass and scattered cactus (Graul, 1975). Historically, these plovers were commonly associated with bison and prairie dog towns. The mountain plover requires expansive dry short-grass prairie such as high plains and semidesert mesas having a high proportion of bare ground (>30 percent) for nesting. Typical associated plants include blue grama, buffalo grass, and scattered cacti or forbs. They feed primarily on insects (ants, beetles, grasshopper, crickets, etc.) and spiders. In New Mexico, the species nests from April through July and may be found nesting in open plains, mesas, or dry playas (lake bed flats). They commonly nest in or near prairie dog towns. Other sites that attract plovers for nesting, but may be in harms way, include farm fields, highway/powerline rights-of-way, and stock tanks. Historically, the mountain plover was most likely a common breeding bird in the Pecos and Staked Plains area, but during the past century, human settlement, the eradication of prairie dogs, and the conversion of native prairie to cropland has significantly reduced the suitable habitat for this species, producing a significant decline in the continental population.

Mountain plover (photo by Fritz Knopf)

Evidence of breeding in the vicinity of the refuges, consists of one nest found in May 1899 in Swisher County, which is approximately 5 miles east of Castro County, Texas, and a flock of 150 birds was seen approximately 10 miles northwest of Tatum, New Mexico in July 1937 (Littlefield, 2000). Their present center of breeding abundance is in Montana, Wyoming, and northeastern Colorado (Graul and Webster, 1976).

Muleshoe - The mountain plover has, on occasion, been observed during migration. The three most recent records were all during the spring from Muleshoe NWR (Littlefield, 2000). These may represent birds returning north from southern Texas.

Grulla - None recorded

Snowy Plover (*Charadrius alexandrinus nivosus*) - The interior western snowy plover is a breeding bird of the alkali and saline flats of the western states. Nest sites of the interior western snowy plover typically occur in flat, open areas with sandy or saline substrates; vegetation is usually sparse or absent (USFWS, 1993). The majority of snowy plovers are site faithful, returning to the same breeding site in subsequent breeding seasons. Birds often nest in exactly the same locations as the previous year (USFWS, 1993). Birds winter in habitats similar to those used during the nesting season. Snowy plovers forage on invertebrates in the wet salt pans, spoil sites, and along the edges of salt marshes and salt ponds. Because of their reliance on interior wetland and playa lake habitats, monitoring of snowy plover breeding and wintering populations is a good indicator of the availability and condition of interior wetland habitats.

Muleshoe - The snowy plover is a rare to uncommon migrant in all of Texas, a rare to uncommon summer resident in the northern Texas Panhandle area, and an uncommon winter resident along the Texas coast (Texas Ornithological Society, 1995). Locally, breeding is mostly confined to the saline lakes at Muleshoe NWR, but they have been observed at saline lakes in the surrounding counties.

Grulla - Snowy plovers are considered a summer resident and an occasional winter visitor in the southeastern part of New Mexico, and mainly observed on alkali beds near water (Hubbard, 1978). Most likely, this species occurred at Grulla NWR in the past when water was available in Salt Lake.

Swift Fox - The swift fox historically occurred throughout the Great Plains of North America, from southern Alberta/Saskatchewan Canada, and the United States from Montana to western Minnesota, south to New Mexico and the Texas Panhandle. Swift fox presently occurs throughout its historic range, but populations are disjunct. They are opportunistic predators, scavenging or feeding on small mammals, birds, reptiles, amphibians, fish, insects (especially grasshoppers and crickets), grasses, and berries. Their preferred habitat is plains grasslands and deserts with loose sandy soil, but they may also frequent pastures/rangelands, farm fields, and fence rows. Prairie development, prey reduction caused by habitat modification and prairie dog control programs, and indiscriminate predator control programs are major causes for its decline.

Swift foxes are known to occur in the Panhandle region of northwest Texas east to Menard County (Davis and Schimidly, 1994). It is listed as a furbearer in seven states including New Mexico and Texas and legally harvested in these states. Available harvest data from Texas is limited, but it shows an annual harvest of between 300 to 500 animals. New Mexico shows a significant decrease (95 percent) in the swift fox harvest in recent years. In New Mexico, the species is primarily found on Plain-Mesa Grassland and Desert Grassland habitat, commonly on soft soils that support large rodent populations such as kangaroo rats. Swift fox occur in eastern New Mexico; however, they are not found in cultivated areas of Curry or eastern Roosevelt Counties (Harrison and Schmitt, 1998).

Both refuges are within the range of the swift fox and may provide potential habitat, but this species has not been documented on either refuge.

Texas horned lizard (*Phrynosoma cornutum*) - This species' population trend is declining. The historic range of the Texas horned lizard includes Arizona, Arkansas, Colorado, Kansas, Louisiana, Missouri, New Mexico, Oklahoma, Texas and Mexico (Fed. Register 1994). It ranges from south central U.S. to northern Mexico and is found in arid and semiarid habitats in open areas with sparse vegetative cover throughout much of Texas, Oklahoma, Kansas, and New Mexico. Currently, it is state listed in Texas as a threatened species. Populations no longer exist in east Texas, are probably declining in north and central Texas, and appear stable in south and west Texas. It inhabits flat, open, generally dry country with little plant cover, except for bunchgrass and cactus. Strictly terrestrial, this lizard can bury itself in loose soil that is sandy, loamy or rocky. It seeks shelter under rocks (Garrett et.al 1987). The most important food item is ants, although beetles can also be an important food and other small invertebrates can also be consumed (Hammerson 1981, Pianka et. al 1975, Stebbins 1954). Pesticides, loss of habitat, the displacement of red ants by fire ants, and other causes are suspect in this species' decline (TPWD, 2000).

<u>Muleshoe</u> - Texas horned lizards have been observed on the refuge, but little is known about its abundance and distribution.

<u>Grulla</u> - Although this species may occur in Roosevelt County, New Mexico, it has not been documented on the refuge.

Texas horned lizard (photo courtesy of USFWS)

3.4 Socioeconomic Environment

3.4.1 Archaeological, Cultural, and Historical Resources

Over 11,000 years ago the area known as the High Plains was home to the Paleo-Indian Culture at Blackwater Draw. These people represent the oldest widely accepted Paleo-Indian culture located in the New World. During the past two thousand years the climate of east-central New Mexico has been getting dryer, thus the reason for being sparsely populated. The Comanche Indians were relatively late arrivals in this area of the High Plains, arriving around 1700. They used this arid High Plains, called by the first Spaniard explorers Llano Estacado, as their hunting grounds living mostly off the thousands of buffalo. The last Comanches were rounded up in 1874 and taken to a reservation at Fort Sill, Oklahoma. After this, the Comanche Indians were gone from the High Plains and it was then safe for cattlemen to set up ranches in the area.

Archaeological, cultural, and historic resources are protected by Federal law (Appendix G). The Service is responsible for surveys of areas affected by refuge management, and for the protection, preservation, and/or mitigation of any affected resource.

<u>Muleshoe NWR</u> - No comprehensive cultural resource surveys have been conducted on the refuge and, at this time, no significant historic, prehistoric, or cultural resources have been identified. However, various people in the

past have commented on Native American artifacts that were found on the refuge before it was established. In recent years pottery chards have been found on the service roads below the rock outcroppings. There are probably a number of undesignated archaeological sites on the refuge, particularly around the lakes.

Grulla NWR - At present, there is only one area of known archaeological significance on the refuge. In 1996, an extensive bison bone bed site was exposed from wind action eroding the surface sediments along the northwestern portion of Salt Lake. Researchers from Eastern New Mexico University in Portales conducted archeological field surveys, and data collection on bison age, sex, and possible cultural involved human exploitation patterns of the bison herd. Data suggested the bison were probably mired annually over a period of years and salvaged by humans as the opportunity arose. Bones of over 300 bison are believed to be in the lake bed. Carbon dating testing of horn sheaths revealed the time period to be in the early 15th century. The bone bed and lake margin were also surveyed for cultural remains and material. Stone artifacts were found in proximity of some of the bison remains. Should other resources be discovered, the refuge will incorporate measures to insure that such resources are protected for possible future study and investigative research.

Bison bones discovered in Salt Lake date back to the 15th Century (photo by Don Clapp)

Field investigations focused on identifying bison age and sex ratios and cultural involvement (photo by Don Clapp)

3.4.2   Land Use / Current Management

Muleshoe
The refuge is located in the southern half of Bailey County, Texas. Early in the 20th century the immense ranches began to break up, and in 1909 organized farming was introduced to this area of the High Plains. Large scale irrigation began in the late 1940s which resulted in the current mainstay of Bailey County, farming and agricultural related business. This county is the second smallest county in Texas, consisting of 827 square miles. In total, about 150,000 acres are irrigated. About 60 percent of the

land base is used for cropland, whereas the other 40 percent is used for livestock production. A belt of tallgrass prairie and shrubs, known as the Muleshoe Sandhills, traverses the northern portion from west to east. North of these sandhills, croplands are extensive, consisting primarily of irrigated corn, soybeans, and vegetable crops, whereas crops to the south consist mostly of dryland cotton, wheat, and milo. Since the mid 1980s, several of the area's milo fields have been sown to grasses under the Federal Conservation Reserve Program, resulting in fewer feeding areas for cranes. Cattle and livestock is the largest industry in Bailey County. Much of the land base in Bailey County not planted in crops is heavily grazed.

Blackwater Draw crosses the county in a west to east direction immediately north of the sandhills, after entering Texas from New Mexico southeast of Clovis. Before the advent of irrigation and subsequent lowering of the water table, the draw received water from freshwater springs and flowed at least in years when precipitation was adequate. Yellow House Creek reaches south of Muleshoe NWR in the southeast corner, and angles toward the southeast into Cochran County. In addition to these two drainage systems, there are about 598 playas. Most are small, wet weather water bodies, but several larger saline lakes occur in the southern portion. These include White Lake, Paul's Lake, Goose Lake, Baileyboro Lake, Monument Lake, and Coyote Lake. Because of excessive underground water pumping for agriculture, these springs are now mostly dry.

In Bailey County, as in all counties of that area, soil erosion is a serious concern, particularly in regions with extensive cotton production. Much of the cropland south of the sandhills falls within the erosion category of more than 75 tons/acre/year (General Accounting Office, 1995). In localized areas, wind and water erosion have already removed much of the topsoil exposing caliche layers, thus decreasing soil productivity (Littlefield, 2000).

Grulla

This refuge is located in the northeast part of Roosevelt County, New Mexico, adjacent to the State line. Roosevelt County, which encompasses 2,457 square miles, is an agricultural county with more than 453,670 acres of cultivated crop land and 1,082,360 acres of rangeland. Roosevelt County leads New Mexico in the production of corn, milo, wheat, peanuts, alfalfa, and potatoes. The county is also the third leading milk producer in the state.

The refuge is surrounded by rangeland and agricultural land that is privately owned. Crops grown near the refuge include wheat, peanuts, cotton, and some milo.

Part of the lake bed of Salt Lake on Grulla NWR is classified as "saline land" which means that it must be kept in public ownership as long as that classification holds. Adjacent landowners are interested in a land exchange with the refuge. By acquiring land around the lake perimeter, a more regular boundary can be formed outside of the lake bed which would allow fencing. A fenced boundary would prevent cattle from roaming into the lake bed where they often get stuck.

Croplands

No crops are raised on either refuge; however, crops grown on the adjacent farmlands influence sandhill crane and waterfowl use on these refuges.

Various studies of sandhill crane use on the High Plains indicate that the amount of grain sorghum (milo) grown in the surrounding area is a factor in the selection of roost lakes by cranes. These birds also utilize adjacent winter wheat fields for feeding and resting, and cotton fields for daytime roosts.

The amount of surrounding cropland has been reduced as a result of the Conservation Reserve Program (CRP). The CRP was authorized by the 1985 Farm Security Act to reduce agricultural production on highly erodible lands. The program is administered by the U.S. Department's Farm Service Agency. It was initiated in Bailey County in 1987. Landowners receive annual payments for planting qualified erodible acres to grasses. The landowners are required to control weeds in the CRP lands and must adhere to other restrictions such as not haying or removing the grasses by other means. Program periods last for 10 years. Acreage was last initiated into the program in 1997. Before the CRP there were 545,000 acres of the farm land in Bailey County. Since 1987 over 100,000 acres, 35 percent of Bailey County, was in CRP. The Muleshoe NWR is nearly completely surrounded by CRP lands for several miles in all directions except to the north where a few fields on adjacent private land are normally planted to wheat.

Sandhill cranes feeding in milo fields adjacent to the refuge (photo by Don Clapp)

Sandhill cranes foraging on crops planted on private lands can result in damage to production. The refuge provides assistance with this problem by lending scare devices to local private land owners (local farmers, ranchers, and feedlots) that request them. The refuge currently has 6-8 of these devises available for loan.

Water Management and Quality

Water is the fundamental component for providing habitats for waterfowl, neotropical birds, other migratory birds, and resident wildlife. The refuges do not have direct control over most factors affecting water quality and quantity. Local and regional water use, over time, has lowered the groundwater aquifer which has affected the groundwater resources throughout the area.

Muleshoe NWR

Historically, the refuge provided habitat for thousands of migrating and wintering waterfowl and other wetland-dependent wildlife. The Ogallala Aquifer has provided a substantial amount of surface water to the area through springs and seeps. This aquifer has dropped over 80 feet since 1970. This is a result of pumping water from the aquifer for urban and agricultural use beyond the aquifer's ability to recharge. The drop in the aquifer has dried up springs that fed the playas and saline lakes. With less water to provide habitat, waterfowl use has decreased. The lowering of the water table and the increased cost associated with pumping may result in a regional shift to dryland agriculture and grazing in the future.

The refuge wetlands are entirely dependent on rainwater and runoff. The State of Texas ruled that the water flowing into the refuge is dispersed groundwater and not subject to a claim of water rights. There are two springs on adjacent private lands that supply water to the north of upper Paul's Lake. Future efforts will focus on protecting springs and seeps providing water to the refuge and developing alternative water sources for refuge wetlands.

The main water source for Upper Paul's Lake is Grundy's Spring, which is located on private land adjacent to the lake (photo by Don Clapp)

Wetlands on Muleshoe NWR have the capacity to provide approximately 1,000 surface acres of habitat. The three major lakes on the refuge are Paul's Lake, White Lake, and Goose Lake. The year round water in Paul's Lake is provided by an underground spring located on private land. The other two lakes hold water from runoff provided by precipitation and irrigation drain water from adjacent lands. These three lakes have been divided into six impoundments by dikes built in the late 1930s. Of the six units on the refuge, only the upper side of Paul's Lake holds water all year. Waterfowl primarily use Upper Paul's Lake where water depths usually range from two to four feet during the winter season. White Lake and Lower Goose Lake do not hold water for long periods. All lakes, except Upper Goose Lake and Paul's Lake, are heavily alkaline. Prior to the early 1960s, Upper Goose Lake provided the most reliable amount of wetland habitat until construction of an upstream dam on private land captured the runoff. Since then, this lake holds water only after heavy rains. Sandhill cranes roost on all refuge lakes when water is present. The refuge plans to acquire an easement to protect the spring feeding Paul's Lake. There is little potential to develop additional wells on the refuge. Attempts to locate other reliable water sources for these lakes during the past 60 years have been unsuccessful.

The National Atmospheric Deposition Program supported by the U.S. Geological Survey is conducting an Acid Rain Deposition Study on Muleshoe NWR, initiated in 1985. A precipitation station was set up on the refuge, and refuge personnel have been collecting pH and conductivity data. Data from the year 2000 have a PH range of 4.74 to 7.18 and specific conductance measurements from 4.8 to 53.9 (Scott Dossett, pers comm).

Grulla NWR
There is limited potential for water development on this refuge. Salt Lake only holds water occasionally. Normal rainfall provides insufficient runoff for this large basin to maintain water on a regular basis. What water does find its way to the lake is lost through evaporation and seepage through the lake's sand bottom.

There is one potential area of a point source pollution problem for Grulla NWR. Several years ago, the county buried cans of pesticides and other contaminants in a dry wash approximately one-half mile west southwest of Grulla NWR. Surface erosion through heavy precipitation could transport contaminants into the wetland habitat.

Grazing

Historically, grazing by large bison herds maintained the grasslands in a natural condition. Livestock grazing is now a habitat management tool used to enhance, support, and achieve established wildlife management objectives. Controlled cattle grazing can duplicate the effects of bison, elk, and pronghorn on grasslands by removing dead vegetation and providing hoof cultivation. This aerates the soils and re-seeds native plants which prevents plant stagnation and promotes plant succession. Improved range conditions from effective grazing practices can provide habitat conditions that are desirable for a wide diversity of animal populations.

Muleshoe

The refuge has historically had some form of a grazing program since its early years. Refuge records show that in the late 1930s when the refuge was established, refuge grasslands were severely over-grazed by previous landowners. During the early 1940s a refuge grazing program was initiated. A local livestock owner that had previously grazed the refuge lands when they were privately owned was selected as the grazing permittee and allowed to graze cattle on the refuge year round.

Cattle grazing has occurred in the area since before the refuge was established (photo by Don Clapp)

In the early 1980s, Service personnel re-evaluated the refuge's grazing program. The result was the creation of seven grazing units comprising a total of 4,466 acres. The seven units ranged in size from 474 acres to 859 acres. Grassland composition comprised one unit of primarily grama grasses, two units of mostly alkali sacaton (cattle do not prefer to graze alkali sacaton if other grasses are present), and the remaining four units consisted of a mixture of grama grasses, alkali sacaton as well as a mixture of other native grasses including buffalograss, vine mesquite, western wheatgrass, sand dropseed, and silver bluestem. Some of these units included woody plants such as honey mesquite (mesquite is spread by grazing during periods when the seed pods are mature), four-winged salt bush, and sand sage.

The modified grazing program was a rest rotation system using electric fencing. The unit fencing allowed livestock to enter refuge lake shores and riparian areas. Watering sites were situated near either end of the units to distribute grazing utilization. Two grazing units were rested each year with none of the remaining units being grazed during the same time of the year two years in succession. The grazing period was reduced to six months for the dates of May through October. The permit was renewed each year to the same permittee as long as the permittee met refuge grazing specifications. The same grazing permittee was allowed to graze cattle (a cow calf operation) on the refuge since it was established until 2000. The maximum number of livestock allowed was set at 80 AUM's. Grazing was regulated by the Refuge Manager. This was correlated with grassland condition. If grass conditions were poor for the entire six month season, AUM numbers would be lower than 80 or no grazing would be allowed at all. If grass conditions became poor during the grazing season, the permittee was notified either to discontinue grazing altogether or to reduce the number of AUM's.

Grassland condition was monitored by grassland enclosures, individual unit grass composition sites, grass clipping weight measurement comparisons, and pre and post grazing evaluation of individual units conducted by the Refuge Manager and U.S. Department of Agriculture Grassland Specialists.

The refuge's grazing program has continued to exist in this form although active grazing has not been conducted since the year 2000. Present refuge planning (the proposed action) includes grassland evaluation to include fire as a management objective and to use a revised grazing program decreased in acreage by more than 50 percent and utilized objectively as a management technique in conjunction with prescribed burning when and where either management technique is deemed appropriate by the refuge Manager. The revised grazing program will include only primary species grasses in individual units and will include livestock and wildlife watering sites at each end of individual unit in order to strive for optimum utilization of refuge grasslands by both livestock and wildlife. The grazing period will be from April through September.

The objective of the refuge's proposed grazing plan is to decrease the number of grazable acres from 4,466 to 2,217 (reduced from 77 to 38 percent of the refuge acreage). The refuge's available acres in the proposed prescribed burning plan will consist of 1808 acres (31 percent of refuge acreage). The remaining 1,733 acres includes the refuge headquarters, campground and wildlife observation areas, and the refuge's three playa lakes. The four proposed grazing units will only be burned when any plant management other than grazing is required. Each of the four units have a watering site at either end in order to disperse livestock utilization. Presently the existing grazing units (see Map 6) are fenced to allow cattle to enter the refuge lakes and other riparian areas. The proposed grazing program will modify unit fences for restriction of livestock from these areas in order to enhance wildlife habitat (see Map 7).

Two of the proposed units consist primarily of alkali sacaton grasses. These alkali sacaton grasses primarily grow adjacent to refuge lakes in alkaline soils. Although these grasses are monotypic in the areas they are found, they are important in preventing wind erosion of the light soils in which they grow. Since few other plants grow in these alkaline areas, alkali sacaton does provide habitat for some grassland birds and other wildlife such as raptors, rodents, badgers, foxes, and coyotes.

Alkali sacaton grasses are less palatable than grama and other refuge grasses for livestock grazing. Cattle will graze these grasses when they are succulent. This normally occurs in the spring and fall although sacaton grass is not usually as palatable in the fall as during the spring. This varies according to the time rainfall is received during the grazing season. Grazing on these alkali sacaton units will be scheduled for the time periods that grass utilization will be most effective for management purposes.

The other two units in the proposed grazing plan consist primarily of grama grasses and other native grasses. These units are the refuge's best examples of natural grass stands. Little mesquite or other invasive plants are evident in these areas. This is partly due to the soil types of these areas. Fire would normally not be required as a management tool in these units as long as grazing was conducted. According to most range management authorities, these grama grasses do not normally respond well

Muleshoe National Wildlife Refuge

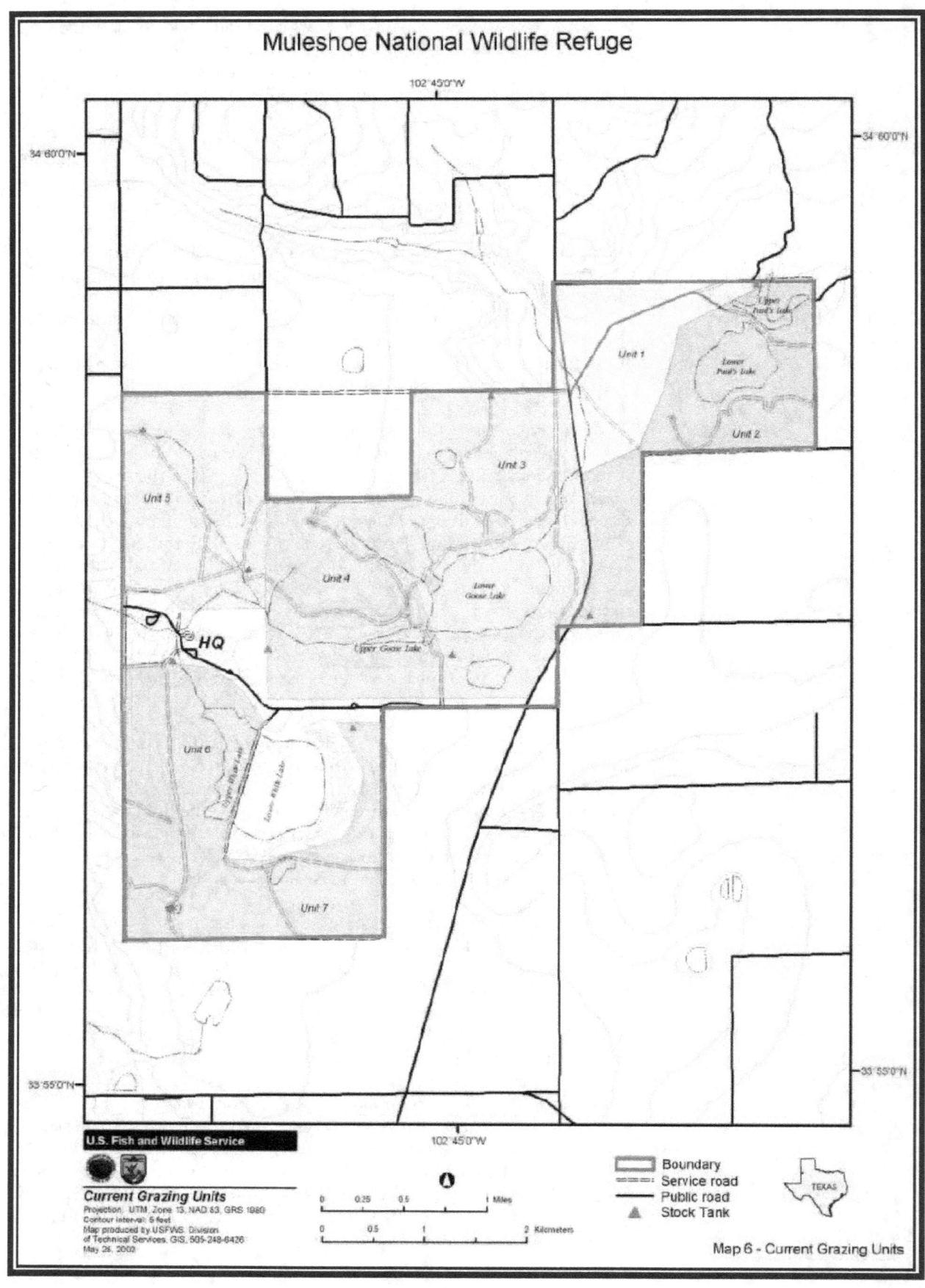

U.S. Fish and Wildlife Service

Current Grazing Units
Projection: UTM, Zone 13, NAD 83, GRS 1980
Contour interval: 5 feet
Map produced by USFWS, Division
of Technical Services, GIS, 505-248-6426
May 26, 2002

Boundary
Service road
Public road
Stock Tank

TEXAS

Map 6 - Current Grazing Units

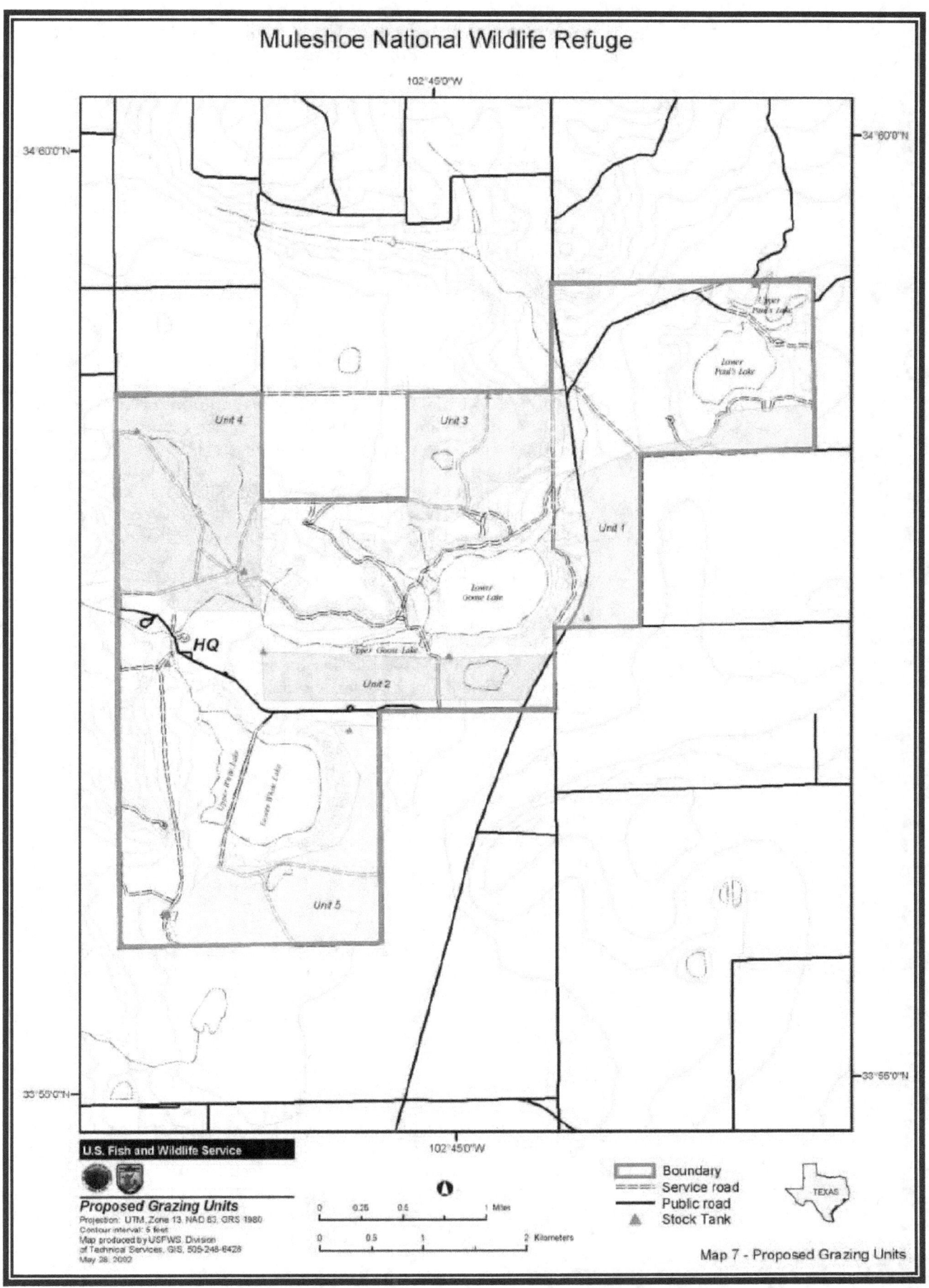

Muleshoe National Wildlife Refuge

102°46'0"W

34°60'0"N

Unit 4

Unit 3

Upper Pauls Lake

Lower Pauls Lake

Unit 1

Lower Goose Lake

Upper Goose Lake

HQ

Unit 2

Upper White Lake

Lower White Lake

Unit 5

33°55'0"N

102°45'0"W

U.S. Fish and Wildlife Service

Proposed Grazing Units
Projection: UTM, Zone 13, NAD 83, GRS 1980
Contour interval: 5 feet
Map produced by USFWS Division
of Technical Services, GIS, 505-248-6428
May 28, 2002

0   0.25   0.5   1 Miles
0   0.5   1   2 Kilometers

Boundary
Service road
Public road
▲ Stock Tank

TEXAS

Map 7 - Proposed Grazing Units

to prescribed burning depending upon available soil moisture before and after burning occurs. Properly managed grazing in these grama grass units has proven to be beneficial for wildlife habitat by providing open areas for wildlife travel and creating plant diversity.

There are 10 stock tanks that provide water to livestock on the refuge (shown on Maps 6 & 7). These watering areas are also important for wildlife and would likely be maintained in all the management alternatives. Four of the tanks are supplied by windmills. The other six tanks are supplied through an underground pipeline from the domestic well, which is the sole source of water for the headquarters and residence. Another well was dug in 1997 to separate the livestock waters from the domestic water supply; however, water from this new well is very saline and has not been used to date.

Permittee selection for refuge grazing will be conducted by sealed bid in order to avoid possible land owner conflicts regarding the selection procedure. It is beneficial to the refuge to maintain the same permittee over several grazing seasons. It is also a beneficial to retain a permittee that maintains a cow herd, as opposed to an operator that grazes stocker or replacement cattle that are taken to market annually. Replacement cattle are new to the area each year and tend to be difficult to hold in fenced areas. On the other hand, a mature cow herd generally consists of the same animals each year and tend to be gentle and easier to manage and hold in fenced areas. Bid selection would designate cow herds only. Cattle owners, especially those with cow herds, prefer to rent the same pastures year after year. This is also a benefit to the refuge since permittees having grazing lands for only one year are not as apt to be as efficient managers as those returning the following year. Bid selection would state a term of allowed selection, preferably three years or more. Management options such as numbers of AUM's and whether to graze or not depending upon grassland conditions would still be in place. Selection requirements would also demand that the qualified bidder be an active cattle owner and operator and have base operations within a reasonable distance (20 or 30 mile radius) from the refuge.

Grulla

There is no managed grazing program on the refuge. However, cattle from adjacent private lands have grazed on Grulla NWR since 1969 when the land was acquired from the BLM. There is difficulty fencing the refuge because of the irregular boundary and limited access points to the refuge. Currently, approximately 570 acres of the refuge's 900 acres of grassland is being actively grazed. Some parts of the refuge are considered over-grazed. Approximately 200 acres on the east end of the refuge was fenced in 1985 to restrict trespass grazing from this area. Other segments of the refuge boundary on both sides of the lake have cross fences or adjacent farm fields which serve to keep cattle off the refuge.

Fire Management

Fire was a natural factor on most wildlands and probably no range site with its associated plant community has developed without being influenced by fire (Vallentine, 1971). Relative to the specific historical role of fire in the shortgrass prairie and more specifically, the Texas Panhandle Region, it is clear that historical fire occurrence, or absence thereof, has been the single most pronounced factor in the development and shaping of these ecosystems

(Humphrey, 1962; Stoddart and Smith, 1955). Sauer (1950) has gone so far as to propose that the primary cause of grassland development and maintenance was fire, and not climate. According to Sauer, "grasslands occur where a combination of conditions, primarily climate and topography, make possible the reoccurrence of periodic fires. In part, this theory would explain why grassland areas and prairies are maintained naturally as such, even though they are climatically capable of growing woody plants or even trees."

One can only speculate as to the historical frequency of fire that was required to keep the grassland brush free. A 1984 study of the subject in the Northern Great Plains between 1940 and 1984 (Higgins, 1984) indicates that lightning caused an average of one fire per year per 650 square miles, a fairly significant occurrence. According to Chandler et al. (1983), the fire frequency for the true shortgrass prairie of the southeast United States is estimated to be between one and twelve years. The regular, recurring nature of fire in the region has been otherwise well documented by Stewart (1955) and Hanson (1939). However, due to the lack of trees in the area, historical fire frequency data from tree ring analysis is not readily available and therefore the historical fire occurrence prior to record keeping is difficult to reconstruct. According to Humphrey (1962), historical fires set by lightning and Native Americans were an annual occurrence in the tallgrass prairie, east of the 100th meridian, but were not recorded as often in the more arid shortgrass prairie. He attributes the reason for this as the diminished precipitation with progress westward and that the greater severity of droughts provided less fuel at most times, and in some years produced too little plant growth for fire spread. This fact is supported by studies conducted by Sharrow and Wright (1977), which suggest that damage to soil and grasses as documented by repeated burning frequencies of less than five years would have prevented the evolution of the shortgrass prairie as it exists today (reference to current species composition and density).

What is perhaps most obvious at Muleshoe and Grulla NWRs, when refuge lands are compared to lands more heavily frequented by fire, is the accumulation of invaders and brush species in the absence of fire, as well as the accumulation of unnatural dead, aboveground biomass. At Muleshoe NWR, it is the prevalence of honey mesquite (*Prosopis glandulosa*), and broom snakeweed (*Xanthocephalum sarothrae*) on upland sites that indicate an absence of fire from the ecosystem.

Muleshoe
Recent fire records at Muleshoe NWR date back to 1962 with large gaps in the records from 1966 through 1983. Unquestionably, these records do not accurately reflect total fire occurrence. The most recent ten year fire occurrence history for the refuge, 1989 through 1999, reflects an occurrence of six wildfires for 153 acres burned, an average of 0.6 fires per year. With respect to fire size, the relatively large average fire size is indicative of the flashy fuels and models present on the refuge. Final fire size would normally have been much larger except for fire breaks within and immediately adjacent to the refuge, and the fact that most fires were aggressively fought once discovered. Although most fires occurred from March through August of each year, fires occurred in all months of the year.

The alkali sacaton grass has been burned on an as needed basis since stands of older grass tend to become clumped with bare soil exposed between clumps. Although few other plant species will grow in the highly alkaline soils surrounding the refuge playa lakes, the burning rejuvenates these dense grass strands.

Controlled burning (500 acres) was last conducted on the refuge in 2000. Grazing of the sacaton grasses during the spring and fall alleviates the need for controlled burning. Controlled burning of the other grasses such as blue grama, sideoates grama, and buffalo grass has not been conducted.

Grulla
No fire records were found for Grulla NWR.
Prescribed burning has not been a part of the habitat management on the refuge and is not likely to be used in the foreseeable future. Small tracts of grasslands and irregular boundaries are contributing factors for not conducting prescribed burning on the Grulla NWR.

Fire Management Plan
A current, Service approved, Fire Management Plan (FMP) exists for the Muleshoe NWR. It also pertains to Grulla NWR and 620 acres of fee title inventory lands, all administered by the Muleshoe NWR. Inventory lands will be referred to as refuges for the remainder of this text. Any specifics regarding all refuge lands will be covered in individual prescribed burning proposals. The comprehensive FMP will be implemented as part of a holistic approach to management in the High Plains region. The plan meets the fire management planning and policy requirements of the Service as specified in 621 FWS and Departmental Manual 620. These policies recognize the natural or unnatural occurrence or absence of fire as an integral factor influencing all ecosystems. The plan was reviewed and approved with an understanding and acceptance of these policies and the enabling legislation which created the refuges.

This plan was written to address the suppression of wildfire and the use of management ignited (prescribed) fire for accomplishing resource management objectives. The thrust of the plan is to document the occurrence and habitat requirements of species which occur in all Service administered lands as well as the historical and current fire regimes of the southern high plains region of Texas and New Mexico. The plan also provides recommendations for managing fire and the schedule, operational procedures, and fiscal resources required for complete implementation of these recommendations. It must be emphasized that for purposes of overall refuge administration, the Service manages each land tract discussed in this plan as a separate refuge unto itself, within the greater Refuge System. However, for fire management purposes and for purposes of describing suppression and prescribed fire strategies, the refuges are referred to collectively throughout the plan as the High Plains Fire Management Complex, or simply Complex. Fire management unit descriptions and prescribed burning prescriptions and frequencies, as described within the text, apply equally to all Service administered lands. The intent of the FMP is to operationally bind all units as one with respect to fire management operations and program administration.

Significant decisions and findings contained within the plan are as follows:

- Historically, fires occurred frequently within the region. Prior to modern day farming and irrigation practices, these fires had the potential to exceed many thousands of acres in size. Fires which occur today can best be described as fast moving, moderate to high intensity surface fires. These fires can and have occurred at any time of year.

- Lightning caused fires are a routine natural phenomena within the southern plains and historically, probably had a major ecological influence in the maintenance of some shrubfree grasslands within the Complex. According to fire records, these fires are thought to contribute approximately 20 percent of the total fire occurrence.

- Appropriate Management (suppression) Response (AMR) is to be implemented, aggressive initial attack and immediate suppression strategies will be employed within and in immediate proximity to the Complex lands (and within the urban interface).

- The construction of a fuelbreak network in all the refuges is required in order to effectively implement the FMP. Existing physical barriers will be utilized whenever possible, some existing fuelbreaks will require maintenance and some new fuelbreaks will require construction within all the units.

- Prescribed fire will be used throughout the Complex to reduce hazardous fuels and to accomplish specific resource management objectives, especially invasive plant species control and wildlife habitat management. The frequency of control and the number of acres managed by prescribed burning will vary depending upon management decisions based on factors which include but are not limited to climate and current management objectives.

- The Complex will host a comprehensive fire management program with participation required at all levels within the Service. Although the operational involvement of regular, on site field station employees will be limited due to staff size, authorized support roles will be assumed by refuge personnel. This involvement is critical to the long-term implementation of the program. On site refuge staff will be responsible for long-term direction, some program administration, and for providing supervisory and approval authority for all actions taken by the District Fire Management Officer (DFMO). Most operational aspects will be charged to the DFMO and staff. The Fire Management District (FMD) presently responsible for fire operations for the Complex is the Wichita Mountains NWR. The planned fire management strategy for the Complex is to retain a staff of at least three seasonal fire crew members stationed at the Muleshoe NWR for the purpose of providing initial fire suppression response and to conduct or assist in conducting prescribed burns. This fire crew would be responsible for all Muleshoe NWR Complex fires including Buffalo Lake NWR. Not only is it critical to have firefighting personnel present for immediate wildfire suppression, it would benefit the prescribed burning in order to be able to burn immediately whenever optimum burning conditions prevailed. When not needed for Muleshoe NWR and Buffalo Lake NWR, the crew would be available to assist the Regional Fire Districts in fire suppression or management activities as required. Both Muleshoe NWR and Buffalo Lake each presently have 200 gallon fire suppression pump units mounted on one ton trucks.

Muleshoe National Wildlife Refuge

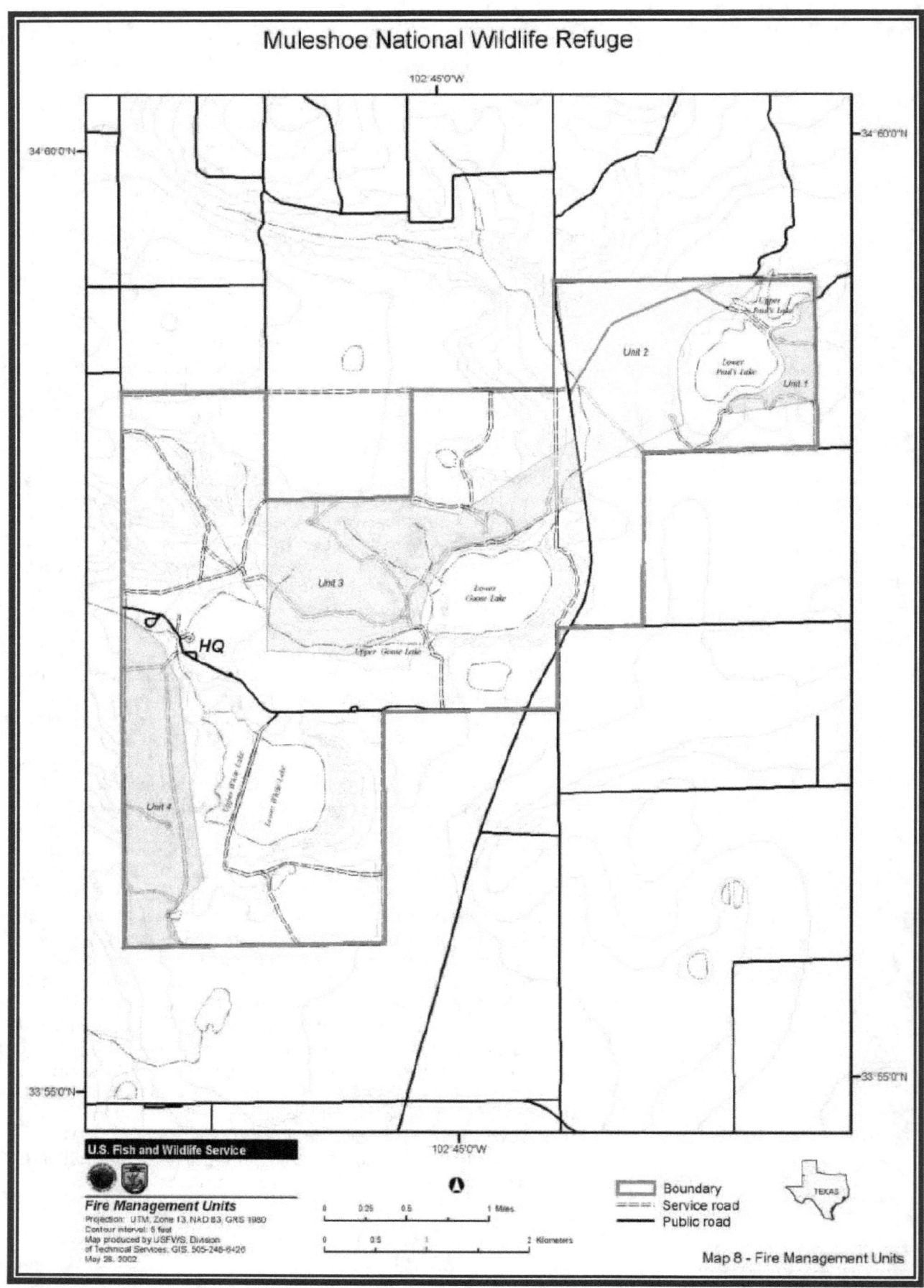

- Interagency communications and cooperation is essential for the full and effective implementation of this plan. The Complex will maintain cooperative agreements with local, state, and other federal agencies as a means of providing for initial attack fire suppression actions and some assistance in prescribed burning.

The first full year of plan implementation is scheduled for FY2004. The implementation schedule of the rotational prescribed fire program proposed in the FMP was initiated in the spring of CY 2000. Proposed Fire Management Units are shown on Map 8.

Fee Title Lands and Easements

In 1997, 640 acres of fee title or inventory transfer lands became the management responsibility of the Muleshoe NWR. The Service received these tracts of land from the Farm Service Administration (FSA), Department of Agriculture. These lands came to the FSA through foreclosure, voluntary conveyance, or conservation easements. Acquisition of these lands by the Service was the result of Farm Bill guidelines that specified establishment of wetland conservation easements or fee title wetlands. Two tracts are 80 miles from the refuge in Hale County and one tract is 130 miles away in Dickens County near Lubbock. These lands are primarily composed of playa lakes, grasslands, and retired farmlands. Tract 10 is 160 acres of native grasses and shrubs. Tract 11 consists of 325 acres of native grasses and shrubs, and two intermittent playa lakes. Tract 12 is 160 acres containing an intermittent lake and fallow farm lands and facilities, with current vegetation composed of native and exotic species. The refuge also has six conservation easement areas in Lubbock County and other surrounding counties. The terms of the easements vary with each parcel, but generally disallow development such as farming and building structures. Most of the easements encompass areas with playa lake beds.

Inventory Land near Spur, Texas (photo by Don Clapp)

The Service Realty Division has completed ownership history and other research on these parcels with funds from the Ecological Service Division. Most of the parcels, particularly the easements, need ground surveys completed and placement of survey markers and boundary signs. The Service has currently invested limited funds and no management efforts on these parcels. The managers occasionally visit the parcels they can locate to check that no development has occurred, and the farmers continue to be in compliance with the agreement. Without appropriate survey markers, refuge managers are uncertain as to the exact location of many of the easements they are responsible for.

The Service is responsible for the protection of resources on both the fee title and easement lands and the maintenance of these properties. Presently nothing can be done regarding management of the two tracts in Hale County, pending resolution of title transaction difficulties.

Land Protection

Muleshoe

A parcel of private land on the north side of Muleshoe NWR has a spring that feeds into Paul's Lake providing habitat for migratory birds. Protection of this valuable water source should be a high priority. The challenge will be to facilitate the means to engage that protection. Some options include purchasing an easement interest or working out some type of agreement with the private land owner regarding the flows. In addition, the refuge would benefit if lands adjacent to the current boundary that could provide important wildlife habitat became available for sale. Purchases of interests in land or water rights would only be done from willing sellers. The Service could first pursue discussions that would result in expansion of the refuge boundary and eventual acquisition of smaller parcels adjacent to the existing refuge boundaries. Secondly, priorities would include water sources, buffer zones or filter strips around playas on FSA fee title lands and easements. Any future proposals to acquire or exchange lands would require separate NEPA and other policy compliance.

Grulla

Improvement of access for management purposes and wildlife observation opportunities at Grulla NWR is a priority. Currently, the refuge boundary is irregular and intersects the Salt Lake bed. The Service could pursue discussions that would lead to a purchase of interest in land adjacent to Salt Lake and on the perimeter of the refuge would move the boundary from the lake bed to solid ground that would enable fencing. However, the Service could and should also investigate how agreements with adjacent land owners might help with the access question.

Possibilities may exist for conducting a land exchange with landowners adjacent to Grulla NWR. An exchange would provide the refuge a strip of solid land around the lake bed that would allow the boundary to be fenced. The adjacent landowners would benefit by this land exchange, as fencing would prevent cattle from trespassing into the lake bed. Any future proposals to acquire or exchange lands would require separate NEPA and other policy compliance.

Depending upon the size of any potential purchase of an interest in lands (i.e. fee simple or easement), such action might be within the discretionary authority of the Regional Director and not subject to the larger boundary expansion procedures.

Wilderness Review

The Wilderness Act of 1964 created the National Wilderness Preservation System. This system sets aside federal lands having wilderness qualities in protected status for preservation. The National Wilderness Preservation includes federal lands managed by the National Park Service, Bureau of Land Management, Forest Service, and Fish and Wildlife Service.

Areas nominated for Wilderness designation must exhibit special characteristics listed in the Wilderness Act (U.S.C. 1121). Such an area:

> "...(1) generally appears to have been affected primarily by the forces of nature, with the imprints of man's work substantially unnoticeable; (2) has outstanding opportunities for solitude or primitive and unconfined

type of recreation; (3) has at least five thousand acres of land or is of sufficient size as to make practicable its preservation and use in an unimpaired condition; and (4) may also contain ecological, geological, or other features of scientific, educational, scenic, or historic value."

Designated Wilderness areas are set aside for preservation through strict limitations on use of mechanized transportation or tools. Motorized vehicle use is generally prohibited within Wilderness, as is use of power tools. Exceptions to these restrictions are typically allowed only for emergency or other unusual conditions, on a case-by-case basis.

Per the policies of the National Wildlife Refuge System Improvement Act of 1997, all refuge CCPs must include a review of the refuge's potential for Wilderness designation. There is little potential for Wilderness designation of lands within either refuge, for the following reasons.

Muleshoe

The refuge encompasses a total of 5,809 acres. Although much of it exemplifies preagricultural conditions of the shortgrass prairie habitat of the High Plains and it has been designated as a registered landmark (The High Plains Natural Area), it has been determined that the refuge does not conform to the definition of a wilderness, as described in the Wilderness Act of 1964. The area has been noticeably affected by humans (roads, grazing, and other management activities). There are no extensive undisturbed areas that provide for outstanding solitude and possibly primitive recreational opportunities. In addition, designation of a wilderness area that meets the standards of the Wilderness Act (+/- 5,000 acres) could potentially conflict with other land management goals and priorities of the Service focused on providing suitable wildlife habitat for migratory birds and resident wildlife.

Grulla

This refuge encompasses only 3,236 acres, considerably less than the 5,000 acre general minimum endorsed in the Wilderness Act. Opportunities for recreation on the refuge are also limited due to the lack of access and the barren/featureless nature of the area. The refuge also lacks opportunities for solitude due to the adjacent farm lands and highway. These human developments, as well as past and ongoing cattle trespass, limit the refuge's wilderness potential.

Research

This section details research that has been conducted on the refuge. Although no new specific research proposals have been identified, there are opportunities to investigate proposals for bird research and monitoring; habitat restoration and enhancement; grazing impacts, fire ecology, specifically long-term studies of ecological response of plant and animal species diversity and abundance to prescribed fire and grazing; and cooperative studies to measure water and chemical movement from the surface to the aquifer. The refuge will develop a Strategic Research Plan (see section 6.4.3) that will describe the research needed to support management goals and objectives.

The National Atmospheric Deposition Program supported by the U.S. Geological Survey is conducting an Acid Rain Deposition Study on Muleshoe NWR, initiated in 1985. A precipitation station was set up on the refuge, and refuge personnel have been collecting pH and Conductivity data (as an indication of salinity or TDS-total dissolved solids) on the precipitation collected. The refuge was chosen as a control because no problems had been identified in the area.

A study of hydrological assessments of broom snakeweed and sideoats grama grass on a discrete range site and soil series was conducted by a PhD student at Texas Tech University in Lubbock, Texas. This assessment includes comparing successional levels on range condition classes with infiltration runoff in broom snakeweed and sideoats grama grass sites, sedimentation rates on discrete range sites, and soil series. Field work for this study was initiated in 1992 and completed in 1994. Findings of the research contributed to data regarding hydrologic and edaphologic processes relating to rangeland watersheds. The following conclusions were determined: Infiltration rates are usually greater and sediment concentration rates lower among broom snakeweed and grama grass clumps and bare ground areas, in comparison to established vegetation stands.

During the 1970s, an exposed mammoth tusk was discovered in one of Muleshoe's dry lakes. Recently, an extensive bison bone bed site was exposed in Salt Lake on the Grulla NWR. Researchers from Eastern New Mexico University in Portales conducted archaeological field studies on this site. The area has a unique geology and analysis of pollen samples taken from the lake sediments indicate new evidence regarding the age of the glacier lake basin sediment. This area holds a great opportunity for further research and there is much interest in continuing various investigations at these sites.

A study was initiated in 1998 on the distribution and use of habitat by breeding shorebirds in the Playa Lakes Region of Texas and the evolution and maintenance of monogamy in American avocets. The objectives of this study are to (1) determine species composition and distribution of breeding shorebirds in the Playa Lakes Region of Texas, (2) examine macro- (i.e., wetland scale) and micro- (within wetland) habitat selection by individual shorebird species during the breeding season, (3) examine factors affecting nesting success and nest site selection of the most numerous breeding shorebird species, and (4) develop conservation and management plans for breeding shorebirds.

A study was initiated in 1999 on the distribution and use of habitat by lesser sandhill cranes breeding in Siberia and wintering in the Playa Lakes Region of Texas. Objectives of this study include determining the distribution of sandhill cranes breeding in Siberia and wintering in the Texas South Plains and examining the feeding habits of wintering cranes.

A study to investigate the movement of water and chemicals from the land surface to the water table in the southern High Plains aquifer system is currently being conducted by the U.S. Geological Survey. The purpose is to measure the movement of water from the land surface to the water table in the Ogallala Aquifer and to determine downward velocities and recharge rates within the aquifer system. This study is expected to continue for five years. Data will be compared with that from irrigated sites on private lands. Information will be used to determine how both natural and human-applied water travels through the unsaturated zone and recharges the aquifer system.

Other Special Places

Muleshoe NWR does not have any research natural area, but the entire refuge consists of exceptional shortgrass prairie habitat and is part of the High Plains Natural Area, designated as a National Natural Landmark of the Great Plains Natural Region administered by the Department of Interior's National Park Service. Its unique features include shallow, flat bottomed depressions called playa lakes and shortgrass grama grasslands. The refuge provides partially pristine examples of what the surrounding area was like before agricultural development.

There are no research natural areas or other special areas on Grulla NWR.

3.4.3 Public Use and Wildlife-Dependent Recreational Activities

The National Wildlife Refuge System Improvement Act of 1997 recognizes six wildlife-dependent public uses including hunting, fishing, wildlife observation, photography, environmental education and interpretation that are to be given priority on refuges when determined to be compatible. Except where otherwise mandated by law, the Service must determine whether a particular use is compatible with refuge resources before permitting it. Compatibility determinations are normally made by the refuge manager, in accordance with guidelines developed by the Service. Under these guidelines, a compatible use is defined as one that "will not materially interfere with or detract from the purposes for which the refuge was established." Compatible uses support refuge purposes, or may have a neutral effect. In making a compatibility determination, the refuge manager must first determine if the use is compatible with refuge purposes strictly on biological grounds. After making such a determination, the refuge manager must further consider applicable laws, Service policy, and public opinion (Lee, 1986).

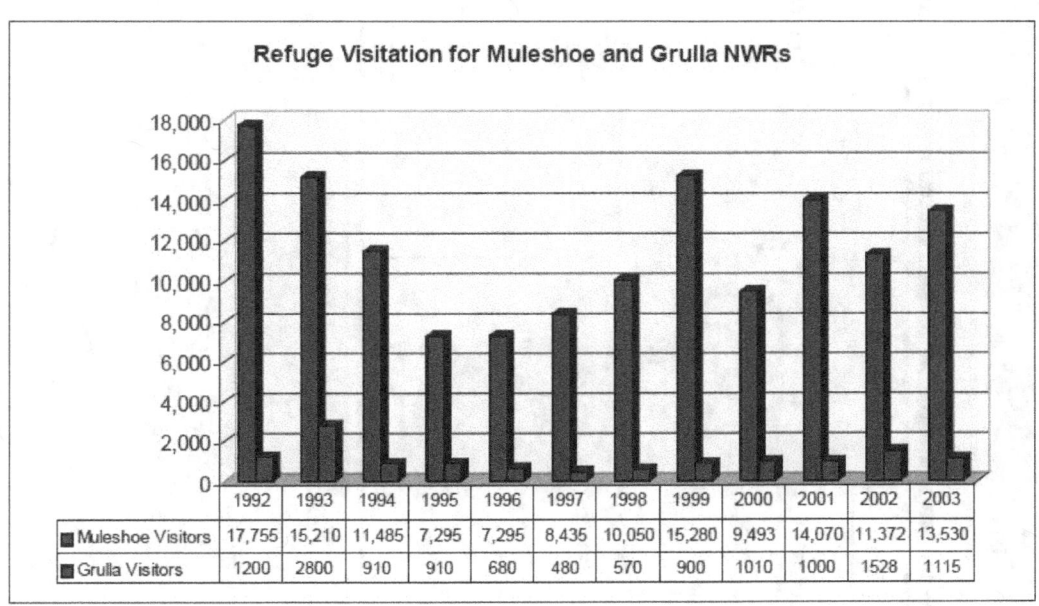

	1992	1993	1994	1995	1996	1997	1998	1999	2000	2001	2002	2003
■ Muleshoe Visitors	17,755	15,210	11,485	7,295	7,295	8,435	10,050	15,280	9,493	14,070	11,372	13,530
■ Grulla Visitors	1200	2800	910	910	680	480	570	900	1010	1000	1528	1115

In 2001, Muleshoe NWRs total visitor use was 15,000. During the 1990s, the average visitation at Muleshoe NWR was 11,338. Public use areas are illustrated on Map 9. Grulla NWR has received as many as 2,800 visitors in one year (1993), but average visitation from 1992 to 2000 was 1,051 visitors

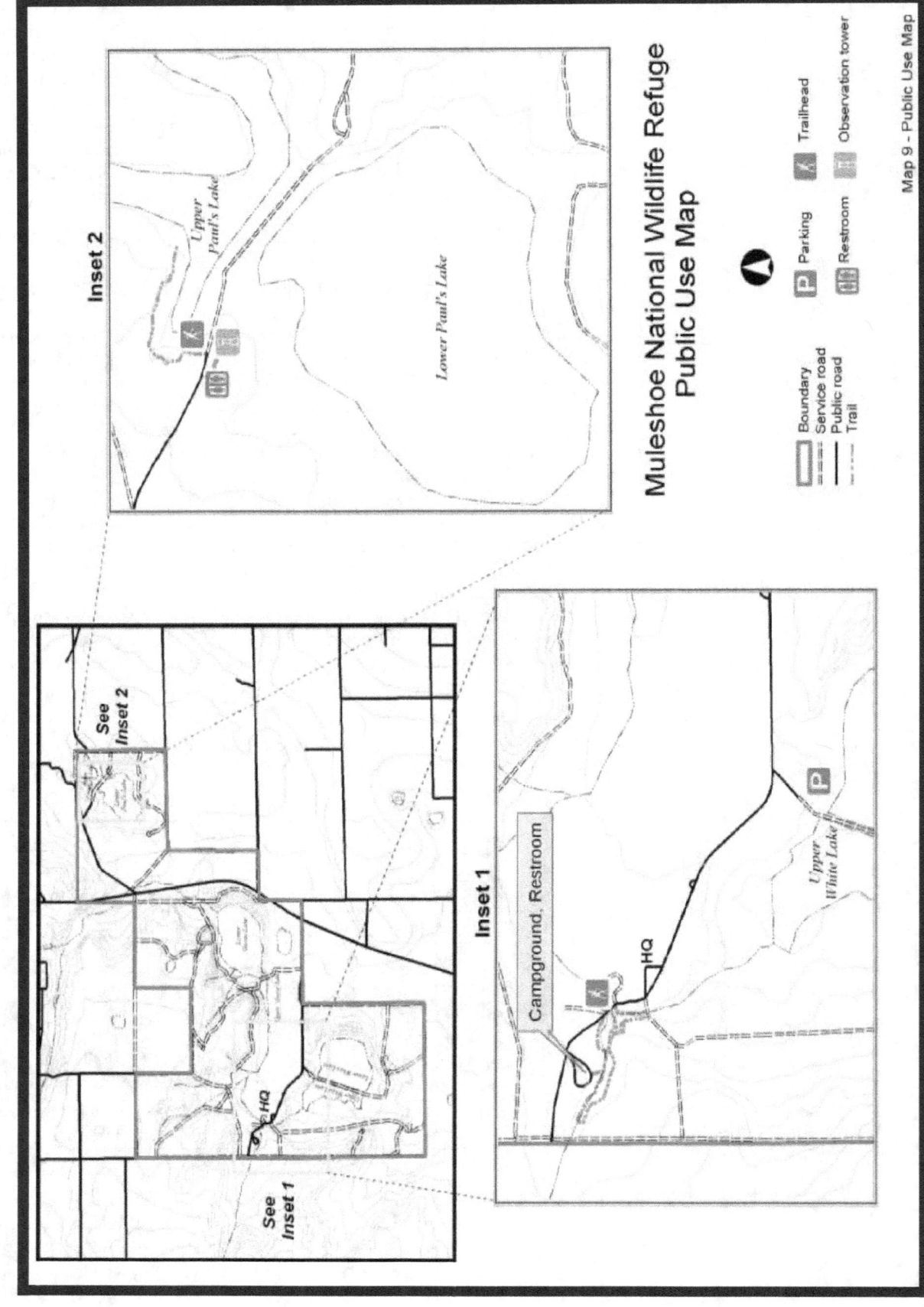

Muleshoe National Wildlife Refuge
Public Use Map

Inset 2

Upper Paul's Lake

Lower Paul's Lake

Inset 1

Campground, Restroom

Upper White Lake

HQ

See Inset 2

See Inset 1

HQ

Boundary
Service road
Public road
Trail

P Parking
Restroom
Trailhead
Observation tower

Map 9 - Public Use Map

The Refuge campground and picnic area attracts occasional wildlife-oriented camper throughout most of the year (photo by Don Clapp)

for the purpose of observing wildlife by walking or using motorized vehicles. Most people drive from Portales, New Mexico (30 miles west of the refuge). The refuge is a draw to many students from Eastern New Mexico University in Portales, New Mexico.

Hunting

Hunting has never been allowed on either refuge, but sandhill crane hunting does occur on adjacent private lands. The sandhill crane hunting season around the Muleshoe NWR lasts three months, from mid-November through mid-February. The New Mexico season is shorter and since there is a lack of available water, hunting does not typically occur around Grulla NWR.

Since hunting is one of the six priority wildlife-dependent public uses on national wildlife refuges, the TPWD requested that the refuge complete a compatibility determination on potential hunting opportunities. Through this compatibility determination (see Appendix F), it was determined that waterfowl and/or sandhill crane hunting on the refuges would harass the birds and/or deter them from using the area, which would materially interfere with the purpose of the refuges.

Limited hunting of common resident species was considered. For Muleshoe NWR, it was determined that hunting certain wildlife species would be compatible with the purpose of the refuge. Further investigation (in cooperation with TPWD) into whether current populations could sustain hunting; whether there is public demand for this activity; and whether a hunting program could safely be implemented on the refuge is necessary before deciding the type and extent of hunting opportunities that should be allowed on the refuge.

Grulla NWR lacks suitable populations, acreage, habitat, access, and personnel to sustain a hunting program. Therefore, the Service is not proposing that this refuge be open to hunting at this time.

Fishing

As a result of the unpredictable water supply and frequent drought, there are no recreational fishing opportunities at either refuge. In recent years stocking fish at Paul's Lake (Muleshoe NWR) and opening the area to public fishing has been considered. Recent water testing has indicated that the water could often be saline during mid summer and only salt tolerant fish species would be appropriate if stocking were implemented.

Wildlife Observation and Photography

Muleshoe
Wildlife viewing, photography, hiking, and camping are the recreational opportunities provided by the refuge. Approximately 20 percent of all visits occur during November and December, primarily for crane viewing. Over 95 percent of the wildlife viewing occurs at Paul's Lake, White Lake, and the prairie dog town exhibit. The parking area at White Lake is used by visitors when water and birds are present. There are two interpretive signs at this site. An overlook was constructed at Paul's Lake and opened to public access. Closed areas of the refuge are open to wildlife observation by special

permission. Photography is permitted in areas open to the public and by special permission throughout other parts of the refuge.

The refuge maintains a small eight site campground and picnic area located near the refuge headquarters. Providing this campground on the refuge is considered appropriate due to the remote location of the refuge and the lack of other over-night facilities in the area. This benefits the public by facilitating early morning crane viewing and other bird watching opportunities. Campground use is the highest during the fall months. The campground is the only exception to the refuge daytime use only regulation. The refuge provides potable water, vault toilets, picnic tables, and fire grills. There is also a fire pit in the center of the campground area. The use of fire is prohibited when conditions are extremely dry. Primary users include Boy Scout troops, tent campers, and retirees with travel homes. These facilities require minimal funding and staff time as they currently exist.

At various points on the refuge, entrance, interpretive, regulatory (boundary and traffic control), and informational signs have been installed to guide the public. Continued maintenance of existing signs, as well as installing additional ones as needed, aid in keeping refuge violations minimal.

The new wildlife observation platform at Paul's Lake has greatly enhanced wildlife viewing opportunities on the Refuge (photo by Don Clapp)

Refuge visitors observing sandhill cranes at Paul's Lake (photo by Donald R. Clapp)

Muleshoe NWR is identified as a stop on TPWD's Great Texas Wildlife Trails and the High Plains Birding Trail. For further information on these sites, please visit the following web-sites: http://www.tpwd.state.tx.us/birdingtrails/sites.htm#westheart and http://www.worldnaturetrails.com/nature_trails/tx_wildlife/muleshoe/

Grulla
The majority of public use at Grulla NWR pertains to wildlife and wildland observations. The primitive status of the refuge limits the potential for developing recreational opportunities at this site.

Public use improvements at Grulla NWR include one entrance road, parking area, and entrance signs. Since this is the only access point to the lake, visitors will occasionally walk over the grasslands to reach Salt Lake's shoreline. There is one small interpretive site on Grulla NWR accessed by a .8 mile road constructed between New Mexico Highway 88 and the interpretive area. The site includes parking pull-ins for five cars, a bare earth 175 ft. walking trail leading to a small self-guided interpretive area, and overlook. The two interpretive signs at the overlook area have recently been stolen. Funding has been requested for sign replacement.

Environmental Education and Interpretation

An office visitor center was constructed at Muleshoe NWR in 1982, with some exhibits being completed in 1986. The current displays consist of a few mounted photographs, a banding return map, and two display cases with bird mounts. The foyer of the office is open 24 hours a day and contains an orientation map of the refuge, a registration podium, and a leaflet dispenser. There are exhibits along Paul's Lake road and at the overlook. There are also several proposed projects to upgrade the interpretive program of both refuges including wayside exhibits and an informational exhibit at the Muleshoe NWR campground/picnic site.

Refuge staff provide few environmental education programs and outreach efforts. The Refuge Manager and Refuge Administrative Technician are involved with interpretation on a limited basis. An average of three to four programs per year are presented to scout groups, civic organizations, and school groups.

The Refuge Manager commonly provides interpretive programs to local school groups (photo by Glenda Copley)

Law Enforcement

<u>Muleshoe</u> - There is currently no law enforcement officer at Muleshoe NWR. The Refuge Manager has established a Memorandum of Understanding (MOU) with the state and county law enforcement authorities to include patrolling for Muleshoe. Because of the remote location of these two refuges, few violations occur. Most impacts of public use involves violations of refuge regulations such as disturbing wildlife, removing plants, littering, and vandalism.

<u>Grulla</u> - Enforcing refuge regulations is difficult because of the distance to Muleshoe NWR. Generally, the law enforcement incidents at Grulla NWR include vandalism at the parking lot as a result of its remote location, and trespass by people riding ORVs on the dry lake bed and hunters unaware of the boundary. These problems could be reduced with adequate posting and regular patrols.

3.4.4 Other Socioeconomic Features

Muleshoe NWR

The refuge is located in Bailey County, Texas, approximately 20 miles south of the town of Muleshoe. The town of Muleshoe is the county seat. Bailey County was a sparsely settled area of huge cattle ranches, but early in the 20th century, the immense ranches began to break up, and in 1909, organized farming was introduced to this area of the High Plains. Large scale irrigation began in the late 1940s which resulted in the current mainstay of Bailey County; farming and agricultural related business. The largest industry in Bailey County is cattle and ranching. Bailey County has the largest livestock sale facility in the region. Approximately 58,600 acres were planted with sorghum and 16,200 were planted with corn, the two major field crops in the county (National Agriculture Statistics Service, 1998 data). Other crops include cotton, various grains, and vegetables. The town of Muleshoe, organized in 1926, was named for the muleshoe brand of a famous early ranch. It has a total population of 4,530 people (2000 Census Data). Today, the town of Muleshoe is the only population center remaining in the county and is a center for marketing and shipping for the High Plains agricultural products. Other smaller communities in the area include Bula, Enochs, Maple, Goodland, Needmore, Stegall, Circleback, Baileyboro, Fairview, and Progress. Activity at these areas has, in the past, centered around cotton gins, but as several have ceased operation in recent years, a number of these hamlets are now virtual ghost towns.

Muleshoe NWR is one of the main attractions advertised for the area. The refuge is within 120 miles of two large cities. Amarillo, Texas has a population 173,627 and is approximately 120 miles northeast of the refuge. Lubbock, Texas, which is approximately 80 miles to the southeast of the refuge, has a population of 199,564 (2000 Census Data). Although the refuge draws attention from these areas, visitors are primarily from Clovis, New Mexico (population 45,044), and Portales, New Mexico (population 18,447), which are both about 50 miles from the refuge. In the past, visitors from 29 states including Texas and New Mexico, as well as three to four foreign countries, have signed the register at refuge headquarters. Visitors are drawn to the refuge to participate in nature related activities. The main wildlife-dependent recreational opportunities provided by the refuge are wildlife viewing and photography. Because of the refuge's remote location and limited facilities, Muleshoe NWR does not attract large numbers of visitors. However, refuge visitors do generate some revenue for the local economy. Over 12,000 people visit the refuge annually, the majority in the fall, to observe cranes.

The refuge's annual budget is approximately $200,000. The refuge receives money from the local economy in the form of grazing fees. The annual grazing revenues received by the refuge are approximately $4,080 for a total of 480 AUMs (80 AUMs/month) for a six month grazing period. The majority of the annual operating budget is recycled into local businesses through purchases of equipment and supplies, as well as contracts for local labor to accomplish refuge projects. The refuge provides some local employment (3 permanent employees live in or near Muleshoe and when funding is available the YCC program provides work and income for a limited number of youths within a 30 mile radius of the refuge). In addition, the refuge staff makes available educational opportunities for local schools and universities.

Through fees collected by the Refuge System, the Service returns to Bailey County annual revenue sharing monies. As required by the Refuge Revenue Sharing Act 1935 (16 U.S.C. 7145:49 Stat. 383, as amended), the Service annually compensates the county for federal land taken off the tax rolls. Monies for these federal payments to counties come from revenues derived from the nationwide sale of refuge products and privileges. These funds are distributed based on one of the following three formulas to provide the highest return to the county:

Seventy-five cents per acre, or

Twenty-five percent of the net revenue received from the operation of the refuge, or

Three-fourths of one percent of the appraised value of the property, which must be reappraised by the Service every five years (usually this is the one applied).

Full funding of this program requires annual appropriations from the U.S. Congress, which has the option of funding the program at levels lower than 100 percent. The funding level approved has decreased in recent years, as reflected by the decreased payment presented in the table above.

The Service pays an annual revenue sharing payment to Bailey County for the lands encompassing Muleshoe NWR, and to Dickens County for 160 acres of inventory transfer lands from the Department of Agriculture. There are approximately 485 acres in inventory transfer lands that are in the process of being transferred to the Service; the status of this land transfer is uncertain, as closing has been delayed due to back taxes owed. Revenue sharing payments will be provided to Hale County for these lands in the future.

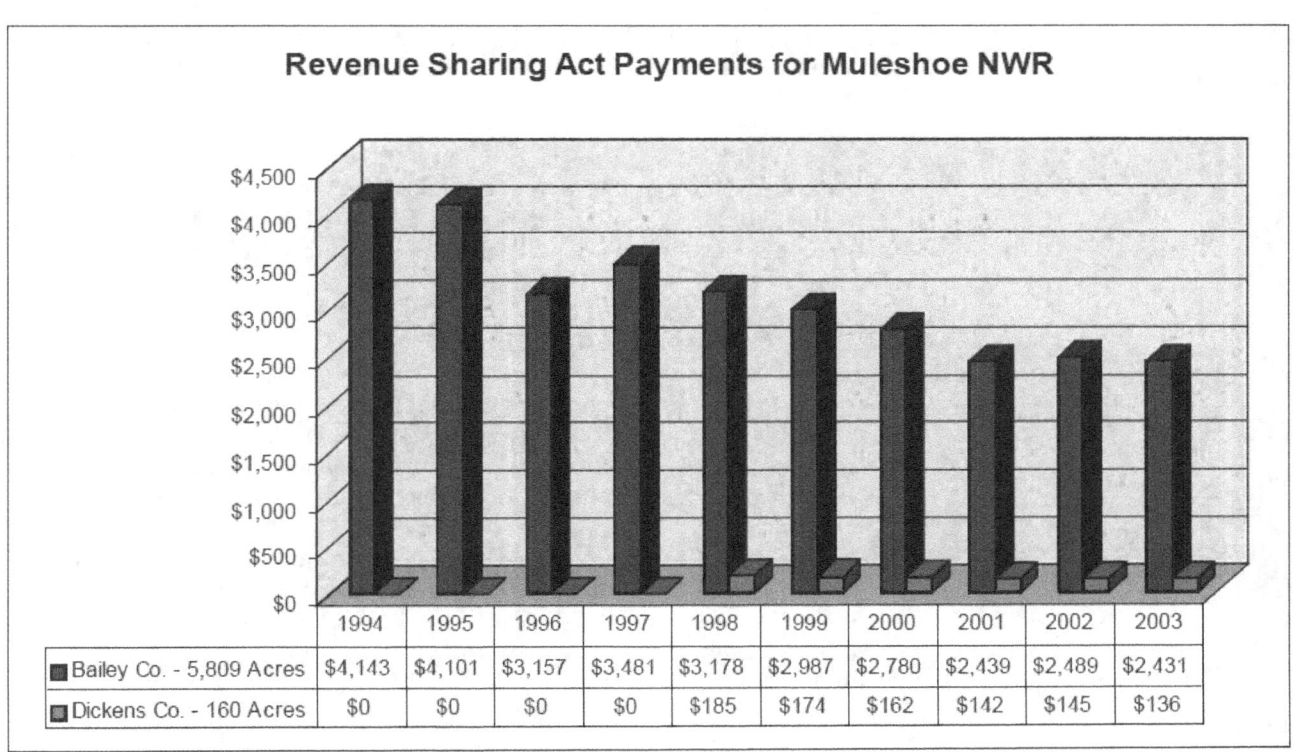

Revenue Sharing Act Payments for Muleshoe NWR

	1994	1995	1996	1997	1998	1999	2000	2001	2002	2003
Bailey Co. - 5,809 Acres	$4,143	$4,101	$3,157	$3,481	$3,178	$2,987	$2,780	$2,439	$2,489	$2,431
Dickens Co. - 160 Acres	$0	$0	$0	$0	$185	$174	$162	$142	$145	$136

Grulla NWR
This refuge is located in Roosevelt County, New Mexico near the small town of Arch, New Mexico. The operation of Grulla NWR has very little social and economic effect on surrounding communities except the farming area within 30 miles. With no employees stationed at the refuge and limited public access, impacts to the community include few depredations by sandhill cranes on agricultural crops, cattle from adjacent private lands trespassing and grazing within the refuge in some areas, destruction of soil quality on private lands adjacent to the refuge by alkali dust blown from the lake bed, and occasional sandhill crane hunting around the refuge boundary.

Revenue sharing payments are not provided to Roosevelt County for Grulla NWR as this refuge is considered an overlay of lands from the BLM.

Population

Muleshoe
According to the 2000 census data from the U.S. Census Bureau, the state of Texas had a population estimate of 20,851,820. Among the 50 states, it is ranked second only to California for the most populated. The population of Texas was approximately 7.4 percent of the total U.S. population. Between 1990 to 2000, the estimated rate of change for Texas was 22.8 percent, compared to the national rate of change at 13 percent. Texas has 254 counties. Approximately 6,594 residents live in Bailey County. Bailey County is one of 19 counties in the state with a population under 10,000. The population change in this county between 1990-2000 was estimated at a negative 6.7 percent. The 2000 census data indicate that 50.3 percent of county's population is white nonhispanic, 47.3 percent is Hispanic, and the remainder is Black, American Indian or Asian.

Grulla
According to the 2000 census data from the U.S. Census Bureau, the state of New Mexico had a population estimate of 1,819,046. The population of New Mexico was less than one percent of the total U.S. population. Between 1990 to 2000, the estimated rate of change for New Mexico was 20 percent, compared to the national rate of change, which was 13 percent. New Mexico has 33 counties. Approximately 18,018 residents live in Roosevelt County. Roosevelt County is one of 15 counties in the state with a population under 20,000. The population change in this county between 1990-2000 was estimated at 7.9 percent. The 2000 census data indicate that 62.7 percent county's population is white nonhispanic, 33.3 percent is Hispanic, and the remainder is Black, American Indian, or Asian.

Regional Economic Profile (Growth)

The average annual personal income total for Bailey County from 1994 through 1998 was $135,633,000. The average annual per capita income generated from 1994 through 1998 was $20,012. Farm income generated 20 percent of the personal income reported in 1997 and 1998.

The county's primary source of income is private employment. By industry, farming provided 19.3 percent of the income; the government (military, federal, state, and local) provided 17 percent; retail trade provided 15.9 percent, services provided 12.7 percent, and agricultural related services (including forestry and fishing) provided 9.2 percent.

Table #2 - Bailey County Personal Income accounts data for 1997 and 1998.

Bailey County	1997	1998
County population (number of persons)	6,769	6,846
Per capita personal income (dollars)	$20,684	$21,331
Personal income	$140,095,000	$146,031,000
Nonfarm personal income	$112,267,000	$116,465,000
Farm income	$27,828,000 (19.8%)	$29,566,000 (20.2%)

The county's agricultural statistics indicate that the acreage of land in farms decreased by 6 percent, from 432,939 acres in 1992 to 408,936 acres in 1997. The average farm size also decreased by 13 percent between 1992 and 1997. The number of full-time farming operations decreased by 2 percent from 304 farms in 1992 to 299 farms in 1997. The market value of agricultural products sold increased by 146 percent, with livestock sales accounting for 79 percent of the market value and crop sales accounting for the remainder. Statistics indicate that although the farming operations have decreased slightly in the past few years, the market value for agricultural products sold has more than doubled (USDA, Texas Agriculture Statistics Service, 1997).

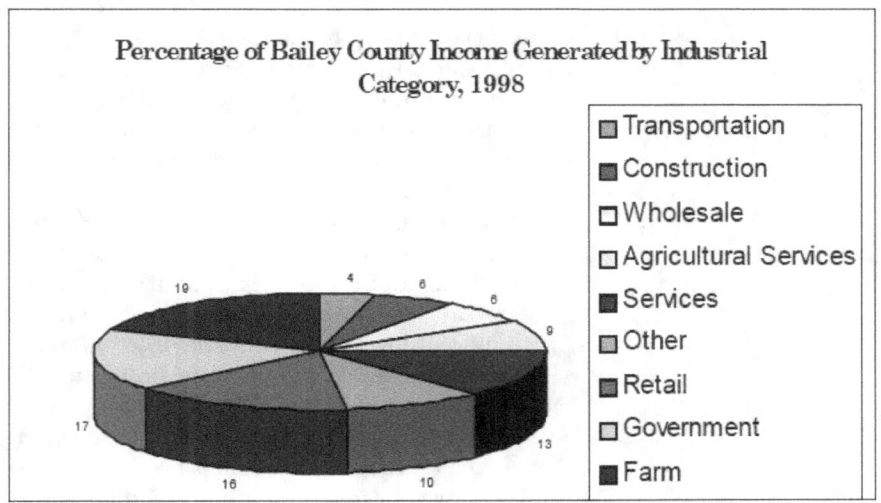

4.0 REFUGE ADMINISTRATION

The full potential of both refuges has not been realized. For a long time, lack of adequate staff has meant that opportunities for program enhancement have languished. Maintenance of existing programs and facilities has been the full-time endeavor of the existing staff. In order to enhance current programs and initiate new activities, additional staff positions will be required.

4.1 Refuge Staffing and Facilities

Muleshoe
Current staffing at this refuge consists of the following positions:

• Refuge Manager	GS-12	PFT
• Administrative Technician	GS-7	PFT
• Engineering Equipment Operator	WG-8	PFT

Current staffing is adequate to perform minimal maintenance and operation programs as these programs currently exist. To initiate many of the tasks proposed in this CCP, additional permanent, seasonal or part-time staff will be necessary, particularly for the increased efforts such as research and monitoring following upgrading of refuge grazing and prescribed burning programs.

Muleshoe NWR headquarters consists of an office building that was constructed in 1982. The old office building has been remodeled into volunteer quarters. There is also a permanent residence, approximately 1,400 sq. ft., constructed in the 1930s. These quarters are also used to house volunteers. Other facilities include a two bay garage/shop, three bay equipment storage building, a small oil shed and two above ground fuel tanks, a metal building used to store wood and carpentry tools, a concrete block storm shelter near the residence, a concrete block structure used to house the water pump and storage tank, and another concrete block building to store exploder guns used to prevent depredation. Except for the office and shop, which were build in 1982, most of these structures were built in the 1930s. Muleshoe NWR also has a campground/picnic area with two vault toilets and a redwood, universally accessible wildlife viewing overlook and toilet at Paul's Lake.

An entrance sign is located along the entrance road to Muleshoe NWR headquarters. An interpretive sign is located at the public viewing overlook at Paul's Lake and White Lake. Additional interpretive and informational kiosks at the entrance to the refuge, Paul's Lake, and White Lake would provide the public with more knowledge of the area and enhance their visit. Placement of boundary informational and regulatory signs on Muleshoe and Grulla NWRs are minimal and need to be improved. There are approximately 16 miles of exterior boundary fence and 14 miles of interior fencing (which includes 6 miles of temporary electric fence and 8 miles of permanent barbed wire fence) at Muleshoe NWR. Roads on the refuge consist of 4.65 miles of public roads, 27 miles of interior service roads (used only for refuge management purposes), and 19.05 miles of boundary/fire break roads.

Grulla

Grulla NWR is administered from Muleshoe NWR; therefore, no personnel are stationed at the refuge. Grulla NWR has an entrance sign, a five car pull-in parking area, and a 175 ft. trail leading from the parking area to a small self-guided interpretive area and overlook. Two interpretive signs were located at this site but were recently stolen. The visitors experiences at this site could be enhanced by upgrading the parking area, providing a toilet, and developing an informational kiosk of the refuge. The only roads available are 1.5 miles of fire lanes and the 0.8 mile entrance road. There is also a refuge gate at a pasture fence through private property at the northwest portion of the refuge.

Only a small portion of the refuge boundary is currently fenced. Approximately three miles of fence has been built by adjacent landowners for grazing cattle and 1.6 miles of fence has been built by the YCC in 1985 around the public use area. Most of this fence meets Service standards. The remainder of the 17.5 mile refuge perimeter is unfenced. Acquisition of sufficient land to allow access on solid land between the fence and the lake is necessary before fencing can be completed. To initiate many of the tasks proposed in this CCP, additional seasonal or part-time staff will be necessary, particularly for the increased efforts such as boundary fencing.

4.1.1 Volunteer Program

There is no formal volunteer program. However, Muleshoe NWR has benefitted from various volunteers over the years who have completed work activities pertaining to maintenance, landscaping, and public use. A volunteer has also lived in the refuge house since January 1995, primarily to provide security to refuge facilities. In addition, members of the Llano Estacado Audubon Society of Lubbock, Texas, regularly contribute refuge wildlife census information. At Grulla NWR, a volunteer that lives in Arch, New Mexico, maintains precipitation records and reports general observations of waterfowl and sandhill crane numbers in the area.

4.2 Memorandums of Understanding (MOU) and Other Agreements

4.2.1 Current Agreements

Interagency cooperation is critical to the successful implementation of the FMP. Mutual aid and joint decision making will occur between different wildland fire suppression agencies on all suppression incidents in close proximity to the refuge boundary, primarily in the Mutual Threat Suppression Zone. Agreements with the following agencies will be maintained to facilitate these suppression actions and the implementation of the prescribed fire program on the refuges.

- Bailey County Volunteer Fire Departments, Muleshoe Fire Department, and the Texas Forest Service: This agreement describes the assistance provided by the state, city and county fire services to Muleshoe NWR. It also addresses cost reimbursement, training, prescribed burning support, etc.

- Roosevelt County Volunteer Fire Departments, Portales Fire Department, and New Mexico State Division of Forestry: This agreement describes the assistance provided by the state, city, and county fire services to Grulla NWR. It also addresses cost reimbursement, training, prescribed burning support, etc.

- Joint Powers Operating Plan: The Operation Plan for Albuquerque Zone (Service, BLM, National Park Service (NPS), Bureau of Indian Affairs (BIA), State Forestry, and the USFS) describes how to request fire resources to be used on the refuges and for other services required such as weather forecasting, communications, record keeping, etc. Automatic extended fire attack resources are also activated through the agreement.

- Memorandum of Understanding (MOU) with the state and county law enforcement authorities to include patrolling for Muleshoe.

In addition to the interagency cooperation that the refuge will receive via formal agreement, a close working relationship has already been developed with the Lake Meredith National Recreation Area. Discussions between the DFMO and the Fire Management Officer (FMO) for the National Recreation Area have provided a foundation for cooperation between the two agencies as it relates to prescribed fire implementation and the staging of severity resources within the immediate area for the purpose of coordinating a mutual initial attack response to Muleshoe NWR and the National Recreation Area.

In addition, the two offices have established protocols for the exchange of fire weather data, dispatch information, and the joint use of the Lake Meredith Step-up Plan.

4.2.2   Future Agreements

Cooperative agreements with other firefighting agencies and jurisdictions will be developed and approved for a maximum shelf life of five years. They will be reviewed annually by the DFMO and cooperator in accordance with the approved presuppression plan.

4.3 Other Land Management

4.3.1   Contaminants

Muleshoe - This refuge is situated in an area where no contaminant sources discharge directly into its boundaries. The nearest contaminant source is a closed unauthorized solid waste disposal site, located approximately 10 km south-southwest of the refuge. Waste buried at the site includes household trash and automotive waste. Surface water run-off from this site may drain into White Draw, which is the only viable surface water pathway into the refuge; however, the distance of the site from the refuge makes it unlikely that contaminants enter the refuge.

Grulla - There is one potential point source pollution problem for Grulla NWR. Several years ago, the county buried cans of pesticides and other contaminants in a dry wash approximately one-half mile west and southwest of Grulla NWR. Surface erosion through heavy precipitation could transport contaminants into the wetland habitat.

4.3.2   Disease Prevention and Control

The refuges are part of the Playa Lakes Disease Council, in cooperation with the Texas Parks and Wildlife Department and Texas Tech University Department of Wildlife Management. Muleshoe NWR coordinates with Buffalo Lake NWR in investigating waterfowl disease incidents in the Playa Lakes Region, which includes the Texas Panhandle, Eastern New Mexico, and the South Plains.

4.4 Other Administrative Considerations/Approaches

<u>Texas State Highway Department</u> - A 100-300 foot right-of-way for state highway 214 passes through Muleshoe NWR for about 4 miles.

<u>Bailey County Electric Cooperative</u> - A recorded easement for a pole-supported 69KV transmission line passes through Muleshoe NWR adjacent to the west edge of the highway right-of-way for about 4 miles. A 7.2KV overhead distribution line runs from the refuge back gate to headquarters.

<u>Five Area Telephone Cooperative, Inc.</u> - An underground telephone line runs from the Muleshoe NWR back gate to headquarters.

<u>Cultural Resources</u> - To comply with the Department and Service policy, the refuge will follow established policies and procedures in the following areas: 1) refuge construction projects; 2) law enforcement; 3) visitor use; 4)special use permits, research referral and other uses; 5) reporting new cultural resources; 6) reporting maintenance, stabilization, and protection needs; 7) National Register nominations, and 9) archives and collections.

Management actions will be evaluated for their potential impacts on archeological and cultural resources. This will include examination of sites slated for road and other facility development to ensure that archeological and historical resources are not damaged by these developments. Where resources are located, the refuge will preserve these in place to the extent possible.

<u>Research and Investigations</u> - Natural science information is necessary for the proper management of any wildlife refuge. It is the policy of the Service and this refuge to encourage and support research and management studies in order to provide scientific data upon which decisions regarding management of the refuge can be based. The refuge will also permit the use of refuge lands for other scientific investigations when compatible with the purposes for which the refuge was established. Priority will be given to studies that contribute to the enhancement, protection, and management of native wildlife and their habitats. Examples of studies completed to date are included under *Research* in section 3.4.2.

<u>Mineral, Oil, and Gas Resources and Economic Uses</u> - Under Executive Order 7214, all lands of the Muleshoe NWR are withdrawn lands reserved for the protection of wildlife and as such are classified as "closed lands" and eliminated from leasing consideration (from 1983 memo denying an oil and gas application). The Grulla NWR is covered by oil and gas leases. If oil and gas drilling occurs, normal Service regulations, policies, and guidelines for gas and oil exploration and extraction will be followed (50 CFR 29 and 31).

5.0 REFUGE MANAGEMENT DIRECTION: GOALS, OBJECTIVES, AND STRATEGIES

The following goals, objectives, and strategies are the Service's response to the issues and concerns expressed by the planning team and the public, and unless otherwise noted in the text, expected to be implemented throughout the 15 year term of this plan. Due to the fact that the refuge CCP and FMP are working documents, modifications to the following objectives and strategies are anticipated. Ultimately, these proposed actions are designed to assist in the achievement of both the purposes of the refuge and the mission of the National Wildlife Refuge System.

5.1 Natural Diversity and Ecosystem Management

Goal 1: Provide habitat and manage for migrating and wintering waterfowl, sandhill cranes, other migratory birds, threatened and endangered species, and other species of concern by implementing appropriate management strategies.

Rationale for Goal: Through implementation of biological programs and wildlife management activities, provide quality habitat components that sustain natural population levels of waterfowl, sandhill cranes, and other migratory birds, and benefit native flora and fauna including threatened and endangered species and other species of concern. Management programs include fire suppression and prescribed fire to promote vegetative diversity, mechanical and biological control of exotic weeds and other invasive plant species, grazing for management of grasslands (at Muleshoe NWR only), avian disease prevention and control, and the protection of alternative water sources to provide quality wetland habitats. Habitat inventories and monitoring are integral components of the biological program providing valuable long-term information on dynamic habitats and animal communities. Recently (fall 2003) Buffalo Lake NWR hire a full-time biologist, who will also work on Muleshoe and Grulla NWRs. A consistent effort needs to be focused on biological inventory and monitoring data. A systematic approach to obtaining needed resource information is paramount for making and evaluating decisions affecting the refuge's biological resource program.

<u>**Objective 1**</u>: Document the diversity of native flora on refuge lands through a comprehensive vegetation map of Muleshoe and Grulla NWRs by 2006.

Rationale for Objective: Documentation is needed to provide baseline information of the existing species diversity of refuge habitats. This information will allow refuge management to measure the changing conditions of the ecological integrity and identify areas that may support greater diversity through management activities.

Strategy: By 2006, develop a vegetation baseline map that delineates the distribution and acreage of native grassland, disturbed grassland, and wetland habitats. This information will be used to develop and update habitat inventory data and determine management needs. (RONS #00002)

Strategy: Through Service contracting, generate GIS overlay maps of the natural resources on refuge lands and update information as appropriate. (RONS #00002)

Objective 2: Develop a comprehensive biological data base for Muleshoe and Grulla NWRs; revise and update the refuge biological program including wildlife inventory plans using the most current information, prepare habitat management plans for Muleshoe and Grulla NWRs by 2006.

Rationale for Objective: For step-down plans to be accurate and effective in guiding management decisions and activities, a comprehensive biological data base is necessary. The step-down plans would include a compilation of available data, specific objectives, monitoring for long-term information on dynamic biological communities, and criteria to evaluate management actions. These plans, as well as this CCP and the FMP, are integral components of the refuge's biological program. By identifying refuge needs through a systematic approach, these plans guide future refuge operations by providing justification for funding.

Strategy: Hire a full time Refuge Biologist and seasonal biological technician by 2010. (MLS RONS #0002, #00004, and #00006)

Strategy: Develop a comprehensive wildlife data base for the refuges. Initiate specific surveys or inventories to collect data on grassland birds, small mammals, reptiles, amphibians, and aquatic invertebrates of Muleshoe and Grulla NWRs habitats by 2007. Monitor the status of key plant and animal species as an indicator of the quality and health of the ecosystem. (MLS RONS #0002, #00004, and #00006)

Strategy: Continue to conduct special biological surveys as requested (mourning dove call counts, coordinated sandhill crane survey, May migratory bird counts, North American Breeding Bird Survey, and other special surveys). (MLS RONS #0001)

Strategy: Compile reptile, mammal, and amphibian lists and implement long-term monitoring of key indicator species. (MLS RONS #0001)

Strategy: Compile and review current available species specific literature, Central Flyway and other geographically appropriate population data, and other information to revise and update the wildlife inventory plan written in 1988 with current species population objectives for Muleshoe and Grulla NWRs. (RONS #0001)

Strategy: Review PIF Plans for Texas and New Mexico and where appropriate incorporate recommendations for key indicator species. (RONS #00004)

Strategy: Develop habitat monitoring programs as part of the grassland management plan for prescribed burn areas, grazing units, and areas managed to remove invader plant species; document results of management actions and evaluate these in terms of habitat objectives; and amend habitat management plans when monitoring and evaluation data support adjustments. (MLS RONS #00002 and #00006)

Strategy: Continue to upgrade computer data filing system with capabilities to properly store, retrieve, and archive biological data; develop data management systems to analyze data and report summaries; statistically analyze biological survey data if appropriate to determine population trends periodically; and adjust population objectives into wildlife inventory plans as appropriate. (RONS #00001)

Strategy: Continue to review and incorporate as appropriate national, international, and regional plans for fish and wildlife and determine how the refuge can best contribute to the management of priority species. (Central Plains Shorebird Conservation Plan, Central Prairie Waterbird Conservation Plan, North American Waterfowl Management Plan, Texas and New Mexico PIF Plan, and regional and physiographic area plans.)

Strategy: Enhance methods to transfer biological data summaries and analysis externally through publications, symposia presentations, biological reports, annual narratives, or other forms of information transfer.

Objective 3:   Continue and improve protection strategies for populations of rare and declining species (including endangered and threatened species and species of concern) and maintain or improve their habitats on refuge and adjacent lands.

Rationale for Objective: The bald eagle, interior least tern, whooping crane, and mountain plover are endangered, threatened, or proposed species that have been recorded (infrequently or as transient migrants) on or near these refuges. Between one to three bald eagles use the refuge during the winter months, relying on waterfowl and small mammals as their primary food source during their stay. Black-tailed prairie dogs (a candidate species) were abundant on the refuge and on adjacent lands; expansion of the nine prairie dog colonies on the refuge has been controlled in the past. Presently, only one small town of prairie dogs remains on the refuge. This population represents the only survivors of a bubonic plague outbreak in the summer of 2000. Future conditions and/or land acquisitions may lead to other state or federally listed species occurring within refuge boundaries.

Strategy: Monitor populations of special status of species (endangered, threatened, candidate, state listed, etc.) to identify their presence, population levels, and distribution. (MLS RONS #00001)

Strategy: Design and implement projects in a manner that minimizes or avoids impacts to threatened and endangered species and their habitats. Protection of threatened and endangered species will be ensured through project design and compliance with Section 7 of the Endangered Species Act. Consultation with the Service's appropriate Ecological Services Field Office will be conducted for projects and actions that may affect threatened and endangered species.

Strategy: Obtain known locations of federal and state listed species from Texas and New Mexico Natural Heritage Program data bases in a format suitable for GIS software (Edwards Plateau Ecosystem Plan).

Strategy: Protect and enhance black-tailed prairie dog colonies, monitor existing and new colonies, and implement natural methods to restrict expansion of colonies onto adjacent private lands. Manage the grazing program to protect areas with prairie dog colonies. The additional staff position of a biologist or refuge Operation Specialist (ROS) is needed to implement this program. (MLS RONS #00001)

Strategy: Implement prescribed burning as directed in the FMP. Place emphasis on limited prescribed burns to enhance prairie dog habitat and monitor initial results. Based on analysis of initial burn impacts, modify prescribed burns as necessary for maximum benefits.

Objective 4: Implement waterfowl management activities to provide migrating and wintering habitat for a minimum of 10,000 lesser sandhill cranes, 150 Canada geese, and 3,000 ducks. When possible, address and incorporate the goals of the North American Waterfowl Management Plan, Central Flyway, and regional plans into refuge habitat and inventory plans.

Rationale for Objective: Historically, the refuge provided habitats for over 300,000 waterfowl and nearly 100,000 lesser sandhill cranes as well as other marsh, water, and shore birds. The refuge wetlands depend entirely upon runoff for water. Waterfowl numbers later ranged around 200,000 until the mid 1970s. During recent years, waterfowl numbers have declined sharply. During migration periods, counts may reach 4,000, but wintering duck populations normally remain around 700 with only occasional sightings of Canada geese and snow geese. Although the refuge held 250,000 cranes during the winter of 1981 and populations of nearly 100,000 cranes before and after that time, lesser sandhill crane numbers have dropped sharply due to the lowering of the Ogalala aquifer and implementation of the CRP (which resulted in many acres of small grain crops being replaced by grasses). In recent years peak crane migration numbers are around 16,000 while winter refuge populations range from 5,000 to 8,000.

At Grulla NWR, waterfowl and other migratory bird numbers have normally been quite low due to the instability of lake water levels. During some years, several hundred migrating ducks and shorebirds may use Salt Lake depending upon available water. Crane numbers vary from a few hundred to several thousand depending upon water conditions.

Protecting water sources to provide valuable wetland habitat is critical in managing for waterfowl and crane populations as well as many other wetland-dependent migratory birds.

Strategy: Obtain baseline biological information and incorporate data, update methodologies, and adjust migratory bird population objectives into wildlife inventory plans and habitat management plans as appropriate. (MLS RONS #00001)

Strategy: Protect the refuge's use of water from a spring located on adjacent private land as a reliable water source for maintaining approximately 80 acres of wetland habitat in Upper Paul's Lake on Muleshoe NWR for migrating and wintering waterfowl.

Strategy: Investigate developing a well, pumping groundwater, and developing an impoundment designed to capture rainfall and water from seeps or springs adjacent to Paul's Lake.

Strategy: Determine if acquisition of 320 acres of adjacent properties is possible; investigate the use of water from available wells to create impoundments providing wetland habitats at Grulla NWR. (GR RONS #0001)

Strategy: Provide low grass resting/loafing areas around Muleshoe NWR lakes for lesser sandhill cranes and waterfowl by removing mesquite and salt cedar with a mechanical dozer tractor and blade. (MLS RONS #00006)

Strategy: Implement prescribed burning as an alternative method for setting back succession, retarding mesquite encroachment on grasslands, and maintaining vegetative diversity and vigor.

Objective 5: Manage refuge grasslands using the most effective methods available to maintain the natural range of diversity in the native short and mid-grass prairie habitat type that occurs on the refuge. Enhance ecosystem integrity on 3,725 acres of native grasslands through natural plant succession and land management programs such as prescribed fire, grazing, and removal of invasive and invader plant species; and implement vegetation monitoring to document changes as a result of management activities.

Rationale for Objective: Before the area was settled in the late 1800s, Muleshoe NWR and the surrounding area supported native shortgrass prairie. Fire was historically a significant factor in maintaining shortgrass prairie and much of the woody vegetation encroachment can be attributed to absence of fire, either wild or prescribed. The grass was used by native wildlife, especially the American bison and black-tailed prairie dogs. Much of Muleshoe and Grulla NWRs remain in native grass dominated by blue grama and buffalo grass. To date, the refuge has managed these grassland habitats primarily through livestock grazing to increase plant diversity and vigor. Prescribed burning has been used on a limited basis, but there are opportunities to enhance the use of this management tool. The refuge manages the grasslands to stimulate species diversity and to provide habitats for sandhill cranes, grassland-dependent birds, and resident wildlife. Cranes historically fed on grasslands and still do occasionally. When the cranes arrive in the fall, they forage on young winter wheat plants on adjacent private lands. During the winter, they prefer the high proteins of the waste grain from harvested milo. Cranes foraging in unharvested grain fields can become a nuisance to many private landowners. When the milo fields are being tilled, the cranes revert back to wheat forage prior to migrations north in February and March. Cranes roost near the refuge's shallow saline lakes during the night, and occasionally loaf in the open stands of mixed grasses near lakes. Agricultural practices in the area have changed in recent times. Most area farmers now grow cotton when there is enough spring moisture because it is a much more lucrative crop compared to grains. The cotton crops; however, provide no forage value for cranes. During dry spring conditions, milo is usually planted.

Recommendations for the Pecos and Staked Plains (PIF Physiographic Area 55) recognize that a careful grazing regime with some rest and rotation that allows moderate fuel buildup for occasional fires will provide long-term benefit both to land managers and birds. By enhancing the quality of adjacent grasslands and providing a diverse mix of native grasses and wildlife watering sites, the refuge would provide habitats for lesser prairie chickens, quail, and other resident birds, small mammals, and deer, as well as a forage base for raptors. With the current issues in the grassland regions, the refuge needs a holistic approach to habitat management. The grazing, prescribed burning, and animal damage control programs require revisions with long-term monitoring strategies addressed.

Intense grazing of fewer acres, control of invading woody vegetation, and the protection of prairie dogs are management activities that will be emphasized in the High Plains region. To enhance habitats for wildlife and improve overall land stewardship on private lands, techniques for improved grassland management will be encouraged through the HPPs with private landowners. Prescribed fire will be used where appropriate as an alternative or in addition to grazing.

Strategy: Hire a full-time biologist to develop a habitat management plan to identify areas to be managed to restore grassland diversity and enhance populations of species at risk. (MLS RONS #00002 and #00004)

Strategy: Delineate specific areas to be targeted for habitat restoration using light grazing to improve the species diversity. (MLS RONS #00002)

Strategy: To augment the use of grazing as a tool for habitat restoration, install wells to upgrade the livestock watering system with stock tanks at each end of specific grazing units to move the cattle through these units quickly to obtain the desired habitat outcome. (MLS RONS #00002)

Strategy: Implement the FMP. Use prescribed fire to burn at least 150 acres of monotypic alkali sacaton every three years. Use prescribed burns to enhance targeted areas of mixed grasses periodically after grazing units are evaluated and revised. Work with the DFMO to accomplish fire management objectives. (MLS RONS #00002)

Strategy: Mechanically remove invader species such as mesquite, invasive species such as salt cedar, and other exotics or shrubs on 150 acres of grassland every three years. Implement a long-term prescribed fire program to assist in accomplishing this strategy. (MLS RONS #00006)

Strategy: Control and/or eradicate existing infestations of invasive species, and prevent the introduction of new infestations through ongoing monitoring and control. Work with RO Invasive Species Coordinator to develop and begin implementing an Integrated Pest Management Step-down Plan by 2005.

Strategy: Establish vegetation monitoring transects, particularly in grazing units and burn areas to determine plant vigor and changes in plant communities resulting from management activities. (MLS RONS #00001 and #00002)

Strategy: Hire two temporary employees to repair and make alterations to grazing units. (MLS RONS #00002)

Strategy: Provide technical assistance to landowners that support reliable wildlife management practices that are economical, legal, and biologically sound (Edwards Plateau Ecosystem Plan).

Strategy: Investigate additional opportunities for research and monitoring to determine the methodologies that are best suited to restore and enhance short and mid-grass prairie habitats on the refuge.

Objective 6: Implement a long-term (10 year) monitoring program for indicator species of migratory songbirds, shorebirds, and other nongame birds to determine density and population response to management. Incorporate population and habitat objectives developed for priority species in refuge wildlife and habitat management programs by 2008.

Rationale for Objective: The PIF plan for New Mexico and Texas provides an avifaunal analysis identifying priority groups of species with indicator species for management and monitoring consideration. The PIF plan will provide information for determining population objectives for priority species and specific refuge habitats. The following species have been identified by the New Mexico and Texas PIF plans as priority species or species of high responsibility and may occur as migrants or breeding birds within the habitats of Muleshoe or Grulla NWRs: snowy plover, mountain plover, grasshopper sparrow, Cassin's sparrow, chestnut-collared longspur, McCown's longspur, short-eared owl, scissor-tailed flycatcher, loggerhead shrike, Spague's pipit, and ferruginous hawk. The PIF plan identifies the habitats of these species as a priority for active restoration and protection.

Strategy: Hire a biologist to conduct breeding bird surveys to monitor grassland birds on the refuges. (MLS RONS #00001 and #00004)

Strategy: Acquire project funding for the implementation of long-term monitoring (monthly point count and area counts) of birds and PIF priority species to document species diversity, population levels, and trends. (MLS RONS #00001 and #00004)

Strategy: Partner with the Audubon Society of Lubbock and universities to conduct surveys to document occurrence of indicator species (specific PIF priority species for the area).

Strategy: Increase or reestablish riparian vegetation around upland springs and seeps at Upper Paul's Lake. This involves removal of some salt cedar in these areas.

Strategy: As part of the grassland management plan, target specific grasslands areas to restore vegetative diversity and develop wells for watering areas to optimize habitats for grassland birds such as scaled quail, bobwhite quail, chestnut-collared longspur, and lesser prairie chickens. (MLS RONS #00002 and #00004)

Strategy: Coordinate with the Regional biologists to receive information on PIF grassland species focus groups and new or recommended methods for wildlife or habitat surveys, monitoring, and evaluation; incorporate new information, and amend wildlife and habitat management plans as appropriate. (MLS RONS #00001, #00002, and #00004)

Strategy: Analyze and evaluate fire effects on targeted species, first by research of available scientific data, then by monitoring impacts of limited prescribed burns. Adjust prescribed burning program to provide maximum benefits to targeted species.

Objective 7: Enhance populations of lesser prairie chickens and other upland bird species on Muleshoe NWR through habitat restoration of 200 acres of native grasslands.

Rationale for Objective: There have been a few sightings of prairie chickens on the refuge in recent years. From 1987 until 1995 a small breeding site adjacent to the Refuge south of White Lake was used by as many as 12 cock pheasants. During 1988, a prairie chicken brood was observed near Lower White Lake and another brood was observed near Paul's Lake. A few active breeding sites have been located about one mile north of the Refuge. Native grasslands on the refuge and adjacent private lands can provide breeding habitat for these birds with the appropriate mix of tallgrass, forbs, and shrub components. Overgrazing and the invasion of weeds and woody vegetation result in less desirable grassland habitat conditions. Lesser prairie chickens are considered an indicator species reflecting grassland conditions. Recently, this species has shown a consistent decline in the High Plains region which has sparked concern by the Service, state agencies, and the public. In response to these concerns, the High Plains Private Land Partnership is being developed to improve the functionality of the grasslands in an effort to restore the climax prairie system. Managed grazing can create an increased distribution of tallgrass, forbs, and shrubs with sufficient overwinter residual vegetation throughout grazing units to encourage leking. Additionally, more emphasis will be focused on population surveys and monitoring to identify the population of these birds on the refuge and adjacent private lands.

Strategy: Hire a full-time biologist and seasonal biological technician to monitor and survey populations of lesser prairie chickens and survey areas that can be enhanced to provide habitat characteristics that will encourage prairie chicken breeding by creating lek habitats. (MLS RONS #00001 and #00004)

Strategy: Mechanically remove 50 acres of woody vegetation and restore 200 acres of native grassland habitats. (MLS RONS #00006)

Strategy: Through the FMP, establish a long-term program of prescribed burning to limit woody vegetation and enhance prairie chicken habitat.

Strategy: Provide a water storage system for wildlife watering sites in upland grassland areas. (MLS RONS #00002)

Strategy: Investigate and facilitate creative partnerships to encourage adjacent landowners to enhance habitats and promote conservation of sensitive species. Provide technical assistance to landowners (Edwards Plateau Ecosystem Plan).

Objective 8: Secure and protect existing water sources and pursue alternative water sources to support wetlands on Muleshoe and Grulla NWRs.

Rationale for Objective: Muleshoe NWR has no streams or draws to supply water. The wetlands are primarily dependent on rainwater and runoff from adjacent grasslands. A spring located on private property adjacent to the refuge provides water for Upper Paul's Lake. Wetlands on Muleshoe NWR have the capacity to provide 1,000 surface acres of habitat. Salt Lake on Grulla NWR holds water only occasionally. Normal rainfall provides insufficient runoff for this large basin to maintain water on a regular basis. Water in the lake basin is quickly lost through evaporation and seepage through the sand bottom. Future efforts regarding the refuges' resources will focus on pursuing special agreements to protect seeps or springs providing water for wildlife habitats on the refuge and investigating the potential for new sites to develop wells to provide additional water for wildlife.

Strategy: Obtain an easement for protecting the spring on private land which supplies water to Upper Paul's Lake on Muleshoe NWR.

Strategy: Request assistance and coordinate with the Service's Water Resources Division to investigate appropriate sites for developing groundwater wells.

Strategy: Coordinate with the Service Realty Division and Technical Services to work with the Texas Water Commission, Texas Natural Resource Conservation Commission (TNRCC), and New Mexico State Water Engineers Office to obtain water right permits associated with pumping groundwater from new wells at Muleshoe and Grulla NWRs to enhance wetland habitats.

Strategy: Review and evaluate the development of water sources for the purpose of dispersing cattle into alternating grazing areas for habitat restoration. (MLS RONS #00002).

Strategy: Pursue the participation of Muleshoe and Grulla NWRs in a wetland recovery study on heavily grazed, palustrine emergent wetlands on federally owned wetlands in New Mexico (Edwards Plateau Ecosystem Plan).

Strategy: Work with NRCS and landowners to identify sites that qualify for the wetlands reserve program and assist in preparation of wetland reserve plans (Edwards Plateau Ecosystem Plan).

Strategy: Conduct the prescribed burning program in a manner that will have a neutral or positive effect on water quality.

Objective 9: By 2006, establish dialogue with area universities (Eastern, UNM, Texas Tech, Texas A&M, etc.) and other institutions to develop research that will improve the biological or archaeological database of the refuge and contribute to habitat restoration and management activities.

Rationale for Objectives: Additional knowledge regarding refuge wildlife, habitats, and archaeology will contribute to better resource management decisions on refuge lands, as well as decisions affecting components of the Edwards Plateau Ecosystem. Research priorities on major ecosystem issues center on habitat restoration, the reestablishment of native aquatic and terrestrial communities, and monitoring the wildlife and plant responses to management and restoration activities.

Strategy: Work with RO biologist and archaeologist to identify research needs, information gaps, and management studies that would help meet the needs of the refuge in making better management decisions affecting the natural resources of Service lands and the public involved in recreation or educational activities.

Strategy: Continue to fill information gaps regarding distribution and abundance of flora and fauna and seek opportunities to conduct studies that meet high priority research needs. (MLS RONS #00001 and #00004)

Strategy: Utilize U.S. Geological Service's Biological Research Division including university cooperative research units for technical assistance in designing and conducting studies.

Strategy: Set up specific research projects through the fire program to monitor and evaluate fire effects of wildfire and prescribed burns. Initial focus will be on impacts of various burn dates, burn frequency in a specific area, and climatic influences altering desired outcomes.

5.2 Cultural Resources

Goal 2: Identify, protect, and interpret the prehistoric and historic cultural resources on Muleshoe and Grulla NWRs for the benefit of present and future generations.

Rationale for Goal: At present, there has been only one known archaeological discovery at Grulla NWR. An extensive bison bone bed was exposed from wind action. Carbon 14 analysis of the horn sheaths dated them to the early 15th century. Archaeological field surveys were conducted of this site by researchers from Eastern New Mexico University. Stone artifacts indicating human cultural involvement were also present along some of the lake beds.

<u>**Objective 1:**</u> By 2010, survey for archaeological sites on current refuge lands and future acquisitions to obtain baseline archaeological information. Monitor known sites for disturbance or deterioration. Ensure all refuge management activities are in compliance with ARPA.

Rationale for Objective: A Cultural Resources Overview and Assessment will provide the refuge with contextual information about the prehistoric and historic information available including past and current archaeological and ethnographic investigations at the refuge and surrounding region, a compilation of existing site records, and maps of these sites. The assessment will also provide recommendations for future cultural resource management options and research directions for the refuge.

Strategy: By 2008, prepare a Cultural Resources Overview and Assessment of the refuge that includes a synthesis of the existing archaeological, ethnohistoric, and historic information presented within the regional context of the prehistory and history of the area.

Strategy: Conduct a comprehensive cultural resource survey of the refuge including GPS mapping of archeological and historic sites.

Strategy: Protect all cultural resources on refuge lands as mandated under ARPA, including appropriate law enforcement measures.

Strategy: Avoid damage and deterioration to cultural resources that would result from erosion, abandonment, or neglect.

Strategy: Work with RO archaeologist to develop a contract with universities to do surveys, research, and obtain information that would meet the needs of the refuge in making better management decisions affecting the archaeological resources on Service lands.

5.3 Land Protection

Goal 3: Protect the area's resource values through land protection strategies that protect tracts of land with desirable habitats. Strategies could include agreements with private land owners, and consideration of developing a boundary expansion proposals for eventual purchase of fee title and less than fee title interest in adjacent lands.

Rationale for Goal: Protecting natural resources on federal lands requires the Service to establish easements or partnerships with private landowners. These efforts may involve land acquisition of parcels to augment resource protection. In particular, many water resources on private lands adjacent to the refuge affect the quality of refuge habitats.

Objective 1: Pursue land protection strategies involving private land adjacent to the refuges (approximately 350 acres at Grulla NWR and 370 acres at Muleshoe NWR), which are necessary to improve boundary management at both refuges, increase opportunities for management and protection of wildlife habitat, and provide additional public access.

Rationale for Objective: Currently, Grulla NWR has one public access point. The boundary is not completely fenced, and cattle from adjacent lands roam free on the refuge. In order to protect the natural resources of Grulla NWR from cattle trespass and human disturbance, fencing is required. The boundary of Grulla NWR is partially unfenced because the boundary line goes through the Salt Lake bed which can be very muddy and unstable. Currently, there is only one access point to refuge lands from a public road. All other access points require permission for entry through private land. Landowners adjacent to Grulla NWR have approached the Service offering to exchange land along the perimeter of the Salt Lake bed to provide a more regular boundary on solid ground for the purpose of fencing cattle out of the lake bed. The landowners benefit by this exchange because fencing would prevent their cattle from roaming and getting bogged down in Salt Lake. At Muleshoe NWR, land adjacent to the north boundary of the refuge has recently become available for sale. The refuge would benefit from acquiring this land. It would allow the refuge to straighten the boundary and acquire agricultural lands that could be used to grow crops to feed migrating sandhill cranes.

Strategy: Determine suitable tracts to propose to private land owners as the subject of an access and/or fencing agreement; or subject of acquisition of interest in lands by purchase or exchange. Conduct boundary surveys and measurements in cooperation with adjacent land owners in order to develop and a proposal for acquisition and participate in the development of acquisition proposals and appraisals.

Strategy: Establish contact with adjacent land owners to determine the most appropriate approach for remedying boundary access and maintenance issues, identify interest in a land exchange and coordinate with landowners during the acquisition process.

| Strategy: | Work with Planning Division and Land Acquisition Review Committee for the eventual preparation of a preliminary project proposal leading to development of a Land Protection Plan for Grulla NWR. |

Strategy: Work with Realty Division to pursue acquisition (long range purchase or easement) of land adjacent to Muleshoe NWR that would improve wildlife management opportunities and boundary management.

Objective 2: Establish a bi-annual review process for Farm Service Agency (FSA), formerly the Farmer's Home Administration, inventory lands to protect, maintain, and enhance native biological communities by 2008.

Rationale for Objective: The refuge is responsible for three tracts of land encompassing 640 acres of fee title lands or inventory transfer lands through the FSA, Department of Agriculture, from bankrupt farmers. All tracts have recently been surveyed by the Service under contract. Two tracts are 80 miles from the refuge in Hale County and one tract is 130 miles away in Dickens County, 60 miles east of Lubbock. Only the tract in Dickens County has a clear title. The two tracts in Hale County are still in litigation due to back taxes owed. The refuge also has six easement areas in Lubbock County and other surrounding counties. These lands are primarily composed of playa lakes, grassland, and retired farmlands. Although the Service is responsible for the land management and protection of resources on these tracts, without specific funding these lands remain in a custodial administrative status. Most of these parcels have been ground surveyed, but placement of survey markers or boundary signs is not completed. It is possible that adjacent landowners may complain about the Service's lack of weed control on these lands affecting their farming operations.

Strategy: Propose funding to conduct ground surveys and establish survey markers on fee title inventory lands and conservation easements.

Strategy: Propose funding to install boundary signs on Service fee title inventory lands.

Strategy: Remove existing buildings and other structures.

Strategy: Implement weed control on fee title lands.

Strategy: Evaluate individual parcels for suitability for prescribed fire to achieve weed control and promote vegetative diversity. Include these parcels in the habitat management and fire management plans.

Strategy: Determine the Service's policy for public use, grazing, and other activities on these parcels and complete the appropriate compatibility determinations if necessary.

Objective 3: Maintain and install 32 miles of boundary fences at Muleshoe and Grulla NWRs to protect the refuge habitats from disturbance by humans (both refuges) and overgrazing by trespass cattle (Grulla only). This includes 27 miles of fence maintenance at Muleshoe and 5 miles of new fence construction at Grulla.

Rationale for Objective: Fencing the Grulla NWR boundary is critical in an effort to protect wildlife, archaeological sites, and natural resources from disturbance by humans and livestock grazing trespass. Fencing will prevent overgrazing on refuge lands and possibly decrease vandalism, violations, and disturbance by people.

Strategy: Post boundaries with signs and supports to Service standards, replace wooden posts, and remove sand accumulating from high winds along fence. (GR RONS #00001)

Strategy: Install road culvert along entrance road of Grulla NWR to allow access into fenced area of refuge for maintenance of boundary signs and fences.

Strategy: Prevent overgrazing and human violations/disturbance on Grulla NWR by replacing three miles of boundary fence and construct 13.5 new miles of boundary fence (if adjacent lands are acquired to allow it) with four strand barb wire, metal line posts, and wooden H braces/corner posts. (Maintenance Management System (MMS) projects)

Objective 4: Develop a proposal for review by the Regional Office to better protect area lands that have important water sources (i.e., springs on adjacent lands) by 2010.

Rationale for Objective: Muleshoe and Grulla NWRs have no water rights from adjacent lands. These refuges receive water for lakes and wetland impoundments from precipitation and runoff. Since these refuges were established primarily to provide habitat (wetlands) for migrating and wintering waterfowl, sandhill cranes, and other migratory birds, water is a key component to the successful accomplishment of the refuge purposes. The potential for developing wells on the Muleshoe Refuge capable of producing the quantities of water necessary to develop or enhance wetlands is doubtful. Several wells have been drilled since the refuge was established, and the results have been mostly poor. It is therefore imperative that the Service protect existing water sources, develop alternative water sources, and establish easements with other agencies or private landowners for the protection of off refuge water sources. Private parcels adjacent to the Refuge boundaries of Muleshoe and Grulla NWRs may have water sources (wells or springs) that provide or have the potential to provide water for wildlife. Establishing easements or acquiring these parcels could benefit the resources of both refuges.

Strategy: Pursue acquisition of a private parcel or easements adjacent to the Grulla NWR boundary. Based upon the size of the acquisition proposed, a boundary expansion proposal may not be necessary and may be under the Regional Director's discretion. This land would provide access to the lakeshore from an adjacent highway, as well as protecting grassland wildlife habitat presently used for grazing by adjacent landowners. (GR RONS #00002)

Strategy: Obtain an easement to protect the spring located on private land and supplying water to Upper Paul's Lake on Muleshoe NWR. Based upon the size of the acquisition proposed, a boundary expansion proposal may not be necessary and may be under the Regional Director's discretion.

Strategy: Implement Partners for Wildlife, Playa Lakes Joint Venture, and other private land programs with surrounding landowners to protect seeps and springs on private lands and enhance wetlands and native mixed grass habitats for wildlife.

Strategy: Seek partnerships with individuals or private organizations interested in opportunities to restore, enhance, or to protect desirable wildlife habitats and natural resources (Audubon, Ducks Unlimited, The Nature Conservancy, etc.).

5.4 Public Use, Education, and Outreach

Goal 4: Further the public's interest and involvement with Muleshoe and Grulla NWRs through wildlife interpretation, education/outreach programs, and quality wildlife-dependent recreational opportunities.

Rationale for Goal: Increasing the public's involvement and appreciation of fish and wildlife resources can be achieved through current and informative interpretive materials, interactive environmental education, demonstrations of management practices, and quality recreational experiences. Several factors will determine the level of future public interest and visitation to Muleshoe and Grulla NWRs: improved directional and informational signs, outreach programs to increase public awareness of the refuges, interactive displays to draw and engage visitors at proposed facilities, and improved public access points, specifically to Grulla NWR.

Objective 1: Provide interactive visitor services and enhancing current visitor facilities, increase public contacts, and better secure public use areas on Muleshoe and Grulla NWRs.

Rationale for Objective: In 2001, approximately 15,000 people visited Muleshoe NWR for wildlife viewing, photography, and camping. Almost 20 percent of visits occur during November and December, primarily for crane viewing. The public's awareness of the unique value and significance of the Edwards Plateau Ecosystem would be further enhanced with exhibits at the refuge headquarters. Existing interior wildlife displays and outdoor exhibits can be upgraded with new information focusing on many of the ecosystem issues. Efforts will be made to bring public attention to areas within the refuge that demonstrate the beneficial effects of prescribed fire and management activities for improving the species diversity and habitat conditions.

The majority of public use at Grulla NWR pertains to wildlife and wildland observations during wet periods. The primitive status of Grulla NWR limits the potential for developing recreational opportunities of this refuge. Grulla NWR has received as many as 2,800 visitors in one year (1993) but average visitation is around 1,000 visitors for the purpose of observing wildlife by walking or using motorized vehicles. There is one small interpretive site on Grulla NWR that includes a parking area, walking trail, a small self-guided interpretive area (two signs), and an overlook of Salt Lake. Unfortunately, the signs have been stolen and have not been replaced. Occasionally visitors walk over the grasslands to reach the shoreline of Salt Lake. Improvements to this refuge include an entrance road, parking area, and entrance signs.

The refuge's one law enforcement officer had the law enforcement authority dropped in January of 1999. Due to the distance from refuge headquarters at Muleshoe NWR to Grulla NWR, enforcement patrols at Grulla NWR are minimal. Generally, the only law enforcement incidents at this refuge are vandalism at the parking lot due to its remote location. The refuge is in the process of developing an MOU with the state and county law enforcement agencies for assistance with covering refuge lands when necessary.

Strategy: Replace stolen signs at Grulla NWR interpretive area. (MMS project)

Strategy: At Grulla NWR, provide a universally accessible toilet, interpretive and informational kiosk, upgrade the parking area and provide additional informational and regulatory signs where needed. (GR RONS #00002)

Strategy: At Grulla NWR, develop self-touring types of discovery opportunities.

Strategy: By 2007, provide an informational kiosk and vehicle turn out at the entrance road to Muleshoe NWR to orient visitors to this refuge and provide some information about Grulla NWR. (MLS RONS #00005)

Strategy: Provide varied interpretive and interactive opportunities for the visitor, work with the RO to develop an interpretive program focused on the theme "Wildlife of the High Plains" to explain the value of the playa lakes region as a wintering area for migratory birds, particularly sandhill cranes and waterfowl. (MLS RONS #00005; GR RONS #00002)

Strategy: Provide interpretive information to inform visitors of the avian disease problems (avian cholera and botulism) with migratory birds in the playa lake region. (MLS RONS #00005; #00007 GR RONS #00002)

Strategy: Provide interpretive information to inform visitors about native habitat and wildlife such as lesser prairie chickens, quail, other resident birds, prairie dogs, other small mammals, and raptors, as well as the value of water, prescribed fire and other management activities that maintain healthy grasslands.

Strategy: Provide interpretive information to inform visitors about the, historic, pre-historic and cultural resources in the area as well as the geological origins of these wetlands relative to the culture at that time.

Strategy: Concurrent with the initiation of an expanded prescribed fire program, conduct extensive outreach and information dissemination regarding the goals and objectives of the program, benefits to be obtained, and historical effect of fire in the area of ecological concern.

Objective 2: In cooperation with TPWD, develop and improve compatible wildlife dependent recreational opportunities on refuge lands to increase visitation by 10 percent within three years and 20 percent within 10 years.

Rationale for Objective: At Muleshoe, over 95 percent of the public's wildlife viewing occurs at Paul's Lake, White Lake, and the prairie dog town exhibit. The parking area at White Lake is sometimes used when water and birds are present. An overlook was constructed at Paul's Lake and opened to public access. There are two interpretive signs and a universally accessible public toilet at this site. The refuge also maintains a small eight site campground and picnic area near the headquarter office. This site provides potable water, vault toilets, picnic tables, and fire grills. There is a one-mile interpretive birding trail near the refuge campground and a one quarter mile nature trail near the Paul's Lake parking area. Entrance, interpretive, regulatory (boundary and traffic control), and informational signs have been installed to guide the public. The development of a public use plan would identify the refuge needs to better serve the public's recreational and educational experiences with a safe and high quality infrastructure. A public use plan would also provide a site by site analysis with recommendations for enhancing the public use on the refuge with short-term, intermediate, and long-term goals and objectives. A well planned public use program and a maintained infrastructure will greatly enhance the quality of a visitor's recreational and educational experience on the refuge.

Strategy: Work with RO specialist to develop a public use plan by 2006.

Strategy: Propose funding to implement priority projects of the public use plan by 2010.

Strategy: Construct two picnic shelters at the Muleshoe NWR picnic area to provide shade and wind shelter by 2005. (MLS RONS #00003)

Strategy: Develop the following interpretive trails to increase wildlife viewing opportunities: a one and a half mile walking trail from the parking area at Goose Lake (north along the base of the bluff, up a draw, across the top and back down to the parking area) with interpretive panels about the plants, colonial nesting birds, and other wildlife (MLS RONS #00003); complete a one-half mile walking trail between the campground and headquarters with interpretive information about the vegetation. (MMS funding has been requested to install interpretive signs along this trail.)

Strategy: Upgrade the public use facilities (signs, trials, roads, viewing areas, parking lots, and restrooms); protect and maintain the infrastructure at both Muleshoe and Grulla NWRs by 2005 (MMS).

Strategy: Upgrade refuge entrance signs and replace all current signs (including informational, directional, regulation, and boundary signs) on Muleshoe and Grulla NWRs to meet Service standards by 2005. (MLS RONS #00003; GR RONS #00002; MMS)

Strategy: By 2005, in coordination with TPWD, gather the data necessary to evaluate, plan, develop, and establish limited compatible big game, non-game, or upland gamebird hunting opportunities that do not conflict with visitor safety.

Strategy: Pursue land acquisitions or land exchanges to provide other access points for public entry to Grulla NWR. (GR RONS #00003)

Strategy: Work with RO staff in Visitor Services to acquire grants for building facilities and developing interpretive information.

Strategy: Pursue volunteer flex funding to build to build 1-2 RV pads with full hookups, to increase chances of attracting potential volunteers.

Strategy: Refuge staff will seek matching funds and prepare proposals for Challenge Cost Share, Partners in Wildlife, Watchable Wildlife, and other Service flexible funding sources to provide interactive office exhibits, interpretive panels of key refuge/ecosystem issues, and/or the construction of additional wildlife viewing opportunities on the refuge.

Objective 3:   Develop an outreach program that interprets the resources of the area and generates interest in the refuge. Provide five community outreach programs annually by 2010 in the towns of Muleshoe, Morton, Littlefield and Sudan, Texas. These products/activities may include community presentations, community involved habitat restoration projects, and/or refuge staff representation at public events that will foster the public's appreciation and understanding of fish and wildlife resources and the mission of the Refuge System.

Rationale for Objective: Outreach programs are instrumental in developing and expanding public interest in the Refuge System. With funding, the refuge has the potential to increase outreach opportunities. Programs such as presentations, interpretive displays, and interactive educational activities will have the greatest opportunity to provide the public with information about fish and wildlife resources, the Edwards Plateau Ecosystem, and the value of wildlife refuges nationally. The refuge staff provides limited environmental education programs and outreach efforts due to the small staff and the relative isolation of the refuge. The refuge staff currently reaches audiences of 150 to 300. An average of six or seven programs per year are presented to scout groups, civic organizations, or school groups on various refuge related topics or issues. By providing the public with resource information, many individuals may become more aware of resource issues and may be willing to support existing and future conservation activities.

Strategy: Hire a seasonal biological technician to assist with environmental education and outreach programs, wildlife surveys, and habitat projects. (MLS RONS #00001 and #00005)

Strategy: Use the district fire management staff to enhance outreach related to fire and fire effects.

Strategy: Provide media interviews, news releases, and other articles that feature refuge issues/opportunities during peak wildlife observation periods for the local media in Portales, Lubbock, and Amarillo.

Strategy: Advertise and provide special guided tours during peak wildlife observation periods such as a Watchable Wildlife Weekend or weekend nature walks.

Strategy: Purchase a portable display panel and work with RO to develop one to two portable displays to provide information on refuge resource themes such as the value of the refuge habitats to wildlife, and archaeology of the area for use at libraries, schools, fairs, and other special events by 2005.

Strategy: The refuge staff will assist RO specialists in developing and designing outreach materials such as brochures, posters, pamphlets, etc. that identify the unique and significant natural resources of the Edwards Plateau Ecosystem.

Strategy: Expand the refuge volunteer program to recruit volunteers to help with environmental education, interpretive programs, special refuge events and opportunities aimed at fostering wildlife observation on the refuge, wildlife surveys, and habitat restoration projects.

Strategy: Investigate opportunities to expand volunteers into organized groups.

Strategy: The refuge staff will promote resource education in the community by identifying new audiences and providing programs specific to their needs. Develop new partnerships with local education institutions, youth groups, and civic groups for opportunities to provide presentations, refuge tours, instructor led outdoor classrooms, and hands-on wildlife habitat related projects.

Strategy: Work with the RO to obtain funding to develop a teacher led outdoor classroom curriculum package including activities, investigations, and equipment; recruit local teachers and environmental education facilitators to assist with the development of the refuge specific curriculum; and provide workshops demonstrating the use of the curriculum for teachers or informal educators interested in the refuge as an outdoor classroom by 2010.

Strategy: The refuge will continue to provide programs that focus on the following issues: endangered species conservation, aquifers, ecological integrity and habitat, wetland values, and natural resource recreation (Edwards Plateau Ecosystem Plan).

Strategy: Develop a program that can be present coincidently with planned burns, with focus on the historical presence of fire and short and long-term fire effects.

Strategy: In cooperation with Texas Parks and Wildlife Department (TPWD) and others, host workshops with tours and demonstration areas for landowners on successful habitat management practices such as prescribed fire that benefit wildlife communities, grasslands, playa lakes, and cattle grazing operations (Edwards Plateau Ecosystem Plan and HPP).

Strategy: The refuge staff will pursue better cooperation with organizations and other community civic groups such as the Texas Environmental Awareness Network (TEAN), local Chambers of Commerce, Audubon groups, Texas and New Mexico Wildlife Society, and Wildlife Associations, etc. to improve the awareness of the area's natural resources and foster wildlife observation at the refuge (Edwards Plateau Ecosystem Plan).

Strategy: Assist with the preparation and distribution of factual briefing materials on the Ogallala Aquifer (Edwards Plateau Ecosystem Plan).

5.5 Interagency Coordination and Relationships

Goal 5: Maintain or strengthen existing interagency and jurisdictional relationships and establish new partnerships within the community to cooperate on mutually beneficial programs for improving wildlife and habitat resources on the refuge within the High Plains region and within the Edward Plateau Ecosystem.

Objective 1: Participate with other government agencies, NGOs, and private groups in partnerships such as the High Plains Initiative, PIF, Playa Lakes Joint Venture, and Integrated Pest Management that are mutually beneficial and will ultimately benefit the fish and wildlife resources of the refuge and surrounding private lands within the High Plains region and Edwards Plateau Ecosystem.

Rationale for Objective: Fish and wildlife resources, public use, and educational opportunities can all be fostered and enhanced through coordination with state, federal, private organizations, and individual landowners. Because of the value of the refuges to migratory birds, including sandhill cranes in the Central Flyway and The Texas Panhandle, coordinating with the entities that are involved in the management of flyway populations is imperative to the purpose for which these refuges were established. The incidence and spread of waterfowl (avian) disease is also an issue that involves coordination with many entities in the clean up and reestablishment of quality, wetland habitats. Private land initiatives and partnerships are instrumental in improving habitat conditions in a large contiguous area for the benefit of wildlife, particularly sensitive species such as the lesser prairie chicken, mountain plover, black-tailed prairie dog, etc.

Strategy: Coordinate with the Central Flyway Technical Committee, the Service's Migratory Bird Management Office, TPWD, Migratory and Game Bird Program Leader, and others to improve the management of waterfowl, sandhill cranes, and other migratory bird populations and resolve issues such as avian disease and crop depredation.

Strategy: Refuge staff will participate in and encourage private land joint ventures and partnerships involving the cooperation of private stakeholders within the community leading to resource restoration and management activities for habitat enhancement on private lands.

Strategy: Work with county, local, and state highway personnel to repair road signs in the area and seek partnerships in the Adopt-a-Highway and Leave No Trace programs.

Strategy: Participate in, and/or initiate, a local Cooperative Weed Management Area to address invasive plant issues of concern to the refuge and adjacent and nearby landowners.

Strategy: Continue cooperative agreements with the Bailey County Volunteer Fire Departments, Muleshoe Fire Department, Texas Forest Service, Roosevelt County Volunteer Fire Departments, Portales Fire Department, and the New Mexico State Division of Forestry. Utilize the Joint Powers Operating Plan for additional fire assets. Develop a formal agreement for interagency cooperation with Lake

Meredith National Recreation Area of the National Park Service and expand current coordination between the Service and Lake Meredith for local fire operations.

Strategy: Coordinate and continue active participation as part of Interagency Playa Lakes Disease Council with Cannon AFB, Texas Parks and Wildlife Department and others involved in the waterfowl disease contingency plan.

Strategy: Pursue cooperative agreements with Eastern New Mexico University, Texas Technical University, and other institutions to assist the refuge in obtaining biological, archaeological, or other resource information including GIS mapping and research that would serve the best interest of the refuge resources.

Strategy: Pursue opportunities with local businesses, schools, scouts, and other organizations to adopt the refuge for projects or special community programs such as Earth Day, Green Team, etc.

Strategy: Contact the Audubon chapters in Lubbock, Texas, and Portales, New Mexico to conduct bird surveys and assist with future planned wildlife tours.

Strategy: Pursue partnerships with organizations and other community civic groups to help foster wildlife observation at the refuge, assist with nature tours and other public use events (TEAN, the local Chambers of Commerce, Texas Waterfowlers Association, Ducks Unlimited, Texas Fish and Wildlife Society, Wildlife Association, etc.).

Strategy: Develop a Friends Group with the local Muleshoe community to foster a constituency that supports the mission and purpose of the refuge.

5.6 Improvement of Staff, Funding, and Facilities

Goal 6: Develop program support sufficient to provide the necessary staffing, facilities, equipment, and operational funds to accomplish the goals of the refuge and fulfill the mission of the Refuge System.

Objective 1: Provide the funding and the support of the RO staff specialists to accomplish the goals of this plan.

Rationale for Objective: Current staffing levels at these two refuges are adequate to accomplish the essential maintenance and continue established programs. However, they are not adequate to implement goals and objectives set forth in this Plan. Presently, Muleshoe NWR no longer has a law enforcement officer to patrol refuge lands, but must rely on an MOU with cooperating law enforcement agencies. Because of the refuge's remote location, few violations occur and involve minimal violations of refuge regulations such as disturbing wildlife, removing plants, littering, and vandalism. The size, isolation, and issues of these refuges warrants the addition of four full-time employees (Public Use Specialist, Refuge Law Enforcement Officer, maintenance worker, and a biologist) and one seasonal employee (resource specialist in a long- term effort for accomplishing the goals of this plan. To implement the objectives of this plan, the refuge staff will need increased support and assistance of the staff listed above to assist with the revisions of management plans, protecting refuge resources, developing interpretive and educational projects, and providing expertise in current biological and resource information.

Strategy: Use internal mechanisms such as RONS to justify and acquire the additional funding to accomplish the refuge goals by 2018. The additional staff positions include:

Wildlife Biologist	GS 7/9 PFT
Refuge Law Enforcement Officer	GS 5/7/9 PFT
Maintenance Worker	WG 8 PFT
Public Use Specialist	GS 5/7 PFT
Resource Specialists (2)	GS-5/7 Seasonal

Strategy: Pursue agreements with other interested agencies and organizations to assist with the needed personnel (interns, volunteers, co-op students, etc.), volunteer housing and other services, supplies, equipment, and funds to accomplish the refuge goals.

Strategy: Continue maintenance of existing signs and install additional ones, as needed, to keep refuge violations minimal. (GR RONS #00002)

Strategy: Use cooperative agreements, the District Fire Management Staff, and Interagency Agreements to expand the refuge fire program. Refuge staff will be responsible for long-term direction of the program, some program administration, and supervisory and approval authority for all actions taken by the DFMO. As appropriate, refuge staff will obtain necessary qualifications to participate in fire activities.

Strategy: Provide protection (through a Refuge Law Enforcement Officer) for Muleshoe, Grulla, and Buffalo Lake NWRs, and for waterfowl disease surveillance and waterfowl hunters in the Panhandle of Texas. (MLS RONS #00003)

Objective 2: Continue to provide a safe, efficient, and productive work environment for refuge employees and a safe infrastructure for refuge visitors.

Rationale for Objective: Refuge equipment used for habitat improvement projects and to maintain public use and other facilities needs to be upgraded to meet safety standards, and needs to be protected from the weather with appropriate storage facilities. The current staffing level is inadequate to upgrade and maintain the facilities and infrastructure at both refuges. The addition of a seasonal maintenance worker to the staff would enable the refuge to meet many of the objectives identified in this plan. To efficiently perform their duties, all refuge employees need appropriate equipment including vehicles, computers, field equipment, etc. This equipment needs to be upgraded periodically.

Strategy: Revise and update the Station Safety Plan written in 1984.

Strategy: Construct a 40 x 70 ft. metal storage building with a concrete floor to store refuge equipment used in maintaining habitat and public use areas.

Strategy: Install road culvert along entrance road of Grulla NWR to allow access into fenced area of refuge for law enforcement, wildlife surveys, wildfire control, and sign and fence maintenance.

Strategy: Use RONS and MMS to upgrade computers, office equipment, field equipment, and vehicles as needed in order to provide an efficient and productive support system for refuge staff.

Strategy: Coordinate with the DFMO to have available necessary equipment and supplies for presuppression, prescribed burn, and wildfire suppression activities.

6.0 PLAN IMPLEMENTATION

Refuge objectives are intended to be accomplished over the next 15 years. New management activities will be phased in over time. Implementation of these will be contingent upon results of biological inventories, monitoring and evaluation, funding, staffing, and regional and national Service directives. This section identifies resource projects, staffing, partnership opportunities, step-down management plans, and the CCP monitoring and evaluation plan.

6.1 Resource Projects

Listed below is a summary of major resource project needs addressing the goals and objectives of this plan. Each project summary includes planning links to this CCP and a preliminary range of cost estimates for project implementation over the next 15 years. This list only reflects the basic needs identified by the planning team based on available information and is subject to modification depending on future conditions, needs, and cost adjustments.

Project 1.   Habitat Management

Develop habitat management and inventory and monitoring plans for the refuges. This will involve vegetation maps delineating major habitat types on Muleshoe and Grulla NWRs, and an inventory of plant species associated with each habitat. Implement habitat monitoring programs for grassland habitats targeted for restoration activities such as prescribed fire and grazing. As part of the habitat management program, water sources will be protected on Muleshoe NWR to provide at least 600 acres of wetland habitats for migratory birds. Other potential water resources will be investigated and pursued if feasible. Integrate the FMP goals and objectives with those of the CCP to achieve CCP goals and objectives.

Planning Links: Goal 1, Objectives 1, 2, 4, 5, 6, 7, 8, and 9; Goal 3, Objective 2 and 4; Goal 5, Objective 1; Goal 6, Objective 1; Fire Management Plan

Project 2.   Population Management

A current inventory of baseline biological data is needed for both Muleshoe and Grulla NWRs. With this information, wildlife inventory plans can be updated with realistic population objectives. Current inventory and habitat plans are essential for making informed management decisions affecting the refuge resources. Refuge census/surveys to monitor natural population fluctuations will be expanded to include additional inventories determined through a biological review process.

Planning Links: Goal 1, Objectives 2, 3, 4, 5, 6, and 9; Goal 5, Objective 1; Goal 6, Objective 1;
Fire Management Plan

Project 3.   Boundary Protection

Through a combination of strategies inclusive of considering private agreements, purchase from willing sellers of fee title interest, and less than fee title interest in lands adjacent to Grulla NWR the refuge could provide improved access. This would allow proper fencing of boundary line and prevent trespass cattle form entering refuge lands. However, any land acquisition consideration is conceptual only; and, any discussion relative to the expansion of the refuge boundary must undergo separate NEPA compliance. Less than fee considerations must also undergo separate boundary expansion compliance and such would have to be done at a later time.

Planning Links: Goal 3, Objectives 1, 2, 3, and 4; Goal 5, Objective 1; Goal 6, Objective 1

Project 4. Archaeological Survey

Complete a comprehensive archaeological survey of Muleshoe and Grulla NWRs to obtain baseline information for the protection of existing cultural resources. This project is essential to meet cultural resource mandates.

Planning Links: Goal 2, Objective 1; Goal 5, Objective 1; Goal 6, Objective 1

Project 5. Develop and Implement Public Use Plan

Develop a Public Use Plan for these two refuges. Proposed funding to complete tasks outlined in the Plan which may include installation of informational, boundary, and directional signs; developing visitor interpretive displays and exhibits at headquarters; producing environmental education and outreach materials; installing outdoor interpretive signs at wildlife viewing areas; and designing an outdoor classroom curriculum guide with field equipment.

Planning Links: Goal 4, Objectives 1, 2, and 3; Goal 5, Objective 1; Goal 6, Objectives 1 and 2; Fire Management Plan

6.2 Current and Proposed Funding and Personnel

Current Staff:

The refuge has a current staff of three permanent FTEs which has remained the same since the refuges were established.

Refuge Manager	GS-12	PFT
Administrative Technician	GS-7	PFT
Maintenance Worker	WG-8	PFT

In addition, approximately 200 hours of volunteer time has been contributed on an annual basis at Muleshoe and Grulla NWRs, primarily for maintenance and wildlife observation.

Proposed Staff:

To accomplish the goals and objectives of this plan, the following increase in staff would be required:

Wildlife Biologist	GS-7/9	PFT
Refuge Law Enforcement Officer	GS-5/7/9	PFT
Maintenance Worker (Grulla NWR)	WG-8	PFT
Public Use Specialist	GS-9	PFT
Resource Specialist	GS-5/6	Seasonal

Current base funding and other funds:

Total annual budget for the refuge varies depending on the Service priorities for the resource projects each year and the national and regional allocation of RONS

---

and MMS funds. The following is a general breakdown of the annual operation budget of the refuges:

Muleshoe NWR:

Year	O&M 1261*	MMS 1262*	Volunteer	YCC	Grazing 6860*	Fire 9120*	Total
1999	181,200	10,800	0	0	0	0	192,000
1998	142,800	12,000	0	0	0	0	154,800
1997	125,000	5,000	0	0	0	1300	131,300
1996	130,430	14,600	0	0	0	1200	146,230
1995	110,000	22,000	0	0	0	3900	135,900

Grulla NWR:

Year	O&M 1261*	MMS 1262*	Volunteer	YCC	Grazing 6860*	Fire 9120*	Total
1999	0	6,000	0	0	0	0	6,000
1998	0	1,000	0	0	0	0	1000
1997	0	0	0	0	0	0	0
1996	0	4,000	0	0	0	0	4000
1995	0	0	0	0	0	0	0

*Description of funding categories:

> 1261 funds are used for fixed costs for salaries, supplies, etc., mandatory training/travel, operational activities, and routine maintenance.

> 1262 (MMS) funds are restricted to deferred maintenance/replacement of refuge facilities and infrastructure which cannot be accomplished with Operation & Maintenance (O&M) funding.

> 9100 funds are for fire management funding for prescribed fire.

A list of RONS projects can be found in Appendix E.

6.3 Partnership Opportunities

There are many opportunities to partner with state and federal governmental agencies, NGOs, private landowners, and local conservation groups to combine efforts on resource issues or projects that would be mutually beneficial to all with the greatest benefits to the area's natural resources.

- Establish partnerships through cooperative agreements with Eastern New Mexico University, Texas Technical Institute, University of Texas, and other universities to provide seasonal student interns to assist with refuge biological programs, GIS mapping, habitat and maintenance projects, and education/outreach efforts. Once the research needs of the refuge are determined, encourage these institutions to develop proposals to conduct the research.

- Pursue opportunities to strengthen existing partnerships with the New Mexico Game and Fish Department (NMGFD) and TPWD to provide the following mutual benefits: volunteers to share duties associated with public use and maintenance on the refuge, enhanced biological programs and management strategies of habitats and wildlife populations on federal and state lands, shared research opportunities and information that would mutually benefit wildlife management on federal and state lands, improve wildlife-oriented recreation opportunities, and contribute through coordinated efforts to local law enforcement coverage for game violations.

Natural Resource Conservation Service (NRCS) personnel from the South Plains Area sometimes use the Refuge for a NRCS grassland field day to "brush up" on their grassland analysis techniques (photo by Don Clapp)

- Establish partnerships with NRCS and private landowners to participate in the HPP and other initiatives to improve habitat for wildlife by restoring species diversity and the condition of the range through the use of grazing management. Encourage private landowners to participate in initiatives and partnerships to protect, enhance, and restore habitats for priority species (lesser prairie chicken, black-tailed prairie dogs, mountain plover, swift fox, etc.) occurring on their lands.

- Initiate dialogue with private landowners and conservation organizations for land exchanges or land acquisition on Grulla NWR and land protection such as easements for the protection of refuge water sources on Grulla and Muleshoe NWRs.

- Through the Service's Technical Services, coordinate with Texas Water Resources Commission, TNRCC, and TPWD to determine the feasibility of pumping groundwater on new wells (acquiring groundwater rights to pump) and strategies to protect surface water dispersing onto the refuge lands.

- Maintain and strengthen partnerships with private landowners, other Service Divisions such as the Service Migratory Bird Management Division, Buffalo Lake NWR, and other agencies (TPWD- Migratory and Game Birds, Airforce Bases) to improve the management of waterfowl, sandhill cranes, and other migratory bird populations for the resolution of crop depredation by cranes, and prevention and clean up of avian disease outbreaks.

- Pursue opportunities with local businesses, schools, scouts, and other organizations to adopt the refuge for projects or special community programs such as Earth Day, Green Team, etc.

- Pursue partnerships with the Audubon chapters in Amarillo and Lubbock, Texas, and Portales, New Mexico to conduct long-term bird surveys, promote the refuge in the Audubon Adventure Educational Programs for local schools, and assist with future wildlife tours.

- Pursue partnerships with organizations and community civic groups such as TEAN, the local Chambers of Commerce, Texas Waterfowlers Association, Ducks Unlimited, Texas Fish and Wildlife Society, the local Audubon chapters, Wildlife Association, etc. to help foster wildlife observation at the refuge and assist with nature tours or other public use events.

- Continue cooperative agreements with the Bailey County Volunteer Fire Departments, Muleshoe Fire Department, Texas Forest Service, Roosevelt County Volunteer Fire Departments, Portales Fire Department and the New Mexico State Division of Forestry. Utilize the Joint Powers Operating Plan for additional fire assets. Develop a formal agreement for interagency cooperation with Lake Meredith National Recreation Area of the National Park Service and expand current coordination between the Service and Lake Meredith for local fire operations.

Maintaining and developing partnerships will enable the refuge to achieve its goals and objectives, minimize costs, share funding and bridge relationships with other. To maintain and enhance wildlife outside of the refuge, the Service will focus its efforts on continuing to develop partnerships with landowners, the state resource agencies, and interested conservation and sportsmen groups. Although the Service does not have management responsibilities for those lands outside the refuge, it is important to articulate the wildlife resource needs area wide. Collaboration with colleges and universities and with conservation organizations will enable the refuge to carry on its plan for research, monitoring, and education. To create awareness and expand environmental education efforts in the community, partnerships will be established or expanded with organizations and school systems.

6.4 Step-Down Management Planning

The following is an annotated list of step-down management plans that are required for the programs implemented on Muleshoe and Grulla NWRs. Many of the plans have been completed and include compatibility determinations and environmental assessments. The preparation and execution of these plans is dependent on funding and the availability of staff or technical support.

6.4.1 Completed Plans for Muleshoe NWR

The following plans and documents have been completed and are subject to review and periodic updates:

Wildlife Inventory and Monitoring Plan

Describes specific wildlife inventory activities and techniques to be conducted to monitor wildlife populations including specific species population objectives, census/survey methods, data analysis, and reporting requirements. Originally completed in 1968. Last updated in 1988.

Prescribed Burning Plan

Describes the planned use of prescribed fire on the refuge, including purpose of the treatment, location and description of treatment area, alternatives, prescriptions, fire suppression methods, and reporting/monitoring requirements. Completed in 1988.

Law Enforcement Management Plan

Describes refuge law enforcement program guidelines, which includes identification of problems, solutions, objectives and management strategies to achieve effective law enforcement on the refuge. Completed in 1988.

Quarters Management Plan

Refuge has one quarters building which was occupied by the refuge manager until 1996. A volunteer has lived in the refuge house since the manager moved off-site. This plan describes the history of vandalism, theft, wildfire, and visitor emergencies and indicates that it is imperative for someone to live on the refuge. Completed in 1987; should be updated.

Animal Control Plan

Describes control methods for black-tailed prairies dogs and crop depredation by sandhill cranes, waterfowl, and blackbirds. The plan states that both of these animal control programs help to promote good will and cooperation between the refuge and its neighbors. It further states that crop depredation must be controlled to prevent economic loss to farmers and other growers in the area. The justification for controlling prairie dogs was to limit the possibility of transmission of bubonic plague from prairie dogs to refuge staff or visitors and prevent prairie dogs from spreading extensively over the refuge and onto private land. Prairie dogs were controlled until 1995; this portion of the plan is no longer implemented. Plan was completed in 1986; needs to be reviewed and updated.

Station Safety Plan

Describes actions and improvements necessary to make the station facilities and operations compliant with federal occupational health and safety standards and other applicable regulations. Combined with Grulla NWR; originally completed in 1984 and amended with a Continuity of Operations Plan in July 1998.

Sign Plan

Describes signs that will be maintained on the refuge, including entrance, interpretive, regulatory (boundary and traffic control) and information. Completed in 1985.

Waterfowl Disease Contingency Plan

This disease contingency plan is prepared for Muleshoe, Grulla, and Buffalo Lake NWRs and the area known as the Playa Lakes Region. It describes procedures for identifying, reporting, and taking care problems (outbreaks of avian botulism, fowl cholera, etc.) in the region. Completed in 1985.

Interpretation Management Plan

Described actions and improvements that would provide the public with limited interpretive opportunities that are compatible with the refuge and provide them with the opportunity to learn about and understand the wildlife and habitat resources in the area. Completed in 1985 and has been fully implemented, with some modifications and additions.

Grassland Management Plan

A Grazing Plan was originally completed in 1985. That plan stated that the objective of managing grasslands on Muleshoe through grazing was to stimulate habitat diversity and provide roosting and feeding areas for sandhill cranes and raptors. The Grassland Management Plan updated the Grazing Plan with revisions to grazing AUMs, mesquite brush control proposals, and the limited use of prescribed fire. Completed in 1990.

Fire Management Plan

Approved FMPs were completed in 1984 and 2002. The latest FMP details suppression strategies and determines the best use of fire in managing and enhancing the refuge habitat. However, it does not provide specific strategies, conditions, and parameters for the use of fire to accomplish habitat objectives for targeted grassland areas.

6.4.2   Completed Plans for Grulla NWR

Interpretive Management Plan

Described actions and improvements that would provide the public with limited interpretive opportunities that are compatible with the refuge and provide them with the opportunity to learn about and understand the wildlife and habitat resources in the area. Includes site planning for vehicular parking and interpretive area. Completed in 1985.

Station Safety Plan

Describes actions and improvements necessary to make the station facilities and operations compliant with federal occupational health and safety standards and other applicable regulations. Combined with Muleshoe Plan; originally completed in 1984, updated in July 1998.

Fire Management Plan

Completed in 1984. This plan described background of the refuge and concluded that prescribed fire is not a practical management tool at this refuge (at that time).

Law Enforcement Management Plan

Describes refuge law enforcement program guidelines, which includes identification of problems, solutions, objectives and management strategies to achieve effective law enforcement on the refuge. Completed in 1988.

Waterfowl Disease Contingency Plan

This disease contingency plan is prepared for Muleshoe , Grulla, and Buffalo Lake NWRs and the area known as the Playa Lakes Region. It describes procedures for identifying, reporting, and taking care of problems (outbreaks of avian botulism, fowl cholera, etc.) in the region. Completed in 1985.

Wildlife Inventory Plan

Described specific wildlife inventory activities and techniques to be used to monitor wildlife on Grulla, including specific species population objectives, census/survey methods, and reporting requirements. Completed in 1988. Needs to be updated.

Sign Plan

Described signs that will be maintained at the refuge, including an entrance sign, information and regulatory signs, and two interpretive signs at the overlook of Salt Lake. Completed in 1985. This plan has been fully implemented and needs to be updated.

6.4.3   Plans and Documents to be Completed in the Future - Both Refuges

The following plans and documents will be developed and subjected to review and periodic updates.

Public Use Management Plan

Addresses specific wildlife related public recreation issues and needs. This plan will identify opportunities for visitors to enjoy and appreciate fish, wildlife, and other resources. As a result, the public will develop an understanding and appreciation for the mission of the Fish and Wildlife Service and the National Wildlife Refuge System. It will identify appropriate/quality recreational opportunities that are conducted in a safe and cost-effective manner; develop and implement a quality environmental education program; interpret key resources and issues; and build volunteer programs and partnerships with refuge support groups. This plan will incorporate updates of the old interpretive management and sign plans.

Habitat Management Plan

Describes the most appropriate management strategies for habitat protection, enhancement, and restoration; emphasizes specific habitats and areas for management activities; provides monitoring methods and evaluation criteria.

Cultural Resource Management Plan

Identifies areas with cultural historic importance and provides methods for the management of these resources. The Cultural Resource Management (CRM) plan also identifies areas of potential significance and outlines site information so managers can make better decisions regarding development or management activities. A comprehensive cultural resource inventory is a prerequisite to the development of the CRM plan as land management activities, including public access, could impact unidentified or unevaluated resources.

Integrated Pest Management Plan

This plan will describe biological, mechanical, or chemical methods for the most effective control and eradication of exotic weeds, woody vegetation, and specific pests, for the protection and restoration of natural resources and biota of the area. The IPM will be consistent with National Fish and Wildlife Service guidance for development of IPM plans.

Fire Management Plan

A comprehensive FMP will be completed after the CCP is formalized. This plan will supercede previous plans and will guide fire management actions for the planning period and beyond. The FMP will support refuge goals and objectives. It will identify specific strategies, conditions, and parameters for use of fire to accomplish habitat objectives for grassland and wetland areas.

Research Plan

Describes the research needs of the refuge to support management goals and objectives. It will describe and prioritize specific research needs, and these will be reflected in accompanying RONS projects. It will be developed utilizing input from refuge and Regional Office staff, and from researchers knowledgeable about the species and habitats that occur on the refuge.

Hunt Plan

Describes compatible hunting opportunities that may be safely implemented on the refuge. Will be developed in cooperation with TPWD.

6.5 Compatibility Determinations and NEPA Compliance

Compatibility determinations are written to determine that specific uses of the refuge are compatible with the purpose and objectives for which the refuge was established. The Refuge Manager will usually complete compatibility determinations as part of the CCP or step-down management plan process for individual uses, specific use programs, or groups of related uses described in the plan. When we add lands to the Refuge System, the Refuge Manager assigned management responsibility for the land to be acquired will identify (prior to acquisition)the existing wildlife-dependent recreational public uses (if any) that are compatible and will determine whether they will be permitted to continue.

Compatibility determinations in existence prior to the effective date of the compatibility policy will remain in effect until and unless modified and will be subject to periodic reevaluation. We will not initiate or permit a new use of a national wildlife refuge or expand, renew, or extend an existing use, unless we have determined that it is compatible with the purpose of the refuge and is not a public safety issue.

We do not require a compatibility determination for refuge management activities as defined by the term "refuge management activity" except for "refuge management economic activities." Examples of refuge management activities that do not require a compatibility determination include: prescribed burning; water level management; invasive species control; routine scientific monitoring, studies, surveys, and censuses; historic preservation activities; law enforcement activities; and maintenance of existing refuge facilities, structures, and improvements.

NEPA Compliance is involved with these determinations. Recreational Act Funding Analysis was completed to determine that the refuge base funding allocated for recreational use management is adequate to administer and manage the recreational public uses and ensure compatibility.

Compatibility determinations were reviewed for the following public uses at Muleshoe and Grulla NWRs: wildlife observation, photography, camping, picnicking, and grazing. No uses currently being conducted on the refuge were found to be incompatible.

The FMP for the Complex will be included in the NEPA process for the CCP, and the environmental assessment for the CCP will include fire activities planned for the Muleshoe/Grulla Complex.

6.5.1 Compatibility Determinations Completed for Muleshoe NWR:

Compatibility determinations were reviewed for five uses at this refuge: wildlife observation, photography, camping, picnicking, and grazing. No uses currently being conducted on the refuge were found to be incompatible. The compatibility determinations detailed below, which were completed in 1994, were reviewed through the CCP planning process and determined to be current and applicable. In addition, a compatibility determination for Hunting was completed (see Appendix F).

Compatibility Determination and Recreation Act Funding Analysis: Wildlife Observation and Photography, 1994

Determined that these activities are compatible with the goals and objectives of the refuge. The majority of the refuge visitors visit the refuge to view wildlife and to be in a natural environment. Wildlife observation and photography are justifiable wildlife-oriented activities and are compatible with the refuge purposes. (NEPA Compliance: Categorical Exclusion, 1994)

Compatibility Determination for Grazing, 1994

Determined that these activities are compatible with the goals and objectives of the refuge. Refuge grasslands are comprised primarily of grama grasses and alkali sacaton grasses. Grazing is an effective habitat management tool designed to benefit wildlife objectives. (NEPA Compliance: Categorical Exclusion, 1994)

Rest Rotation Grazing Environmental Assessment, 1994

The Environmental Assessment determined that continued livestock grazing as a management tool for refuge grasslands was compatible with the goals and objectives of the refuge. Controlled seasonal grazing of between 80-100 AUMs was determined not to have an adverse impact on the habitat and historical resources of the refuge or on any species of plant and wildlife including the bald eagle, whooping crane, or other state listed species. (NEPA Compliance: Environmental Assessment, Section 7 Biological Evaluation, and Finding of No Significant Impact, 1994.)

Compatibility Determination and Recreation Act Funding Analysis: Camping and Picnicking, 1994

Determined that camping and picnicking at a small designated campground near the refuge headquarters are compatible with the goals and objectives of the refuge. Most visitors that use the campground and picnic area are there for the purpose of wildlife observation. Since the refuge is 20 miles from the nearest motel accommodations, the campground is beneficial to those visitors wishing to view wildlife during the early morning and late evening hours when they are most active. (NEPA Compliance: Categorical Exclusion, 1994)

6.5.2 Compatibility Determinations Completed for Grulla NWR:

Compatibility determinations were reviewed for one use, wildlife observation, at this refuge. The use was Categorically Excluded and a Recreation Fund Analysis was completed. This compatibility determination was reviewed through the CCP planning process and determined to be current and applicable.

Compatibility Determination for Wildlife Observation, 1994

Determined that this activity is compatible with the goals and objectives of the refuge. The majority of the refuge visitors visit the refuge to view wildlife and to be in a natural environment. Wildlife observation is justifiable wildlife-oriented activity that is compatible with the refuge purposes. (NEPA Compliance: Categorical Exclusion, 1994)

6.6 Monitoring and Evaluation of the CCP

The National Wildlife Refuge System Improvement Act requires that the Service monitor fish, wildlife, and plants on refuges in order to establish status and trends of both resident and migratory wildlife. Monitoring is an essential component of this plan, and specific strategies have been integrated into the previously described goals and objectives. All habitat management activities will be monitored to assess whether the desired effect on wildlife and habitat has been achieved. Baseline surveys will be established for species of wildlife for which existing or historical numbers are not well known.

If the plan is to be a useful measure of the achievements of the refuge programs and useful to future refuge managers, documentation needs to be a priority to determine if the objectives are achieved within the time frame of this plan. The existing refuge programs, current data bases, and guidelines for monitoring and evaluation of each step-down program plan needs to be considered in the review, evaluation, and amendments of the CCP. Implementation of the CCP will require periodic review and adjustments to amend the plan so it will continue to be effective as the programs progress.

Where possible, the CCP identified and incorporated monitoring and evaluation activities as objectives or strategies under the general goals for the refuge. Specific guidelines for monitoring and evaluation will vary by program and need to be developed and referred to in the appropriate step-down plan.

6.7 Plan Amendment and Revision

The Muleshoe and Grulla National Wildlife Refuge CCP is a dynamic plan. While it will serve as a guide for overall refuge direction, it will be adjusted to consider new and better information, ensuring that refuge activities best serve the established purpose of these refuges and the mission of the National Wildlife Refuge System. The CCP will be reviewed every five years, and monitored continuously to ensure the developed management actions support the goals and objectives of
Muleshoe and Grulla NWRs.

This CCP will be informally reviewed by refuge staff while preparing annual work plans and updating the Refuge Information Management System (RMIS) database. It may also be reviewed during routine inspections or programmatic evaluations. Results of the reviews may indicate a need to modify the CCP. The monitoring of objectives is an integral part of the plan, and management activities may be modified if desired results are not achieved. If minor changes are required, the level of public involvement and associated NEPA documentation will be determined by the project leader. This CCP will be formally revised at least every 15 years.

REFERENCES

Andrews, R. and R. Righter. 1992. Colorado birds. Denver Mus. Natur. Hist., Denver, CO. 442 pp.

Brown, David E (1989): Arizona Game Birds. The University of Arizona Press and The Arizona Game and Fish Department, Tucson.

Bureau of Economic Geology, 1992. Geologic Map of Texas. Austin, Texas, Scale 1:500,000.

Carter, M.F., W.C. Hunter, D.N. Pashley, and K. V. Rosenberg, 2000. Setting Conservation priorities in the United States: Partners in Flight Approach. The Auk: 117(2):541-548. et al. 2000.

Chandler, C., Cheney, P., Thomas, P. Trabaud, L. And Williams, D. 1983. Fire in Forestry. Volumes 1 and 2. New York; Wiley

Clark, Tim W., et al., 1982. Prairie Dog Colony Attributes and Associated Vertebrate Species. Great Basin Naturalist, Vol.42(4). pp.572-582.

Craig, G. 1986. Peregrine Falcon. *Audubon Wildlife Report 1986.*

Dixon, Charles and James E. Knight 1993. Scaled Quail Habitat Management, Guide L-304. College of Agriculture and Home Economics, New Mexico State University. http://www. Cahe.nmsu.edu/pubs/-I/I-304.html

Davis, William B. and David J. Schmidly. 1994. The Mammals of Texas. Texas Parks and Wildlife; Nongame and Urban Program. 4200 Smith School Road. Austin, TX, 78744

Dechant, J. A., M. L. Sondreal, D. H. Johnson, L. D. Igl, C. M. Goldade, P. A. Rabie, and B. R. Euliss. 1999. Effects of management practices on grassland birds: Ferruginous Hawk. Northern Prairie Wildlife Research Center, Jamestown, ND. Jamestown, ND: Northern Prairie Wildlife Research Center Home Page. http://www.npwrc.usgs.gov/resource/literatr/grasbird/ferhawk/ferhawk.htm (Version 17FEB2000).

DeGraaf, R.M. and Rappole, J. H. 1995. Neotropical Migratory Birds, (Natural History, Distribution, and Population Change) Comstock Publishing Associates, a Division of Cornell University Press, Ithaca and London.

DeHoyo, J. And Elliot, A. 2000. Status and Conservation Action Plan Whooping Crane *(Grus americana).* Summary. in Handbook of the Birds of the World:Volume 3. eds. Lynx edition and the ICBP Barcelona. Section 1.5, Conservation Status. http://www.portup.com/~nacwq/whooping.htm#priority

Ehrlich, Paul R., D.S. Dobkin and D. Wheye. 1988. The Birders Handbook: a Field Guide to the Natural History of North American Birds. Simon and Schuster.

Elmore, F.H. 1976. Shrubs and Trees of the Southwest Uplands. Southwest Parks and Monuments Association.

Finch, Deborah M. August 1992. Threatened, Endangered, and Vulnerable Species of Terrestrial Vertebrates in the Rocky Mountain Region. USDA Forest Service General Technical Report RM-215

Findley, J.S., A.H. Harris, D.E. Wilson, and C. Jones. 1975. Mammals of New Mexico. University of New Mexico Press, Albuquerque, New Mexico. xxii + 360 pp.33

Field Guide to the Birds of North America, Third Edition. National Geographic Society.1999.

Garrett, J.M. and D.G. Barker. 1987. A Field Guide to Reptiles and Amphibians of Texas. Texas Monthly Press, Austin. 225 pp.

Gould, Frank W. 1993. Grasses of the Southwestern United States. University of Arizona Press.

Gould, Frank. W. 1975 . Texas Plants, A Checklist and Ecological Summary. The Texas A&M University System, The Texas Agricultural Experiment Station.

Graul, W.D. 1975 Breeding biology of the Mountain Plover. Wilson Bull. 87:6-31

Graul, W.D. and L.E. Webster. 1976. Breeding status of the Mountain Plover. Condor 78:265-267.

Gustavson, T. C., 1996. Fluvial and eolian depositional systems, paleosols, and paleoclimate of the Upper Cenozoic Ogallala and Blackwater Draw formations, southern High Plains, Texas and New Mexico. Austin, Texas, Bureau of Economic Geology, Report of Investigations No. 239, 62.

Hall, R.S., R.L. Glinski, D.H. Ellis, J.M. Ramakka, and D.L. Base. 1988. Ferruginous Hawk. Pp. 111-118 in R.L. Glinski et al., eds. Proceedings of the southwest raptor management symposium and workshop. Natl. Wildl. Fed. Scien. Tech. Ser. No. 11.

Hall, S. A., and Valastro, S., Jr., 1995. Grassland vegetation in the southern Great Plains during the last glacial maximum. Quaternary Research, v. 40, p. 127-133.

Hammerson, G.A. 1981. An ecogeographic analysis of the herpetofauna of Colorado. PhD. Thesis, University of Colorado, Boulder.

Hanson, H.C. 1939. Fire in land use and management. Am. Midland Naturalist 21:415-434.

Harrison, R.L. and Schmitt, C.G. 1998. Current Swift Fox (*Vulpes velox*) Distribution and Habitat Selection Within Areas of Historical Occurrence in New Mexico. Swift Fox Symposium. USGS Northern Prairie Wildlife Research Center. http://www.npwrc.usgs.gov/resource/1998/swiftfox/page14.htm

Hawks Aloft, Inc. 2000. Nesting, Productivity, and food habits of Ferruginous Hawks as a function of Priaire dog towns in central, western and northwestern New Mexico. Unpublished report for the Bureau of Land Management, Socorro and Farmington District Offices and New Mexico Department of Game and Fish.

Higgins 1984 - USFWS Fire Report

Holliday, V. T., 1995. Stratigraphy and paleoenvironments of late Quaternary valley fills on the southern High Plains. Boulder, Colo., Geological Society of America, Memoir 186, 136 p.

Hubbard, J.P. 1985. Least Tern (*Sterna antillarum*). New Mexico Department o Game and Fish, Handbook Spec. End. In New Mexico BIRD/LA/ST/AN:1-2

Hubbard, J.P. 1978. Revised check-list of the birds of New Mexico. New Mexico Ornithological Society, Publication No. 6

Humphrey, Robert R. 1962. Range Ecology. The Roland Press Co., New York City.

Hundertmark, C.A. 1974. Breeding range extensions of certain birds in New Mexico. Wilson Bulletin 86:298-300.

Iverson, P., A Vohs, and T.C. Tacha. 1985. Distribution and abundance of sandhill cranes wintering in western Texas. J. Wildl. Manage. 49: 250-255.

Jones, J. Knox, et al. 1987. Annotated Checklist of Recent Mammals of Northwestern Texas. In Occasional Papers of The Museum of Texas Tech University. Number 111; 13 pp.

Knowles, C.J., C.J. Stoner, and S.P. Gieb. 1982. Selective use of black-tailed prairie dog towns by mountain plovers. Condor 84:71-74.

Kotliar, N.B., B.W. Baker, A.D. Whicker, and G. Plumb. 1999. A critical review of assumptions about the prairie dog as a keystone species. Environmental Management 24(2)177-192.

Lame, J. 1968. *Ammodramus bairdii* (Audubon), Baird's sparrow. U.S. Nat. Mus. Bull. 237:745-765.

Lewis, J.C. 1995. Whooping crane _in_ The Birds of North America, No. 153. Academy of Natural Sciences, Philadelphia, PA and American Ornithologists' Union, Washington, D.C. 28 pp.

Littlefield, Carrol D. 2000. Birds of Muleshoe National Wildlife Refuge and Surrounding Counties, Texas. Unpublished report. 175 pp.

Mack, R. N. and J. N. Thompson. 1982. Evolution in steppe with few large, hooved mammals. Am. Nat. 119:757-773.

McMahon, C.A., R.G. Frye, and K.L. Brown. 1984. The vegetation types of Texas including cropland. Texas Parks and Wildlife Department. Austin, Texas, unpaged.

New Mexico Department of Game and Fish. 1988. Handbook of Species Endangered in New Mexico, F-580:1-2.

New Mexico Department of Game and Fish. 1990. Checklist of the Native Birds of New Mexico. Santa Fe, New Mexico, 87503. June 30, 1990.

Oberholser, H.C. 1974. The Bird Life of Texas, Vol.2. Univ. of Texas Press, Austin, TX 537pp.

Olendorff, R.R. 1993. Status, biology and management of ferruginous hawks: a review. Raptor Research and Technological Assistance Center Special Report. U.S. Department of Interior, Bureau of Land Management : Boise, ID

Pianka, E.R. and W.S. Parker. 1995. Ecology of horned lizards: a review with special reference to *Phrynosoma platryrhinos*. Copeia 1975(1):141-162.

Regional Economic Information System. 1997. Regional Economic Information for Bailey County, Texas. REIS Texas Home Page: http://govinfo.library.orst.edu/cgi-bin/reis-list?9_05-017.txc

Root, T. 1988. Atlas of Wintering North American birds. University of Chicago Press, Chicago, lL. 312pp.

Sauer, J.R., G. Peterjohn, S. Schwartz, and J.E. Hines. 1995. *The Grassland Bird Home Page. Version 95.0 Patuxent Wildlife Research Center, Laurel, MD*

Sauer, Carl O. 1950. Grassland climax, fire and man. J. Range Manage. 3 (1) :16-21.

Schmutz , J.K. 1984. Ferruginous and Swainson's hawk abundance and distribution in relation to land use in southeastern Alberta. Jour. Wildl. Manage. 48.1180-1187.

Sharrow, Stephen H., Henry A. Wright. 1977. Proper burning intervals for tobosa grass in west Texas based on nitrogen dynamics. J. Range Manage. 30 (5): 343-346.

Seyffert, K.D. 1985. The Breeding Birds of the Texas Panhandle. Bull. Texas Ornithological Society. 18:7-20.

Stebbin, R.C. 1954. Amphibians and Reptiles of Western North America. McGraw-Hill Book Co., Inc., New York

Stebbins, R.C. 1985. A Field Guide to Western Reptiles and Amphibians. Houghton Mifflin Co. Boston.

Stewart, R.E. 1975. Breeding birds of North Dakota. Harrison Smith, Lund Press, Minneapolis, Mn 295pp.

Stewart, 1955. O.C. Why were the prairies treeless? Southwestern Lore. 20:59-64

Stoddart, Lawrence A. and Arthur D. Smith. 1955. Range Management. McGraw-Hill Book Co., Inc. New York City.

Stravers, J.A. and G.L. Garber. 1998. Nest site selection, reproductive success and territory reoccupation of ferruginous hawks in three regions of New Mexico. Unpublished report, Bureau of Land Management, Socorro and Farmington Field Office.

Sutton, G.M. 1967. Oklahoma birds. University of Oklahoma Press, Norman, OK. 674 pp.

Texas Parks and Wildlife Department. 2000. Exploring Texas: The High Plains. http://www.tpwd.state.tx.us/expltx/eft/bison/highplains.htm

Texas Parks and Wildlife Department. 2000. Wildlife Fact Sheets. http://www.tpwd.state.tx.us/nature/wild/birds/htm http://www.tpwd.state.tx.us/nature/wild/animals/htm http://www.tpwd.state.tx.us/nature/wild/reptiles/htm http://www.tpwd.state.tx.us/nature/endang/animals/htm

Texas Tech University. 2000. The Science Coalition. Environment–Water Resources. http://www.texastech.edu/research/water.htm

Texas Ornithological Society. 1995. Checklist of the Birds of Texas, 3rd edition. Printed by Capital Printing, Inc. Austin, Texas, U.S.A.

Thompson, M.C. and C. Ely. 1989. Birds of Kansas, Vol.1, Univ. of Kansas Museum of Nat. History. Public education Series No. 11, Lawrence, KS

Udvardy, M.D.F. 1977. The Audubon Society Field Guide to North American Birds (Western Region). Alfred A. Knopf, Inc. New York.

U.S. Census Bureau. 2000. http:/www.census.gov/www/cen2000.html

U.S. Census Bureau. 1999. State and County Quick Facts. http://quickfacts.census.gov/qfd/states/48000.html

U.S. Census Bureau. 1997. Highlights of Agriculture 1997 and 1992, Bailey County, Texas. http://www.nass.usda.gov/census/census97/highlights/tx/txc009.txt

U.S. Department of Agriculture.. 1997. Texas Agriculture Statistics Service. Census of Agriculture County Profile, Bailey, Texas

U.S. Department of Agriculture, Soil Conservation Service and Forest Service. 1959. Soil Survey Series No. 21. Bailey County, Texas (sections by Robert B. Orton) pp.1-3

U.S. Department of Commerce, Bureau of Economic Analysis. 2000. Regional Accounts Data: Regional Economic Profile, Bailey County, Texas http://www.bea.doc.gov/bea/regional/reis/ca30/48/ca30_48017.htm

U.S. Department of Interior, National Biological Survey and National Park Serice. 1994. Final Draft Accuracy Assessment Procedures, NBS/NPS Vegetation Mapping Program.

U.S. Geologic Survey, 1998. Swift Fox Symposium. Northern Prairie Wildlife Research Center. http://www.npwrc.usgs.gov/resource/1998/swiftfox/htm

U.S. Geologic Survey, 2000. Partners in Flight homepage. Physiographic Area Plan (55) Pecos and Staked Plains. Executive Summary. http://www.blm.gov/wildlife/pl_55sum.htm

U.S. Fish and Wildlife Service. 1935. Detailed Plan. Muleshoe Lakes Migratory Waterfowl Refuge, Bailey County, Texas. Project of the Bureau of Biological Survey.

U.S. Fish and Wildlife Service. 1938. Supplemental Report. Muleshoe Lakes Migratory Waterfowl Refuge, Bailey County, Texas. Project of the Bureau of Biological Survey.

U.S. Fish and Wildlife Service. 1966. Summary of the Proposed Land Acquisition: Grulla National Wildlife Refuge. Internal Memorandum. 5pp.

U.S. Fish and Wildlife Service. 1985. Malheur National Wildlife Refuge Master Plan and Environmental Assessment.

U.S. Fish and Wildlife Service. 1990. Whooping Crane. http://species.fws.gov/bio_whoo.html

U.S. Fish and Wildlife Service. 1993. Endangered and Threatened Wildlife and Plants; Determination of Threatened Status for the Pacific Coast Population of the Western Snowy Plover. 50 CFR Part 17. http://endangered.fws.gov/r/fr93493.html

U.S. Fish and Wildlife Service. 1995. 50 CFR Part 17. Endangered and Threatened Wildlife and Plants; 12-Month Finding for a Petition To List the Swift Fox as Endangered.

U.S. Fish and Wildlife Service. 1993. Endangered and Threatened Wildlife and Plants; Determination of Threatened Status for the Pacific Coast Population of the Western Snowy Plover. http://endangered.fws.gov/r/fr93493.html

U.S. Fish and Wildlife Service. 1994. Environmental Assessment Grassland Management, U.S. Fish and Wildlife Service, Region 2, Muleshoe National Wildlife Refuge, Muleshoe National Wildlife Refuge

U.S. Fish and Wildlife Service. 1994. Endangered and Threatened Wildlife and Plants; Animal Candidate Review for Listing as Endangered or Threatened Species; Propose Rule. Federal Register. November 15, 1994.

U.S. Fish and Wildlife Service. 1994. Edwards Ecosystem Plan. Edwards Ecosystem Team, Albuquerque, New Mexico 15pp.

U.S. Fish and Wildlife Service. 1995. Endangered and threatened species: bald eagle reclassification, final rule. Federal Register 50:35999-36010. July 12, 1995.

U.S. Fish and Wildlife Service. 1999. High Plains Patrnership–Conservation of the High Plains Legacy. 3pp.

U.S. Fish and Wildlife Service. 1999. Endangered and threatened wildlife and plants: propose rule to remove the bald eagle in the lower 48 states from the list of endangered and threatened wildlife. Federal Register 64:36454-36464.

U.S. Fish and Wildlife Service. 1999. Endangered and threatened wildlife and plants: proposed threatened status for the mountain plover. Federal Register 64:7587-7601. February 16, 1999.

U.S. Fish and Wildlife Service. 1999. Endangered and threatened wildlife and plants: final rule to remove the American peregrine falcon from the federal list of endangered and threatened wildlife, and to remove the similarity of appearance provision for free-flying peregrines in the conterminous United States. Federal Register 64:46543. August 25, 1999.

U.S. Fish and Wildlife Service. 1990-2001. Muleshoe National Wildlife Refuge Annual Narrative Reports Calender Years: 1990-2001. Muleshoe National Wildlife Refuge.

U.S. Fish and Wildlife Service. 1990-2001. Grulla National Wildlife Refuge Annual Narrative Reports Calender Years: 1990-2001. Grulla National Wildlife Refuge.

Valentine, John F. 1971 Range Development and Improvements. 2nd Edition. Brigham Young University Press, Provo, Utah. 545pp.

Whitson, T.D., L.C. Burrill, S.A. Dewey, D. Cudney, B.E. Nelson, R.D. Lee, R. Parker. 1991 Weeds of the West. Western Society of Weed Science. Pioneer of Jackson Hole, Publ.

LIST OF PREPARERS

Carol Torrez - Biologist/Natural Resource Planner, Division of Planning, Region 2, U.S. Fish and Wildlife Service, Albuquerque, New Mexico.

Research Management Consultants, Inc. (RMCI):
Louis J. Bridges - Project Scientist/Biologist
J. Paul Wharry - Environmental Scientist IV
C. Anne Janik - Environmental Scientist III
Jeff Fountain - Environmental Scientist III

Contributors:

Thomas P. Baca, Chief, Division of Planning, Region 2, U.S. Fish and Wildlife Service, Albuquerque, New Mexico

John Slown, Biologist/Natural Resource Planner, Division of Planning, Region 2, U.S. Fish and Wildlife Service, Albuquerque, New Mexico

Yvette Truitt, Biologist/Natural Resource Planner, Division of Planning, Region 2, U.S. Fish and Wildlife Service, Albuquerque, New Mexico

Harold Beierman, Refuge Manager, Muleshoe and Grulla National Wildlife Refuges

Jude Smith, Refuge Biologist, Muleshoe, Grulla, and Buffalo Lake NWRs

Don Clapp, Refuge Manager (Retired), Muleshoe and Grulla National Wildlife Refuges.

Rod Krey, Refuge Supervisor OK/TX, NWRS, Region 2, U.S. Fish and Wildlife Service, Albuquerque, New Mexico

Patty Hoban, Biologist/GIS (Mapping), Division of Technical Services, Region 2, U.S. Fish and Wildlife Service, Albuquerque, New Mexico.

April Fletcher, Invasive Species Coordinator, Division of Resource Management, Region 2, U.S. Fish and Wildlife Service, Albuquerque, New Mexico

Kathy Granillo, Regional Refuge Biologist, Division of Resource Management, Region 2, U.S. Fish and Wildlife Service, Albuquerque, New Mexico

Bill Howe, Non-game Migratory Bird Coordinator, Division of Migratory Birds, Region 2, U.S. Fish and Wildlife Service, Albuquerque, New Mexico

David Haukos, Regional Migratory Gamebird Specialist, Division of Migratory Birds, Region 2, U.S. Fish and Wildlife Service, Lubbock, Texas

GLOSSARY

Adaptive Management: Refers to the process in which policy decisions are implemented within a framework of scientifically driven experiments to test predictions and assumptions inherent in management plans. Analysis of results help managers to determine whether current management should continue as is or it should be modified to achieve desired conditions.

Alternative: 1) A reasonable way to fix the identified problem or satisfy the stated need (40 CFR 1500.2); 2) Alternatives are different means of accomplishing refuge purposes and goals and contributing to the System mission (Draft Service Manual 602 FW 1.5).

AUM or Animal Unit Month: A measure of the quantity of livestock forage. Equivalent to the forage sufficient to sustain a 1,000 pound animal (or 1 cow/calf pair) for 1 month during a normal season.

Biological Diversity: The variety of life and its processes, including the variety of living organisms, the genetic differences among them, and the communities and ecosystems in which they occur.

Categorical Exclusion: A category of actions that do not individually or cumulatively have a significant effect on the human environment and have been found to have no such effect in procedures adopted by a Federal agency pursuant to the National Environmental Policy Act (40 CFR 1508.4).

Compatible Use: A wildlife-dependent recreational use, or any other use on a refuge that will not interfere with or detract from the fulfillment of the mission of the Service or the purpose(s) of the refuge.

Comprehensive Conservation Plan or CCP: A document that describes the desired future conditions of the refuge, and provides long-range guidance and management direction for the refuge manager to accomplish the purposes of the refuge, contribute to the mission of the National Wildlife Refuge System, and meet other relevant mandates.

Ecological Integrity: The variety of life forms and their processes, including the variety of living organisms, the genetic differences among them, and the communities and ecosystems in which they occur.

Ecosystem: A dynamic interrelated complex of plant and animal communities and their associated nonliving environment.

Ecosystem Approach: A strategy or plan to protect and restore the natural function, structure, and species composition of an ecosystem, recognizing that all components are interrelated.

Ecosystem Management: Management of an ecosystem that includes all ecological, social, and economic components which make up the whole of the system.

Endangered Species: Any species of plant or animal defined through the Endangered Species Act as being in danger of extinction throughout all or a significant portion of its range, and published in the *Federal Register*.

Environmental Assessment or EA: A systematic analysis to determine if proposed actions would result in a significant effect on the quality of the environment.

Endemic Species: Plants or animals that occur naturally in a certain region and whose distribution is relatively limited to a particular locality.

Exotic or Invading Species (Noxious Weeds): Plant species designated by Federal or State law as generally possessing one or more of the following characteristics: aggressive or difficult to manage; parasitic; a carrier or host of serious insects or disease; or nonnative, new or not common to the United States, according to the Federal Noxious Weed Act (PL 93-639), a noxious weed is one that causes disease or has adverse effects on man or his environment and therefore is detrimental to the agriculture and commerce of the United States and to the public health.

Fauna: All the vertebrate and invertebrate animal species of a determined area.

Federal Trust Resources: A trust is something managed by one entity for another who hold the ownership. The Service holds in trust many natural resources for the people of the United States of America as a result of Federal Acts and treaties. Examples are species listed under the Endangered Species Act, migratory birds protected by the Migratory Bird Treaty Act and other international treaties, and native plant or wildlife found on the National Wildlife Refuge System.

Federal Trust Species: All species where the Federal government has primary jurisdiction including federally endangered or threatened species, migratory birds, anadromous fish, and certain marine mammals.

Fire Regime: A description of the frequency, severity, and extent of fire that typically occurs in an area or vegetative type.

Goals: Descriptive statements of desired future conditions.

Habitat: Suite of existing environmental conditions required by an organism for survival and reproduction. The place where an organism typically lives.

Integrated Pest Management: Methods of managing undesirable species, such as weeds, including: education, prevention, physical or mechanical methods of control, biological control; responsible chemical use; and cultural methods.

Invader Species: Members of the native plant community that become dominant or much more common when a natural regime is disturbed (e.g., native woody species in prairie ecosystems become much more common when fire frequency is decreased by fire suppression programs).

Invasive Species: Non-native species that lack natural controls and tend to aggressively dominate the plant community, often forming extensive monocultures; a plant that has been introduced into an environment or environmental conditions in which it did not evolve, and thus in which it has few or no natural enemies to limit its reproduction and spread. Both invasive and invader species generally reduce diversity and health of ecosystems when they become dominant.

Issue: Any unsettled matter that requires a management decision. For example, public uses, habitat protection needs, conflicts or controversies that are the focus of the planning effort.

Lek: A territory that is held and defended against rivals by males of certain species (such as the prairie chicken) during the breeding season. The male displays within its lek in order to attract females into the lek for mating. Females move among the leks, mating with males to whose displays they respond. Consequently, for a local population of a species , leks are usually grouped together within a breeding area and dominant males tend to occupy the more central lek, where their displays can be seen by the largest number of females.

Migration: The seasonal movement from one area to another and back.

Mission Statement: A succinct statement of a unit's purpose and reason for being.

Monitoring: The process of collecting information to track changes of selected parameter over time.

National Wildlife Refuge: A designated area of land or water or an interest in land or water within the Refuge System, including national wildlife refuges, wildlife management areas, waterfowl production areas, and other areas under Service jurisdiction for the protection and conservation of fish and wildlife, and plant resources. A complete listing of all units of the refuge system may be found in the current *Annual Report of Lands Under Control of the U.S. Fish and Wildlife Service.*

National Wildlife Refuge System: Various categories of areas (land and water) that are administered by the Secretary of the Interior and the U.S. Fish and Wildlife Service for the protection and conservation of fish and wildlife, and plant resources including species that are threatened with extinction; including national wildlife refuges, wildlife management areas, waterfowl production areas.

Native Species: Species that normally live and thrive in a particular ecosystem.

Neotropical Migratory Bird: A bird species that breeds north of the U.S. - Mexican border and winters primarily south of this border.

No Action Alternative: An alternative under which existing management would be continued.

Non-priority Public Use: Any use other than a compatible wildlife-dependent recreational use.

Objectives: Concise statements of what will be achieved, how much will be achieved, when and where it will be achieved and who is responsible for the work. Objectives are derived from goals and provide the basis for determining management strategies, monitoring refuge accomplishments, and evaluating the success of the strategies. Objectives should be attainable and time specific and should be stated quantitatively to the extent possible. If objectives cannot be stated quantitatively, they may be stated qualitatively.

Opportunities: Potential solutions to issues.

Preferred Alternative: This is the alternative determined (by the decision-maker) to best achieve the refuge purpose, vision, and goals; contributes to the Refuge System mission; addresses the significant issues; and is consistent with the principles of sound fish and wildlife management. The Service's selected alternative at the draft CCP stage.

Prescribed Fire: The skillful application of fire to natural fuels under conditions of weather, fuel moisture, soil moisture, etc., that allows confinement of the fire to a predetermined area and produces the intensity of heat and rate of spread to accomplish planned benefits to one or more objectives of habitat management, wildlife management, or hazard reduction.

Priority Public Uses: Compatible wildlife dependent recreational uses (hunting, fishing wildlife observation and photography, environmental education and interpretation) are the priority general public uses of the system and shall receive priority consideration in refuge planning and management.

Proposed Action: The Service proposed action for CCPs is to prepare and implement the CCP.

Public Involvement: The process by which interested and affected individuals, organizations, agencies, and governmental entities are offered an opportunity to become informed about, to express their opinions and participate in the planning and decision-making process of Service actions and policies. In this process, these views are studied thoroughly and thoughtful consideration of public views is given in shaping decisions for refuge management.

Purpose of the Refuge: The purposes specified in or derived from the law, proclamation, executive order, agreement, public land order, donating document, or administrative memorandum establishing, authorizing or expanding a refuge, refuge unit or refuge sub-unit.

Scoping: A process for determining the scope of issues to be addresses by a CCP and for identifying the significant issues. Involved in the process are federal, state, and local agencies, private organizations and individuals.

Special Status Species: Plants or animals that have been identified through either Federal law, State law, or agency policy, as requiring special protection or monitoring. Examples include federally listed endangered, threatened, proposed, or candidate species, state listed endangered or threatened species; U.S. Fish and Wildlife species of management concern and species identified by Partners in Flight program as being of extreme or moderately high conservation concern.

Species: A distinctive kind of plant or animal having distinguishable characteristics and that can interbreed and produce young. A category of biological classification.

Species of Management Interest: Those plant and animal species, while not falling under the definition of special status species, that are of management interest by virtue of being Federal trust species such as migratory birds, important game species, important prey species, or significant keystone species.

Strategy: A general approach or specific action, tool, or technique or combination used to achieve refuge objectives.

Step-Down Management Plan: A plan that provides the details necessary to implement strategies identified in the CCP (Draft Service Manual 602 FW 1.5).

Sound Professional Judgement: A finding, determination, or decision that is consistent with principles of sound fish and wildlife management and administration, available science and resources, and adherence to the requirements of the Refuge Administration Act and other appropriate laws.

Threatened Species -Those plant or animal species likely to become endangered species throughout all or a significant portion of their range within the foreseeable future. A plant or animal identified and defined in accordance with the 1973 Endangered species Act and published in the *Federal Register*.

Trust Species: Species for which the U.S. Fish and Wildlife Service has primary responsibility, including, most federally-listed threatened and endangered species, anadromous fishes once they enter inland U.S. waterways, migratory birds, and certain marine mammals.

Vegetation: Plants in general, or the sum of total plant life in the area.

Vegetation Type or Habitat Type: A category of land based on potential or existing dominant plant species of a particular area.

Vision Statement: A concise statement of the desired future condition of the planning unit, based primarily upon the System mission, specific refuge purposes, and other relevant mandates.

Watershed: The entire land are that collects and drains water into a stream or stream system

Wetlands: Areas such as lakes, marshes, and streams that are inundated by surface or ground water for a long enough period of time each year to support, under natural conditions, plants and animals adapted to thrive in saturated or seasonally saturated soils.

Wilderness Area (or Designated Wilderness Area): An area designated by the U.S. Congress to be managed as part of the National Wilderness Preservation System (Draft Service Manual 602 FW 1.5).

Wildfire: A free-burning fire requiring a suppression response; all fire other than prescribed fire that occurs on wildlands.

Wildland: Lands characterized by natural vegetation and landscapes where man-made structures and alternations are not evident.

Wildlife: Wild animals and vegetation, especially animals living in a natural, undomesticated state.

Wildlife-dependent Recreational Use: A use of a refuge that involves hunting, fishing, wildlife observation and photography, or environmental education and interpretation. The National Wildlife Refuge System Improvement Act of 1997 specifies that these are the six priority general public uses of the Refuge System.

Wildlife Diversity: A measure of the number of wildlife species in an area and their relative abundance.

ABBREVIATIONS AND ACRONYMS

AMR	Appropriate Management Response
ARPA	Archeological Resources Protection Act
AUM	Animal Unit Month
BBS	Breeding Bird Survey
BIA	Bureau of Indian Affairs
BLM	Bureau of Land Management
CCP	Comprehensive Conservation Plan
CRM	Cultural Resource Management
CRP	Conservation Reserve Program
DFMO	District Fire Management Officer
ESA	Endangered Species Act
FSA	Farm Service Agency
FMO	Fire Management Officer
FMP	Fire Management Plan
GIS	Geographic Information Systems
GR	Grulla
HPP	High Plains Partnership
MMS	Maintenance Management System
MOU	Memorandum of Understanding
MLS	Muleshoe
NMGFD	New Mexico Game and Fish Department
NEPA	National Environmental Policy Act
NRCS	Natural Resource Conservation Service
NWR	National Wildlife Refuge
NGO	Nongovernmental Organization
NPS	National Park Service
O&M	Operation & Maintenance
PIF	Partners in Flight
Refuge System	National Wildlife Refuge System
RO	Regional Office
ROS	Refuge Operations Specialist
RONS	Refuge Operating Needs System
Service	United States Fish and Wildlife Service
SGS	Shortgrass Steppe
TEAN	Texas Environmental Awareness Network
TNRCC	Texas Natural Resource Conservation Commission
TPWD	Texas Parks and Wildlife Department
WPA	Work Progress Administration
YCC	Youth Conservation Corps

APPENDIX A - MULESHOE NWR SPECIES LIST

BIRDS

* Nests locally

Hypothetical - refers to sightings or reports of birds that would not normally be expected in an area or for which there is no corroborative detail such as well-written description by someone familiar with the species (such as a photo, recording, etc.) and for which there is some suspicion that the bird may have been misidentified (e.g. by an inexperienced observer, poor sighting conditions, difficult to identify species). Some of them are almost certainly correctly identified but many are probably not and there is not enough information to know which is which.

Loons
Common Loon	*Gavia immer*

Grebes
Pied-billed Grebe*	*Podilymbus podiceps*
Horned Grebe	*Podiceps auritus*
Eared Grebe	*Podiceps nigricollis*
Western Grebe	*Aechmophorus occidentalis*

Pelicans
American White Pelican	*Pelecanus erythrorhynchos*

Cormorants
Double-crested Cormorant	*Phalacrocorax auritus*

Bitterns and Herons
American Bittern	*Botaurus lentiginosus*
Least Bittern (hypothetical)	*Ixobrychus exilis*
Great Blue Heron	*Ardea herodias*
Great Egret	*Ardea alba*
Snowy Egret	*Egretta thula*
Little Blue Heron	*Egretta caerulea*
Tricolored Heron (hypothetical)	*Egretta tricolor*
Cattle Egret	*Bubulcus ibis*
Green Heron	*Butorides virescens*
Black-crowned Night Heron*	*Nycticorax nycticorax*
Yellow-crowned Night Heron	*Nyctanassa violacea*

Ibises and Spoonbills
White-faced Ibis	*Plegadis chihi*

Ducks, Geese, and Swans
Greater White-fronted Goose	*Anser albifrons*
Snow Goose	*Chen caerulescens*
Ross' Goose	*Chen rossii*
Canada Goose	*Branta canadensis*
Brant (hypothetical)	*Branta bernicla*
Tundra Swan	*Cygnus columbianus*
Wood Duck	*Aix sponsa*
Gadwall	*Anas strepera*
Eurasian Wigeon (hypothetical)	*Anas penelope*
American Wigeon	*Anas americana*
American Black Duck (hypothetical)	*Anas rubripes*

Mallard*	*Anas platyrhynchos*
Blue-winged Teal*	*Anas discors*
Cinnamon Teal	*Anas cyanoptera*
Northern Shoveler*	*Anas clypeata*
Northern Pintail	*Anas acuta*
Green-winged Teal	*Anas crecca*
Canvasback	*Aythya valisineria*
Redhead	*Aythya americana*
Ring-necked Duck	*Aythya collaris*
Greater Scaup	*Aythya marila*
Lesser Scaup	*Aythya affinis*
Surf Scoter	*Melanitta perspicillata*
White-winged Scoter	*Melanitta fusca*
Black Scoter (hypothetical)	*Melanitta nigra*
Long-tailed Duck	*Clangula hyemalis*
Bufflehead	*Bucephala albeola*
Common Goldeneye	*Bucephala clangula*
Hooded Merganser	*Lophodytes cucullatus*
Common Merganser	*Mergus merganser*
Red-breasted Merganser	*Mergus serrator*
Ruddy Duck*	*Oxyura jamaicensis*

American Vultures

Black Vulture (hypothetical)	*Coragyps atratus*
Turkey Vulture*	*Cathartes aura*

Kites, Eagles, and Hawks

Osprey	*Pandion haliaetus*
Mississippi Kite	*Ictinia mississippiensis*
Bald Eagle	*Haliaeetus leucocephalus*
Northern Harrier*	*Circus cyaneus*
Sharp-shinned Hawk	*Accipiter striatus*
Cooper's Hawk	*Accipiter cooperii*
Northern Goshawk	*Accipiter gentilis*
Harris Hawk	*Parabuteo unicinctus*
Broad-winged Hawk	*Buteo platypterus*
Swainson's Hawk*	*Buteo swainsoni*
Red-tailed Hawk	*Buteo jamaicensis*
Ferruginous Hawk*	*Buteo regalis*
Rough-legged Hawk	*Buteo lagopus*
Golden Eagle	*Aquila chrysaetos*

Falcons

American Kestrel*	*Falco sparverius*
Merlin	*Falco columbarius*
Peregrine Falcon	*Falco peregrinus*
Prairie Falcon	*Falco mexicanus*

Pheasants and Quail

Ring-necked Pheasant*	*Phasianus colchicus*
Lesser Prairie-Chicken	*Tympanuchus pallidicinctus*
Northern Bobwhite*	*Colinus virginianus*
Scaled Quail*	*Callipepla squamata*

Rails, Gallinules, and Coots

Yellow Rail	*Coturnicops noveboracensis*

Black Rail	*Laterallus jamaicensis*
Sora	*Porzana carolina*
Virginia Rail	*Rallus elegans*
American Coot*	*Fulica americana*

Cranes

Sandhill Crane	*Grus canadensis*
Whooping Crane	*Grus americana*

Plovers

Black-bellied Plover	*Pluvialis squatarola*
Snowy Plover*	*Charadrius alexandrinus*
Semipalmated Plover	*Charadrius semipalmatus*
Killdeer*	*Charadrius vociferus*
Mountain Plover	*Charadrius montanus*

Stilts and Avocets

Black-necked Stilt*	*Himantopus mexicanus*
American Avocet*	*Recurvirostra americana*

Sandpipers and Phalaropes

Greater Yellowlegs	*Tringa melanoleucus*
Lesser Yellowlegs	*Tringa flavipes*
Solitary Sandpiper	*Tringa solitaria*
Willet	*Catoptrophorus semipalmatus*
Spotted Sandpiper	*Actitis macularia*
Upland Sandpiper	*Bartramia longicauda*
Whimbrel (hypothetical)	*Numenius phaeopus*
Long-billed Curlew	*Numenius americanus*
Marbled Godwit	*Limosa fedoa*
Ruddy Turnstone	*Arenaria interpres*
Sanderling	*Calidris alba*
Semipalmated Sandpiper	*Calidris pusillus*
Western Sandpiper	*Calidris mauri*
Least Sandpiper	*Calidris minutilla*
White-rumped Sandpiper	*Calidris fuscicollis*
Baird's Sandpiper	*Calidris bairdii*
Pectoral Sandpiper	*Calidris melanotos*
Dunlin	*Calidris alpina*
Curlew Sandpiper (hypothetical)	*Calidris ferruginea*
Stilt Sandpiper	*Calidris himantopus*
Long-billed Dowitcher	*Limnodromus scolopaceus*
Wilson's Snipe	*Gallinago delicata*
Wilson's Phalarope	*Phalaropus tricolor*
Red-necked Phalarope	*Phalaropus lobatus*
Red Phalarope	*Phalaropus fulicaria*

Gulls and Terns

Franklin's Gull	*Larus pipixcan*
Bonaparte's Gull	*Larus philadelphia*
Ring-billed Gull	*Larus delawarensis*
Herring Gull	*Larus argentatus*
Glaucous Gull (hypothetical)	*Larus hyperboreus*
Common Tern	*Sterna hirundo*
Least Tern	*Sterna antillarum*
Forster's Tern	*Sterna forsteri*

Black Tern   *Chlidonias niger*

Pigeons and Doves
   Band-tailed Pigeon (hypothetical)   *Columba fasciata*
   Mourning Dove*   *Zenaida macroura*
   White-winged Dove   *Zenaida asiatica*
   Inca Dove (hypothetical)   *Columbina inca*

Cuckoos and Roadrunners
   Black-billed Cuckoo   *Coccyzus erythropthalmus*
   Yellow-billed Cuckoo*   *Coccyzus americanus*
   Greater Roadrunner*   *Geococcyx californianus*

Owls
   Barn Owl*   *Tyto alba*
   Great Horned Owl*   *Bubo virginianus*
   Burrowing Owl*   *Athene cunicularia*
   Long-eared Owl   *Asio otus*
   Short-eared Owl   *Asio flammeus*

Goatsuckers
   Lesser Nighthawk (hypothetical)   *Chordeiles acutipennis*
   Common Nighthawk*   *Chordeiles minor*
   Common Poorwill (hypothetical)   *Phalaenoptilus nuttallii*

Swifts
   Chimney Swift   *Chaetura pelagica*

Hummingbirds
   Black-chinned Hummingbird   *Archilochus alexandri*
   Calliope Hummingbird (hypothetical)   *Stellula calliope*

Kingfishers
   Belted Kingfisher   *Ceryle alcyon*

Woodpeckers
   Lewis' Woodpecker   *Melanerpes lewis*
   Red-headed Woodpecker   *Melanerpes erythrocephalus*
   Golden-fronted Woodpecker   *Melanerpes aurifrons*
   Red-bellied Woodpecker   *Melanerpes carolinus*
   Yellow-bellied Sapsucker   *Sphyrapicus varius*
   Red-naped Sapsucker   *Sphyrapicus nuchalis*
   Ladder-backed Woodpecker*   *Picoides scalaris*
   Downy Woodpecker   *Picoides pubescens*
   Hairy Woodpecker   *Picoides villosus*
   Northern Flicker   *Colaptes auratus*

Tyrant Flycatchers
   Northern Beardless-Tyrannulet (hypothetical)   *Camptostoma imberbe*
   Olive-sided Flycatcher   *Contopus cooperi*
   Western Wood-Pewee   *Contopus sordidulus*
   Eastern Wood-Pewee   *Contopus virens*
   Hammond's Flycatcher (hypothetical)   *Empidonax hammondii*
   Black Phoebe (hypothetical)   *Sayornis nigricans*
   Unidentified Flycatcher   *Empidonax spp.*
   Eastern Phoebe   *Sayornis phoebe*

Say's Phoebe*	Sayornis saya
Vermillion Flycatcher	Pyrocephalus rubinus
Ash-throated Flycatcher*	Myiarchus cinerascens
Great Crested Flycatcher	Myiarchus crinitus
Great Kiskadee (hypothetical)	Pitangus sulphuratus
Cassin's Kingbird	Tyrannus vociferans
Western Kingbird*	Tyrannus verticalis
Eastern Kingbird*	Tyrannus tyrannus
Scissor-tailed Flycatcher*	Tyrannus forficatus

Vireos
Bell's Vireo	Vireo bellii
Plumbeous Vireo	Vireo plumbeus
Warbling Vireo	Vireo gilvus
Red-eyed Vireo	Vireo olivaceus

Jays and Crows
Blue Jay	Cyanocitta cristata
Western Scrub-Jay	Aphelocoma californica
American Crow	Corvus brachyrhynchos
Chihuahuan Raven*	Corvus cryptoleucus
Common Raven	Corvus corax

Larks
| Horned Lark* | Eremophila alpestris |

Swallows
Purple Martin (hypothetical)	Progne subis
Tree Swallow	Tachycineta bicolor
Violet-green Swallow	Tachycineta thalassina
Northern Rough-winged Swallow	Stelgidopteryx serripennis
Bank Swallow	Riparia riparia
Cliff Swallow	Petrochelidon pyrrhonota
Barn Swallow*	Hirundo rustica

Titmice
| Black-crested Titmouse | Baeolophus atricristatus |
| Mountain Chickadee | Poecile gambeli |

Verdins
| Verdin | Auriparus flaviceps |

Bushtits
| Bushtit | Psaltriparus minimus |

Nuthatches
| Red-breasted Nuthatch | Sitta canadensis |
| White-breasted Nuthatch | Sitta carolinensis |

Creepers
| Brown Creeper | Certhia americana |

Wrens
Cactus Wren*	Campylorhynchus brunneicapillus
Rock Wren*	Salpinctes obsoletus
Canyon Wren*	Catherpes mexicanus

Carolina Wren	*Thryothorus ludovicianus*
Bewick's Wren*	*Thryomanes bewickii*
House Wren	*Troglodytes aedon*
Marsh Wren	*Cistothorus palustris*

Kinglets and Gnatcatchers
Golden-crowned Kinglet	*Regulus satrapa*
Ruby-crowned Kinglet	*Regulas calendula*
Blue-gray Gnatcatcher	*Polioptila caerulea*

Thrushes
Eastern Bluebird*	*Sialia sialis*
Western Bluebird	*Sialia mexicana*
Mountain Bluebird	*Sialia currucoides*
Townsend's Solitaire	*Myadestes townsendi*
Swainson's Thrush	*Catharus ustulata*
Hermit Thrush	*Catharus guttata*
American Robin	*Turdus migratorius*

Mockingbirds and Thrashers
Gray Catbird	*Dumetella carolinensis*
Northern Mockingbird*	*Mimus polyglottos*
Sage Thrasher	*Oreoscoptes montanus*
Brown Thrasher*	*Toxostoma rufum*
Curve-billed Thrasher*	*Toxostoma curvirostre*
Crissal Thrasher	*Toxostoma crissale*

Pipits
| American Pipit | *Anthus rubescens* |
| Sprague's Pipit | *Anthus spragueii* |

Waxwings
| Bohemian Waxwing (hypothetical) | *Bombycilla garrulus* |
| Cedar Waxwing | *Bombycilla cedrorum* |

Silky Flycatchers
| Phainopepla | *Phainopepla nitens* |

Shrikes
| Northern Shrike | *Lanius excubitor* |
| Loggerhead Shrike* | *Lanius ludovicianus* |

Starlings
| European Starling | *Sturnus vulgaris* |

Wood Warblers
Tennessee Warbler	*Vermivora peregrina*
Orange-crowned Warbler	*Vermivora celata*
Nashville Warbler	*Vermivora ruficapilla*
Virginia's Warbler	*Vermivora virginiae*
Northern Parula	*Parula americana*
Yellow Warbler	*Dendroica petechia*
Yellow-rumped Warbler	*Dendroica coronata*
Chestnut-sided Warbler (hypothetical)	*Dendroica pensylvanica*
Townsend's Warbler	*Dendroica townsendi*
Black-throated Green Warbler	*Dendroica virens*

Hermit Warbler	*Dendroica occidentalis*
Blackburnian Warbler	*Dendroica fusca*
Grace's Warbler (hypothetical)	*Dendroica graciae*
Yellow-throated Warbler	*Dendroica dominica*
Prairie Warbler	*Dendroica discolor*
Blackpoll Warbler	*Dendroica striata*
Black-and-White Warbler	*Mniotilta varia*
American Redstart	*Setophaga ruticilla*
Worm-eating Warbler	*Helmitheros vermivorus*
Northern Waterthrush	*Seiurus noveboracensis*
Kentucky Warbler (hypothetical)	*Oporornis formosus*
Mourning Warbler (hypothetical)	*Oporornis philadelphia*
MacGillivray's Warbler	*Oporornis tolmiei*
Common Yellowthroat	*Geothlypis trichas*
Hooded Warbler (hypothetical)	*Wilsonia citrina*
Wilson's Warbler	*Wilsonia pusilla*
Yellow-breasted Chat	*Icteria virens*

Tanagers

Summer Tanager	*Piranga rubra*
Western Tanager	*Piranga ludoviciana*

Sparrows

Green-tailed Towhee	*Pipilo chlorurus*
Spotted Towhee	*Pipilo maculatus*
Canyon Towhee*	*Pipilo fuscus*
Cassin's Sparrow*	*Aimophila cassinii*
Rufous-crowned Sparrow*	*Aimophila ruficeps*
American Tree Sparrow	*Spizella arborea*
Chipping Sparrow	*Spizella passerina*
Clay-colored Sparrow	*Spizella pallida*
Brewer's Sparrow	*Spizella breweri*
Field Sparrow	*Spizella pusilla*
Black-chinned Sparrow (hypothetical)	*Spizella atrogularis*
Vesper Sparrow	*Pooecetes gramineus*
Lark Sparrow*	*Chondestes grammacus*
Black-throated Sparrow	*Amphispiza bilineata*
Sage Sparrow	*Amphispiza belli*
Lark Bunting*	*Calamospiza melanocorys*
Savannah Sparrow	*Passerculus sandwichensis*
Baird's Sparrow	*Ammodramus bairdii*
Grasshopper Sparrow	*Ammodramus savannarum*
LeConte's Sparrow	*Ammodramus leconteii*
Fox Sparrow	*Passerella iliaca*
Song Sparrow	*Melospiza melodia*
Lincoln's Sparrow	*Melospiza lincolnii*
Swamp Sparrow	*Melospiza georgiana*
White-throated Sparrow	*Zonotrichia albicollis*
White-crowned Sparrow	*Zonotrichia leucophrys*
Golden-crowned Sparow	*Zonotrichia atricapilla*
Dark-eyed Junco	*Junco hyemalis*
McCown's Longspur	*Calcarius mccownii*
Lapland Longspur	*Calcarius lapponicus*
Smith's Longspur	*Calcarius pictus*
Chestnut-collared Longspur	*Calcarius ornatus*

Cardinals and Grosbeaks

Northern Cardinal	*Cardinalis cardinalis*
Pyrrhuloxia	*Cardinalis sinuatus*
Rose-breasted Grosbeak	*Pheucticus ludovicianus*
Black-headed Grosbeak	*Pheucticus melanocephalus*
Blue Grosbeak*	*Guiraca caerulea*
Lazuli Bunting	*Passerina amoena*
Indigo Bunting	*Passerina cyanea*
Painted Bunting (hypothetical)	*Passerina ciris*
Dickcissel	*Spiza americana*

Blackbirds and Orioles

Red-winged Blackbird*	*Agelaius phoeniceus*
Eastern Meadowlark*	*Sturnella magna*
Western Meadowlark*	*Sturnella neglecta*
Yellow-headed Blackbird*	*Xanthocephalus xanthocephalus*
Rusty Blackbird	*Euphagus carolinus*
Brewer's Blackbird	*Euphagus cyanocephalus*
Common Grackle	*Quiscalus quiscula*
Brown-headed Cowbird*	*Molothrus ater*
Hooded Oriole (hypothetical)	*Icterus cucullatus*
Orchard Oriole*	*Icterus spurius*
Baltimore Oriole	*Icterus galbula*
Bullock's Oriole*	*Icterus bullockii*
Scott's Oriole (hypothetical)	*Icterus parisorum*

Finches

Purple Finch (hypothetical)	*Carpodacus purpureus*
House Finch	*Carpodacus mexicanus*
Pine Siskin	*Carduelis pinus*
Lesser Goldfinch	*Carduelis psaltria*
American Goldfinch	*Carduelis tristis*
Evening Grosbeak	*Coccothraustes vespertinus*

Old World Sparrows

House Sparrow	*Passer domesticus*

MAMMALS

Coyote	*Canis latrans microdon*
Gray Fox	*Urocyon cinereoargenteus scottii*
Mule Deer	*Odocoileus hemionus hemionus*
Deer Mouse	*Peromyscus maniculatus*
White-footed Mouse	*Peromyscus leucopus*
Western Harvest Mouse	*Reithrodontomys megalotis*
Plains Harvest Mouse	*Reithrodontomys montanus*
Southern Plains Woodrat	*Neotoma micropus*
White-throated Wood Rat	*Neotoma albigula*
Northern Grasshopper Mouse	*Onychomys leucogaster*
Cotton Rat	*Sigmodon hispid*
Ord's Kangaroo Rat	*Dipodomys ordii durranti*
Silky Pocket Mouse	*Perognathus flavus*
Hispid Pocket Mouse	*Chaetodipus hispidus*
Opossum	*Didelphis marsupialis*
Porcupine	*Erethizon dorsatum*
Bobcat	*Lynx rufus texensis*
Plains Pocket Gopher	*Geomys bursarius*
Yellow-faced Pocket Gopher	*Pappogeomys castanops*
Desert Cottontail	*Sylvilagus auduboni*
Eastern Cottontail	*Sylvilagus floridanus*
Black-tailed Jackrabbit	*Lepus californicus*
Badger	*Taxidea taxus berlandieri*
Striped Skunk	*Mephitis mephitis varians*
Long-tailed Weasel	*Mustela frenata frenata*
Raccoon	*Procyon lotor fuscipes*
Thirteen-lined Ground Squirrel	*Citellus tridecemlineatus*
Spotted Ground Squirrel	*Citellus spilosoma*
Black-tailed Prairie Dog	*Cynomys ludovicianus*
Least Shrew	*Criptotis parva*
Hoary Bat	*Lasiurus cinereus*
Pallid Bat	*Antrozous pallidus*

AMPHIBIANS AND REPTILES

Salamanders
Mole Salamander
Barred Tiger Salamander   *Ambystoma tigrinium mavortium*

Toads
Great Plains Toad   *Bufo cognatus*
Green Toad   *Bufo debilis*
Plains Spadefoot   *Scaphiopus bombifrons*
New Mexico Spadefoot   *Scaphiopus multiplicatus*
Western Spadefoot   *Scaphiopus hammondi*

Frogs
Spotted Chorus Frog   *Pseudacris clarkii*
Plains Leopard Frog   *Rana blairi*

Turtles
Ornate Box Turtle   *Terrapene ornata*
Yellow Mud Turtle   *Kinosternon flavescens*

Lizards
Western Collared Lizard   *Crotaphytus collaris*
Lesser Earless Lizard   *Holbrookia maculata*
Texas Horned Lizard   *Phrynosoma cornutum*

Snakes
Prairie Racerunner   *Cnemidophorus sexlineatus*
Western Hognose Snake   *Heterodon nasicus*
Bullsnake   *Pituophis melanoleucas*
Milk Snake   *Lampropeltis tirangulum*
Western Coachwhip   *Masticophis flagellum*
Prairie Rattlesnake   *Crotalus viridis*
New Mexican MilkSnake   *Lampropeltis triangulun*
Desert Kingsnake   *Lampropeltis getula*
Prairie Ringneck Snake   *Diadophis punctatus*

PLANTS - This list of 289 plants (68 families) found on the Muleshoe NWR was compiled by Tommy Rosson. The nomenclature follows the <u>Manual of the Vascular Plants of Texas</u>, Donovan S. Correll and Marshall C. Johnston.

ASTERACEAE
Ragweed	*Ambrosia spp.*
Cocklebur	*Anthium spp.*
Threadleaf Sagebrush	*Artemesia filifolius*
Fringed Sage	*Artemisia frigida*
Big Sage	*Artemesia tridentata*
Thistle	*Cirsium spp.*
Horseweed	*Conyza canadensis*
Fetid Marigold	*Dyssodia papposa*
Trailing Fleabane	*Erigeron flagellaris*
Blanket Flower	*Gaillardia aristata*
Snakeweed	*Gutierrezia sarothrae*
Gumweed	*Grindelia squarrosa*
Purple Aster	*Haplopappus spinulosus*
Sunflower	*Helianthus annus*
Golden Aster	*Heterotheca spp.*
Dogbane	*Hymenopappus filifolius*
Rydbergia	*Hymenoxys argentea*
White Daisy	*Leucelene ericoides*
Blazing Star	*Liatris punctata*
Skeletonweed	*Lygodesmia juncea*
Purple Aster	*Machaeranthera tanacetifolia*
Lemonweed	*Pectis angustifolia*
Ragwort, Butterweed	*Senecio spp.*
Hopi Tea	*Thelesperma megapotamicum*
Goat's Beard	*Tragopogon dubius*

BIGNONIACEAE
Desert Willow	*Chilopsis linearis*

BORAGINACEAE
Beggars-tick, Stickweed	*Lappula redowskii*

CACTACEAE
Prickly Pear	*Opuntia cymochila*

CARYOPHYLLACEAE
Northern Spleenwort	*Asplenium septentrionale*

CHENOPODIACEAE
Lamb's Quarters	*Chenopodium album*
Common Kocia	*Kochia scoparia*
Prickly Russian Thistle	*Salsola kali*

CONVOLVULACEAE
Field Bindweed	*Convolvulus arvensis*
Ipomea	*Ipomoea leotophylla*

CUCURBITACEAE
Wild Gourd	*Cucurbita foetidissima*

CUPRESSACEAE
One-seed Juniper   *Juniperus monosperma*
Red Cedar   *Juniperus scopulorum*

CYPERACEAE
Bulrush   *Scirpus spp.*
Sedge   *Carex spp.*

ELEAGNACEAE
Russian Olive   *Elaegnus angustifolia*

EUPHORBIACEAE
White Margin Spurge   *Eupgorbia albomarginara*
Fendler's Spurge   *Euphorbia fendleri*
Spurge   *Euphorbia spathulata*
Doveweed   *Croton texensis*

FABACEAE
Alfalfa   *Medicago sativa*
Horn Loco Milk Vetch   *Astralagus missouriensis*
White Sweet Clover   *Melilotus albus*
Yellow Sweet Clover   *Melilotus officinalis*

FAGACEAE
Juniper Oak   *Quercus undulata*

JUNCACEAE
Baltic Rush   *Juncus balticus*

HYPERICACEAE
Common Horehound   *Marrubium vulgare*

LOASACEAE
Stickleaf   *Mentzelia dispersa*

NYCTAGINACEAE
Narrow-leaf Umbrella-wort   *Oxybaphus linearis*

MALVACEAE
Red Globe Mallow   *Sphaeralcea coccinea*

ONAGRACEAE
Scarlet Gaura   *Gaura coccinea*
Velvet Leaf Gaura   *Gaura parviflora*

PINACEAE
Pinyon Pine   *Pinus edulis*
Ponderosa Pine   *Pinus ponderosa*

POACEAE
Crested Wheatgrass   *Agropyron cristatum*
Tall Wheatgrass   *Agropyron elongatum*
Intermediate Wheatgrass   *Agropyron intermedium*
Saunder's Wheatgrass   *Agropyron saundersii*
Western Wheatgrass   *Agropyron smithii*
Slender Wheatgrass   *Agropyron trachycaulum*

Redtop Bentgrass	*Agrostis alba*
Stinkgrass	*Agrostis cilianensis*
Spike Bentgrass	*Agrostis exarata*
Water Bentgrass	*Agrostis emiverticillata*
Carpet Bentgrass	*Agrostis stolonifra*
Big Bluestem	*Andropogon gerardii*
Arizona Three-awn	*Aristida arizonica*
Harvard Three-awn	*Aristida barbata*
Fendler Three-awn	*Aristida fendleriana*
Blue Three-awn	*Aristida glauca*
Red Three-awn	*Aristida longiseta*
Wild Oats	*Avena fatua*
Oats	*Avena sativa*
Pine Dropseed	*Blepharoneuron tricholepis*
Australian Bluestem	*Bothriochloa bladhii*
King Ranch Bluestem	*Bothriochloa ischaemun*
Silver Bluestem	*Bothriochloa saccharoides*
Sideoats Grama	*Bouteloua curtipendula*
Black Grama	*Bouteloua eriopoda*
Blue Grama	*Bouteloua gracilis*
Hairy Grama	*Bouteloua hirsuta*
Weeping Brome	*Bromus frondosus*
Smooth Brome	*Bromus inermis*
Japanese Brome	*Bromus japonicus*
Cheatgrass	*Bromus tectorum*
Rescue Brome	*Bromus unioloides*
Buffalograss	*Buchloe dactyloides*
Prairie Sandreed	*Calamovilfa longifolia*
Field Sandbur	*Cenchrus pauciflorus*
Windmill Grass	*Chloris verticillata*
Feather Fingergrass	*Chloris virgata*
Orchardgrass	*Dactylis glomerata*
Parry Oatgrass	*Danthonia parryi*
Poverty Oatgrass	*Danthonia spicata*
Texas Crabgrass	*Digitaria sanguinalis*
Saltgrass	*Distichlis spicata*
Canada Wildrye	*Elymus canadensis*
Blue Wildrye	*Elymus glaucus*
Russian Wildrye	*Elymus juncus*
Weeping Lovegrass	*Eragrostis curvula*
Plains Lovegrass	*Eragrostis intermedia*
Hairy Tridens	*Erioneuron pilosum*
Arizona Fescue	*Festuca arizonica*
Tall Fescue	*Festuca arundinacea*
Meadow Fescue	*Festuca elatior*
Sheep Fescue	*Festuca ovina*
Red Fescue	*Festuca rubra*
Tall Mannagrass	*Glyceria elata*
American Mannagrass	*Glyceria grandis*
Galleta	*Hilaria jamesii*
Foxtail Barley	*Hordeum jubatum*
Mouse Barley	*Hordeum leporinum*
Little Barley	*Hordeum pusillum*
Prairie Junegrass	*Koeleria pyramidata*
Green Sprangletop	*Leptochloa dubia*
Perennial Ryegrass	*Lolium perenne*

Wolftail	*Lycurus phleoides*
Plains Muhly	*Muhlenbergia cuspidata*
Bullgrass	*Muhlenbergia emersleyi*
Least Muhly	*Muhlenbergia minutissima*
Mountain Muhly	*Muhlenbergia montana*
New Mexico Muhly	*Muhlenbergia pauciflora*
Ring Muhly	*Muhlenbergia torreyi*
Spike Muhly	*Muhlenbergia wrightii*
Creeping Muhly	*Muhlenbergia repens*
False Buffalograss	*Munroa squarrosa*
Indian Ricegrass	*Oryzopsis hymenoides*
Littleseed Ricegrass	*Oryzopsis micrantha*
Bulb Panic	*Panicum bulbosum*
Witchgrass	*Panicum capillare*
Vine Mesquite	*Panicum obtusum*
Scribner's Panic	*Panicum scribnerianuum*
Switchgrass	*Panicum virgatum*
CanaryGrass	*Phalaris spp.*
Timothy	*Phleum pratense*
CommonReed	*Phragmites commonis*
Pringle's Ricegrass	*Piptochaetium pringlei*
Bigelow's Bluegrass	*Poa bigelovii*
Canada Bluegrass	*Poa compressa*
Muttongrass	*Poa fendleriana*
Kentucky Bluegrass	*Poa pratensis*
Alkaligrass	*Puccinellia spp.*
Tumblegrass	*Schedonnardus paniculatus*
Little Bluestem	*Schizachyrium scoparium*
Rye	*Secale cereale*
Knotroot Bristlegrass	*Setaria geniculata*
Yellow Bristlegrass	*Setaria lutescens*
Bottlebrush Squirreltail	*Sitanion hystrix*
Indiangrass	*Sorghastrum nutans*
Johnsongrass	*Sorghum halepense*
Alkali Sacaton	*Sporobolus airoides*
Sacaton	*Sporobolus airoides v. wrightii*
SpikeDropseed	*Sporobolus contractus*
Sand Dropseed	*Sporobolus cryptandrus*
Needle and Thread	*Stipa comata*
Letterman's Needlegrass	*Stipa lettermanii*
New Mexico Feathergrass	*Stipa neomexicana*
Sleepygrass	*Stipa robusta*
Fluffgrass	*Tridens pulchellus*
Wheat	*Triticum aestivum*
Jointed Goatgrass	*Triticum cylindricum*
Six-weeks Fescue	*Vulpia octoflora*

POLYGONACEAE

Smartweed	*Polygonum spp.*
Knotweed	*Polygonum aviculare*
Buckwheat	*Eriogonum annum*

POTAMOGETONACEAE

Pondweed	*Potamogeton spp*

ROSACEAE

Apache Plume   *Fallugia paradoxa*

SALICACEAE
Fremont's Cottonwood   *Populus fremontii*
Narrow-leaf Cottonwoods   *Populus angustifolia*
Godding's Willow   *Salix goddinngii*
Coyote Willow   *Salix exigua*

SCROPHULARIACEAE
Beardstongue   *Penstemon albida*

SOLANACEAE
Nightshade   *Solanum spp.*
Horse Nettle   *Solanum elaeagnifolium*
Wild Nightshade   *Solanum rostratum*

TAMARICACEAE
Salt Cedar   *Tamarix spp.*

TYPHACEAE
Cattail   *Typha angustifolia*

ULMACEAE
Siberian Elm   *Ulmus pumila*

VERBENACEAE
Vervain   *Verbena bracteata*

APPENDIX B - GRULLA NWR SPECIES LIST

BIRDS

*Nests locally

Grebes
Eared Grebe   *Podiceps caspicus*

Bitterns and Herons
Great Blue Heron   *Ardea herodias*
Snowy Egret   *Egretta thula*
Cattle Egret   *Bubulcus ibis*

Swans, Geese, and Ducks
Snow Goose   *Chen caerulescens*
Canada Goose   *Branta canadensis*
Gadwall   *Anas strepera*
American Wigeon   *Anas americana*
Mallard*   *Anas platyrhynchos*
Cinnamon Teal   *Anas cyanoptera*
Northern Shoveler*   *Anas clypeata*
Northern Pintail   *Anas acuta*
Green-winged Teal   *Anas crecca*
Redhead   *Aythya americana*
Ring-necked Duck   *Aythya collaris*
Ruddy Duck*   *Oxyura jamaicensis*

American Vultures
Turkey Vulture*   *Cathartes aura*

Kites, Eagles, and Hawks
Mississippi Kite   *Ictinia mississippiensis*
Bald Eagle   *Haliaeetus leucocephalus*
Northern Harrier*   *Circus cyaneus*
Sharp-shinned Hawk   *Accipiter striatus*
Cooper's Hawk   *Accipiter cooperii*
Swainson's Hawk*   *Buteo swainsoni*
Red-tailed Hawk   *Buteo jamaicensis*
Ferruginous Hawk*   *Buteo regalis*
Rough-legged Hawk   *Buteo lagopus*
Golden Eagle   *Aquila chrysaetos*

Falcons
American Kestrel*   *Falco sparverius*
Merlin   *Falco columbarius*
Prairie Falcon   *Falco mexicanus*

Pheasants and Quail
Ring-necked Pheasant*   *Phasianus colchicus*
Lesser Prairie-Chicken   *Tympanuchus pallidicinctus*
Northern Bobwhite*   *Colinus virginianus*
Scaled Quail   *   *Callipepla squamata*

Rails, Gallinules, and Coots
American Coot*   *Fulica americana*

Cranes
    Sandhill Crane   *Grus canadensis*

Plovers
    Black-bellied Plover   *Pluvialis squatarola*
    Snowy Plover*   *Charadrius alexandrinus*
    Killdeer*   *Charadrius vociferus*

Stilts and Avocets
    Black-necked Stilt   *Himantopus mexicanus*
    American Avocet   *Recurvirostra americana*

Sandpipers and Phalaropes
    Greater Yellowlegs   *Tringa melanoleucus*
    Lesser Yellowlegs   *Tringa flavipes*
    Willet   *Catoptrophorus semipalmatus*
    Spotted Sandpiper   *Actitis macularia*
    Long-billed Curlew   *Numenius americanus*
    Semipalmated Sandpiper   *Calidris pusillus*
    Western Sandpiper   *Calidris mauri*
    Least Sandpiper   *Calidris minutilla*
    Baird's Sandpiper   *Calidris bairdii*
    Pectoral Sandpiper   *Calidris melanotos*
    Long-billed Dowitcher   *Limnodromus scolopaceus*
    Wilson's Phalarope   *Phalaropus tricolor*

Gulls and Terns
    Ring-billed Gull   *Larus delawarensis*
    Black Tern   *Chlidonias niger*

Pigeons and Doves
    Mourning Dove*   *Zenaidura macroura*

Cuckoos and Roadrunners
    Greater Roadrunner*   *Geococcyx californianus*

Owls
    Great Horned Owl   *Bubo virginianus*
    Burrowing Owl*   *Athena cunicularia*
    Short-eared Owl   *Asio flammeus*

Goatsuckers
    Common Nighthawk   *Chordeiles minor*

Tyrant Flycatchers
    Western Kingbird*   *Tyrannus verticalis*
    Scissor-tailed Flycatcher   *Tyrannus forficata*

Larks
    Horned Lark*   *Eremophila alpestris*

Swallows
    Cliff Swallow   *Petrochelidon pyrrhonota*
    Barn Swallow   *Hirundo rustica*

Jays and Crows
American Crow *Corvus brachyrhynchos*
Chihuahuan Raven *Corvus cryptoleucus*

Thrushes
Mountain Bluebird *Sialia currucoides*

Pipits
American Pipit *Anthus rubescens*

Shrikes
Loggerhead Shrike* *Lanius ludovicianus*

Cardinals and Grosbeaks
Blue Grosbeak *Guiraca caerulea*

Sparrows
Brewer's Sparrow *Spizella breweri*
Lark Sparrow * *Chondestes grammacus*
Lark Bunting * *Calamospiza melanocorys*
Savannah Sparrow *Passerculus sandwichensis*
Baird's Sparrow *Ammodramus bairdii*
Grasshopper Sparrow *Ammodramus savannarum*
White-crowned Sparrow *Zonotrichia leucophrys*
Dark-eyed Junco *Junco hyemalis*

Blackbirds and Orioles
Western Meadowlark* *Sturnella neglecta*
Yellow-headed Blackbird *Xanthocephalus xanthocephalus*
Brewer's Blackbird *Euphagus cyanocephalus*

Finches
Pine Siskin *Carduelis pinus*

Old World Sparrows
House Sparrow *Passer domesticus*

Note: Species lists for Mammals, Reptiles and other species have not been compiled for Grulla NWR.

APPENDIX C - THREATENED AND ENDANGERED SPECIES LISTS

TEXAS PARKS AND WILDLIFE ANNOTATED COUNTY LIST OF RARE SPECIES FOR BAILEY COUNTY - Last Revision: December 6, 2002

Birds	Federal Status	State Status
American peregrine falcon (*Falco peregrinus anatum*)	DL	E
Arctic peregrine falcon (*Falco peregrinus tundrius*)	DL	T
Baird's sparrow (*Ammodramus bairdii*)		
Bald eagle (*Haliaeetus leucocephalus*)	T-PDL	T
Ferruginous hawk (*Buteo regalis*)		
Lesser prairie-chicken (*Tympanuchus pallidicinctus*)	C	
Mountain plover (*Charadrius montanus*)	PT	
Snowy plover (*Charadrius alexandrinus*)		
Western burrowing owl (*Athene cunicularia hypugaea*)		
Whooping crane (*Grus americana*)	E	E

Mammals		
Black-footed ferret (*Mustela nigripes*)	E	E
Black-tailed prairie dog (*Cynomys ludovicianus*)	C	
Plains spotted skunk (*Spilogale putorius interrupta*)		
Swift fox (*Vulpes velox*)		

Reptiles		
Texas horned lizard (*Phrynosoma cornutum*)		T

Status Key:
- E - Endangered
- T - Threatened
- PT - Proposed Threatened
- C - Candidate
- DL - Federally Delisted
- PDL - Proposed for Delisting
- "blank"- Rare, but with no regulatory listing status

FEDERAL ENDANGERED, THREATENED, PROPOSED, AND CANDIDATE SPECIES AND SPECIES OF CONCERN IN ROOSEVELT COUNTY. NEW MEXICO
(compiled by the U.S. Fish and Wildlife Service, Region 2)

ENDANGERED
Black-footed ferret *(Mustela nigripes)*

THREATENED
Bald Eagle *(Haliaeetus leucocephalus)*

PROPOSED THREATENED
Mountain Plover *(Charadrius montanus)*

CANDIDATE
Black-tiled prairie dog *(Cynomys ludovicianus)*
Lesser Prairie Chicken *(Tympanuchus pallidicinctus)*
Sand Dune Lizard *(Sceloporus arenicolus)*

SPECIES OF CONCERN
Swift fox *(Vulpes velox)*
Western red bat *(Lasiurus blossevillii)*
American peregrine falcon *(Falco peregrinus anatum)*
Arctic peregrine falcon *(Falco peregrinus tundrius)*
Baird's sparrow *(Ammodramus bairdii)*
Yellow-billed Cuckoo *(Coccyzus americanus)*
Sandhill Goosefoot *(Chenopodium cycloides)*

APPENDIX D - SECTION 7 CONSULTATION

United States Department of the Interior

FISH AND WILDLIFE SERVICE
Ecological Services
WinSystems Center Building
711 Stadium Drive, Suite 252
Arlington, Texas 76011

2-12-04-I-038

November 6, 2003

Memorandum

To: Chief, Division of Planning, NWRS, Regional Office, Albuquerque, NM

From: Field Supervisor, FWS, Ecological Services, Arlington, TX

Subject: Draft Comprehensive Conservation Plan and Environmental Assessment for Muleshoe and Grulla National Wildlife Refuges and Intra-Service Section 7 Consultation (R2/NWRS-PLN)

We have reviewed the Draft Comprehensive Conservation Plan and Environmental Assessment for Muleshoe and Grulla National Wildlife Refuges and believe it adequately addresses the Service's mission and goals. The only comment we have is related to the current status of the mountain plover (*Charadrius montanus*). The draft CCP/EA refers to this species as having "proposed threatened" status under the Endangered Species Act. Recently, the Service withdrew the proposed rule (68 FR 53083, September 9, 2003) and, therefore, the mountain plover no longer has any federal status.

We also concur with the "not likely to adversely affect" determination for listed species with regard to the implementation of the CCP. We have enclosed the signed Intra-Service Section 7 Evaluation Form, which concludes consultation on the proposed action.

We appreciate the opportunity to provide comments on the draft CCP/EA. If you have any questions or comments, please contact Mr. Omar Bocanegra of this office.

Enclosure

INTRA-SERVICE SECTION 7 BIOLOGICAL EVALUATION FORM
MULESHOE NATIONAL WILDLIFE REFUGE

Originating Person: ___Carol Torrez___
Telephone Number: ___505-248-6821___
Date: ___August 6, 2003___

I.   **Region:** Southwest (Region 2)

II.   **Service Activity (Program):** Refuges

III. **Pertinent Species and Habitat:**

The Arlington Ecological Services Office provided Federal and State species lists for Bailey County, Texas (shown in Appendix C of the CCP). All species on that county list were considered; those found not to occur or have potential habitat on the refuge or surrounding area are not discussed. The following species have been documented and/or have potential habitat on Muleshoe NWR

A.   Listed species and/or their critical habitat within the action area:

black-footed ferret (*Mustela nigripes*) - endangered
bald eagle (*Haliaeetus leucocephalus*) - threatened
whooping crane (*Grus americana*) - endangered
interior least tern (*Sterna antillarum*) - endangered

There is no designated critical habitat on the refuge.

B.   Proposed species and/or proposed critical habitat within the action area:

Mountain plover (*Charadrius montanus*) is proposed threatened without critical habitat.

C.   Candidate species within the action area:

Black-tailed prairie dog (*Cynomys ludovicanus*)
Lesser prairie chicken (*Tympanuchus pallidicinctus*)

D.   Include species/habitat occurrence on a map:

For a map of the Refuge please see Map #1 in the draft CCP. The species listed above are not known to breed or typically occur on the refuge; therefore, no map of species/habitat occurrence is available.

The bald eagle is the only listed species that may regularly (but rarely) occur on the Refuge. The interior least tern and whooping crane are migrants or accidental visitors that are infrequently sighted during spring or fall migration. The black-tailed prairie dog is a resident of the refuge (see Map #5). The other species listed (mountain plover and lesser prairie chicken) have potential habitat in the area but have not been documented on the Refuge.

IV.   **Geographic area/station name and background of action:**

Station: Muleshoe National Wildlife Refuge in northwest Texas.

Action: Issuance and implementation of the Comprehensive Conservation Plan for the Muleshoe and Grulla NWRs.

V.   **Location:** See Map #3 in the CCP

A.   Ecoregion Number and Name:

Region 2 Ecosystem #11, the Edwards Plateau Ecosystem

B.   County and state:

Bailey County, Texas

C.   Section, township, and range (or latitude and longitude):

Latitude 33 ° 57'; Longitude 102° 45'

D.   Distance (miles) and direction to nearest town:

Muleshoe NWR is located approximately 20 miles south of Muleshoe, Texas.

E.   Species/habitat occurrence:

Black-footed Ferret - The black-footed ferret historically occurred throughout the High Plains of Texas. However, they have not been observed in Texas, or on the refuge, since 1963. They rely on prairie dogs for food and shelter, living in burrows made by prairie dogs. Almost 90 percent of their diet consists of prairie dogs. Prairie dogs have been reduced in number due to habitat loss, disease, and eradication efforts. Current habitat conditions (specifically limited prairie dog populations) will not support ferrets in the area.

Bald Eagle - The bald eagle is considered an occasional winter and accidental fall migrant throughout Texas. Generally between one to three bald eagles spend the winter months (November through February) on Muleshoe NWR and take advantage of the varied food sources in the area. Bald eagles are opportunistic and will forage on prairie dogs, sick or dead waterfowl and crippled or unretrieved cranes. Their spring migration seems to coincides closely with the spring departure of waterfowl and cranes.

Whooping Crane - Whooping cranes are a common winter resident in Aransas and Matagorda NWRs. Otherwise, whooping cranes are very rare in Texas, other than during migration where they utilize a narrow corridor north of their primary wintering areas. During migration, they feed and roost in a wide variety of habitats, including croplands, large and small freshwater marshes, the margins of lakes and reservoirs, and submerged sandbars in rivers. Rare sightings have been reported in the Muleshoe area, but this species has not been documented on the refuge.

Interior Least Tern - Interior least terns are migratory and breed along the Red, Mississippi, Arkansas, Missouri, Ohio, and Rio Grande river systems. They nest on the ground, on sandbars rivers or lakes or pond edges, typically on sites that are sandy and relatively free of vegetation. Historically, least terns have been reported on the Muleshoe NWR. It is reported that one pair may have nested in 1967, but the species has not been found on the refuge since 1981. In recent years, most of the large saline lakes on the refuge have been mostly dry, which has probably precluded least tern use of the area.

Mountain plover - Mountain plovers are a disturbance-evolved species that breeds in the Plains and gathers in flocks to migrate to their fall wintering grounds. The mountain plover requires expansive dry short-grass prairie such as high plains and semidesert mesas having a high proportion of bare ground (>30 percent) for nesting. Typical associated plants include blue grama, buffalo grass, and scattered cacti or forbs. They commonly nest in or near prairie dog towns. Other sites that attract plovers for nesting, but may be in harms way, include farm fields, highway/powerline rights-of-way, and stock tanks. Historically, the mountain plover was most likely a common breeding bird in the Pecos and Staked Plains area, but during the past century, human settlement, the eradication of prairie dogs, and the conversion of native prairie to cropland has significantly reduced the suitable habitat for this species. The mountain plover has, on occasion, been observed on the refuge during migration. Sightings are typically during the spring when the birds may be returning north from southern Texas. Refuge grasslands, which are typically in good condition with little bare ground, would preclude their use for nesting, however, the dry lake beds could be potential nesting habitat. In addition, the area could be used for foraging during migration.

Black-tailed Prairie Dog - This species lives colonially in shortgrass and mid-grass prairies and grass-shrub habitats. This species is considered a critical link or keystone species, one that plays a key role in the overall health and diversity of the shortgrass prairie ecosystem. Black-tailed prairie populations on the refuge have fluctuated dramatically throughout the years (see Map 5 in Appendix H of the CCP). The refuge's prairie dog towns comprised 500 acres in 1938. Bubonic plague outbreaks occurred in the refuge's prairie dog populations over the years causing the prairie dog numbers to decline sharply only to gradually increase to large numbers until the plague would again reduce their numbers. Outbreaks of bubonic plague have almost completely eliminated refuge prairie dog populations in the 1950s, the 1970s, and as recently as the year 2000. In the mid 1960s, prairie dog towns covered a large amount of the refuge's grasslands, and were particularly evident around refuge headquarters. Presently, the only prairie dog population that exists on the refuge consists of a small town located northwest of Paul's Lake.

Lesser Prairie Chicken - The lesser prairie chicken is an occupant of arid shortgrass prairies interspersed with shinnery oak and sand sagebrush brushlands. This species was formerly abundant within this range, but has dramatically declined during the twentieth century. Loss of habitat is responsible for these declines, especially the conversion of native prairie to cultivated fields. Brush removal within remaining prairies is also a factor, since the oak and sagebrush provide important food and cover throughout the year. Recent increases in this species may be the result of conversion of grassland to Conservation Reserve Program (CRP) grasslands.

Prairie chicken observations on the refuge over the years have always been reported as rare. The first documented prairie chicken sighting on the refuge was in 1938. Other sighting dates on the refuge include: 1943, 1944, 1945, and 1949. Although not seen on the refuge between 1949 and 1981, there were reported sightings on surrounding private lands in 1954 and 1964. In 1981 prairie chickens were again seen on the refuge. Then in 1988, there were several observations. In February 1988, a large flock (110 birds) was observed south of the Lower White Lake near the southern Refuge boundary. Throughout the years, prairie chickens have been seen in the Paul's Lake area, west and north of the Refuge Headquarters, the southeast corner of the refuge, south of White Lake, and on private land southwest and northwest of the refuge. From 1994 through 2002, no prairie chickens have been seen on the refuge or on the site south of White Lake, but an active site is consistently seen one mile north of the refuge's northwest corner (USFWS narratives).

VI.   Description of proposed action:

The proposed action is to implement the Muleshoe and Grulla National Wildlife Refuge Comprehensive Conservation Plan over the next 15 years. The CCP will emphasize native prairie/grassland and wetland ecosystem protection, management and re-establishment within the refuge.

The CCP is divided into a series of goals, objectives, and strategies that will be implemented throughout the 15 year term of this plan. Specific goals associated with the CCP are: 1) to provide habitat and manage for migrating and wintering waterfowl, sandhill cranes, other migratory birds, threatened and endangered species, and other species of concern by implementing appropriate management strategies; 2) to identify, protect, and interpret the prehistoric and historic cultural resources on Muleshoe and Grulla

NWRs for the benefit of present and future generations; 3) to protect the areas's resource values through land protection strategies that protect tracts of land with desirable habitats; 4) to further the public's interest and involvement with Muleshoe and Grulla NWRs through wildlife interpretation, education/outreach programs, and quality wildlife-dependent recreational opportunities; 5) to maintain or strengthen existing interagency and jurisdictional relationships and establish new partnerships within the community to cooperate on mutually beneficial programs for improving wildlife and habitat resources on the refuge, within the High Plains region, and the Edwards Plateau Ecosystem; and 6) to develop program support sufficient to provide the necessary staffing, facilities, equipment, and operational funds to accomplish the goals of the refuge and fulfill the mission of the Refuge System.

The overall management of the refuge will focus on restoring, maintaining and enhancing a healthy prairie ecosystem. Management efforts will be directed toward threatened and endangered species, species of special concern, waterfowl, sandhill cranes, other migratory birds, and resident wildlife that currently and historically occurred on the refuge.

For detailed descriptions of proposed actions (objectives and strategies), please refer to the draft CCP. As a working document, modifications to the objectives and strategies are anticipated. However, if modifications result in changes to the effects analysis, or include actions that are not considered in this document, the Refuge will reinitiate consultation.

VII. Determination of Effects:

A. Explanation of effects of the action on species and critical habitat in items III A, B, and C:

Under the proposed action, management of special status species would continue with habitat protection, protection of individuals from disturbance and expanded monitoring of populations and habitat where necessary. Habitat management activities (grazing, prescribed burning, and invasive species control), as described in the CCP, are designed to maintain or enhance the refuge's prairie habitat. No negative direct impacts on threatened and endangered species are expected to occur. The timing, duration, and magnitude of these activities are not expected to cause disturbance to the species that use the area. Indirect effects of improved grassland conditions should be beneficial. The enhancement of opportunities for wildlife observation, photography, interpretation, and education identified in the proposed action are expected to have little or no effect on the refuge's biological resources, expect to improve the public's awareness and understanding. All proposed public use activities have been carefully planned to avoid unacceptable levels of impact. Any hunting program that may be developed is not expected to have significant effects, because it will only be implemented if it does not conflict with visitor safety or negatively impact other refuge resources. Management activities that could result in temporary disturbance will be implemented in a manner that minimizes impacts (i.e. through seasonal restrictions). Threatened and endangered species are expected to benefit as a result of improved habitat diversity and quality. Those species that are migrants or accidental visitors will also benefit by virtue of the existence of the refuge.

Bald eagle - Eagle use on the Refuge is generally associated with migrating flocks of waterfowl. There are limited areas to perch on the refuge and no known roost sites. No nesting or roosting occurs on the refuge, so no direct effects are anticipated. Impacts as a result of disturbance are expected to be insignicant or discountable. Habitat enhancement activities will likely improve conditions for a number of potential prey species, thereby indirectly improving or providing additional opportunities for bald eagles to capture prey.

Interior least tern, whooping crane, and mountain plover - These species do not breed or typically occur on the refuge. Therefore, implementation of the CCP is not expected to affect these species.

Black-tailed prairie dog - Habitat for the black-tailed prairie dog would be enhanced and protected. If concentrations of prairie dogs build to sufficient levels, the potential to reintroduce the black-footed ferret would be evaluated.

Lesser prairie chicken - Areas of native prairie would be managed to create desirable habitat for the lesser prairie chicken, including prescribed burns designed specifically for prairie chicken habitat nee

B.   Explanation of actions to be implemented to reduce adverse effects:

None anticipated.

Effect determination and response requested: [* = optional]

A.   Listed species/designated critical habitat:

Determination   Response Requested

No effect on species/critical habitat
(species: <u>whooping crane, interior least tern</u>)   __X__ *Concurrence

May affect, is not likely to adversely affect species
 /critical habitat
(species: <u>bald eagle</u>)   __X__ Concurrence

May affect, is likely to adversely affect species
 /critical habitat
(species: <u>none</u>)   _____ Formal Consultation

B. Proposed species/proposed critical habitat

No effect
(species: <u>mountain plover</u>)   __X__ Concurrence

C. Candidate species

No effect
(Species: <u>none</u>)   _____ Concurrence

Is NOT likely to jeopardize candidate species*
(Species: <u>black-tailed prairie dog, lesser prairie chicken</u>)   __X__ Concurrence

* the effects of implementing the CCP on these species should be beneficial

Prepared by: _____   8-14-03
                     Biologist/Natural Resource Planning   Date

Reviewed/Approved by: _____   8-19-03
                     Refuge Manager   Date
                     Muleshoe/Grulla NWR

IX.   **Reviewing ESFO Evaluations:**

A.   Concurrence: ✓   Nonconcurrence: _____

B.   Formal consultation required: _____

C.   Conference required _____

D.   Informal conference required _____

E.   Remarks (attach additional pages as needed):

Tom Cloud _____   _11-5-03_
Signature   Date
Field Supervisor
Arlington Ecological Services Field Office

INTRA-SERVICE SECTION 7 BIOLOGICAL EVALUATION FORM
GRULLA NATIONAL WILDLIFE REFUGE

Originating Person: Carol Torrez
Telephone Number: 505-762-9721
Date: August 6, 2009

I.   Region: Southwest (Region 2)

II.   Service Activity (Program): Refuge

III.   Pertinent Species and Habitat:

        The New Mexico Ecological Services Office provided a species list for Roosevelt County, New
        Mexico (shown in Appendix S of the CCP). The following species have been documented and/or
        have potential habitat on the Refuge:

        A.   Listed species and/or their critical habitat within the action area:

                Bald-headed eagle (Haliaeetus leucocephalus) – delisted

        B.   Proposed species and/or proposed critical habitat within the action area:

                Mountain plover (Charadrius montanus) is proposed threatened without critical habitat.

        C.   Candidate species within the action area:

                Black-tailed prairie dog (Cynomys ludovicianus)
                Lesser prairie chicken (Tympanuchus pallidicinctus)
                Sand dune lizard (Holbrookia arenicola)

        D.   Include species/habitat occurrence map:

                Refuge habitat consists of the 2,300 Salt Lake, which is dry much of the time, and 900 acres of
                native grasses and shrubs. For a map of the Refuge, please see Map #2 in the draft CCP.

                The bald eagle, which can occur more widely during migration and the winter, may use the refuge
                for feeding when water and waterfowl are present in the area. The other species listed above
                are not known to breed or typically occur on the refuge, so no map of species/habitat occurrence
                is available.

IV.   Geographic area or station name and action/program action:

        Station: Grulla national wildlife refuge in south central New Mexico.

        Action: Issuance and implementation of the Comprehensive Conservation Plan for the Muleshoe and
        Grulla NWRs.

V.   Location (See Map #2 in the CCP)

        A.   Ecoregion Number and Name

                Region 2 Ecoregion # 11, the Edwards Plateau Ecosystem

B. County and state

Roosevelt County, New Mexico

C. Section, township, and range (or latitude and longitude):

Latitude 34° 4' 0" Longitude 103° 3' 0"

D. Distance (miles) and direction to nearest town:

Grulla NWR is located approximately 20 miles east of Portales, New Mexico

E. Species/habitat occurrence:

Black-footed Ferret – There is no potential habitat on this refuge and no recorded (historic) sightings in the area.

Bald Eagle – Most wintering and nesting bald eagles in New Mexico are associated with major rivers, lakes, or reservoirs. The lakes give an opportunity to catch fish, and the dead waterfowl and crippled game are a food source. The bald eagle, which can occur on the refuge during migration and the winter, may use the refuge for foraging (when Salt Lake does freeze and large numbers of waterfowl and water are present in the area).

Mountain plover – Mountain plovers are a short-distance, endemic species that breed in the Plains and gather in flocks to migrate to their fall/winter dog grounds. The mountain plover prefers expansive dry short-grass prairies such as high plains and semidesert areas having a high proportion of bare ground (>30 percent) for nesting. Typical associated plants include blue grama, buffalo grass, and prickly pear cactus. In most instances, the species nests from April through July, and may be found nesting in open playas areas, on dry playas (lake beds, too). They primarily nest in or near prairie dog towns. Other sites that attract plovers for nesting, but may be less ideal, include bare fields, highway corridor rights-of-way, and stock tanks. Historically, the mountain plover was most likely a common breeding bird in the Pecos and Staked Plains area, but during the past century, human settlement, the eradication of prairie dogs, and the conversion of native prairie to cropland has significantly reduced the suitable habitat for this species, producing a significant decline in the continental population.

Although Grulla NWR is within the range of the mountain plover, and the dry lake bed and surrounding area do offer some temporarily potential nesting habitat, this species has not been documented in or around the refuge. It is possible that the area could be used for foraging during migration.

Black-tailed Prairie Dog – Prairie dogs have not been documented on the refuge. However, there is a small prairie dog town on private land east of the refuge entrance road.

Lesser Prairie Chicken – The lesser prairie chicken is an occupant of arid shortgrass prairies interspersed with shinnery oak and sand sagebrush (sands) habitats. In New Mexico, the main area of occurrence is on the Pecos and Staked Plains including Roosevelt County, particularly in the vicinity of Portales. Although Grulla NWR is in the vicinity, no prairie chickens have been documented on the refuge and there is limited potential habitat. The 300 acres of vegetation cover on the refuge is dominated by saline components of the playas such as blue grama and buffalo grass, saltbush, and yucca. The nearest known prairie chicken is on private land a few miles southeast of the refuge.

Sand dune lizard – This species occurs in the southern part of Roosevelt County, but it is not known to occur or have potential habitat on or around the refuge.

VIII. **Effect determination and response requested:**   [* = optional]

A.   Listed species/designated critical habitat:

Determination   Response Requested

No effect on species/critical habitat
(species: black-footed ferret)   _____ *Concurrence

May affect, is not likely to adversely affect species
  /critical habitat
(species: bald eagle.)   _X_ Concurrence

May affect, is likely to adversely affect species
  /critical habitat
(species: none)   _____ Formal Consultation

B. Proposed species/proposed critical habitat

No effect
(species: mountain plover)   _X_ Concurrence

C. Candidate species

No effect
(Species: black-tailed prairie dog, lesser prairie chicken,
          sand dune lizard)   _X_ Concurrence

Prepared by: _____   8-14-03
             Biologist/Natural Resource Planning   Date

Reviewed/Approved by: _____   8-19-03
                      Refuge Manager   Date
                      Muleshoe/Grulla NWR

IX.   **Reviewing ESFO Evaluations:**

A.   Concurrence: __✓__   Nonconcurrence: _____

B.   Formal consultation required: _____

C.   Conference required _____

D.   Informal conference required _____

E.   Remarks (attach additional pages as needed)

_____   11/17/03
Signature   Date
Field Supervisor
New Mexico Ecological Services Field Office

Refuge Operating Needs
TIER 1

Station Project Title	Project Number	Project Description	FTEs	Operations Costs ($000)		
				One-Time	Recurring Base	Total 1st Yr
Muleshoe NWR Remove Mesquite Shrubs and Other Invasive Plants	00006	Restore 1,500 acres of natural grassland by controlling the invasion of mesquite and other invasive plants. Overgrazing and the absence of burning before the refuge was established contribute to the encroachment of mesquite shrubs in native grasslands that provide habitat for sandhill crane, lesser prairie chicken, and other wildlife. The refuge grasslands are some of the last remnants of migratory bird grassland habitat in an area that has been predominantly developed for agriculture, and their restoration and protection will play a significant role in the preservation of several migratory bird species.		25	12	37
Muleshoe NWR Restore and enhance lesser prairie chicken populations and other upland bird species	00004	Provide part-time or seasonal staff to contribute to the restoration of lesser prairie chicken populations and other upland bird species in and around the refuge. Individual will research habitat types and restoration techniques, and conduct appropriate management of grasslands. Lesser prairie chicken populations on the High Plains have decreased significantly in the last decade due to habitat loss and degradation.	0.5	33	25	58
Muleshoe NWR Improve Public Use Facilities	00003	Provide a maintenance worker position to enhance visitor services by upgrading and maintaining public use facilities, including wildlife observation platforms, nature trails, and interpretive signs. Existing interpretive facilities are in need of rehabilitation or replacement. Over 13,000 people visit the refuge each year, many to view the refuge's large sandhill crane population. There is limited outdoor recreational opportunities in this remote area along the Texas/New Mexico border communities. The project will assist the refuge in meeting its goals of creating a positive wildlife viewing experience and in providing information to the public regarding wildlife and refuge regulations.	1.0	65	59	124
Muleshoe NWR Restore Upland Habitat	00002	Provide a GS-7 biologist to restore and enhance wildlife habitat on 6,700 acres of refuge grasslands and on 3,000 acres of intermittent wetlands. The refuge's native grasslands are characteristic of the area before agriculture development and require intensive research and management in order to remain a healthy ecosystem. The project will include grassland and wetland monitoring and rehabilitation.	1.0	65	59	124
		Totals	**2.5**	**188**	**155**	**343**

Refuge Operating Needs
TIER 2

Station Project Title	Project Number	Project Description	FTEs	Operations Costs ($000)		
				One-Time	Recurring Base	Total 1st Yr
Muleshoe NWR Expand wildlife monitoring program	00001	Conduct surveys and compile a comprehensive wildlife census database for the refuge. The refuge is in need of essential wildlife data and analysis to enable sound management. Project will enhance wildlife management techniques and provide accurate wildlife inventory data for management planning.	1.0	75	80	155
Muleshoe NWR Expand outreach program	00005	Enhance the wildlife related public education and outdoor recreation programs both on and off the refuge, provide special events, improve contacts with the media, local communities, schools, and other agencies. This project would increase public awareness of conservation and Fish and Wildlife Service goals and contribute to the local economy. This project would best be accomplished through the addition of a recreation specialist.	1.0	75	80	155
Muleshoe NWR Improve waterfowl disease response capabilities	00007	Improve waterfowl disease control response capabilities by expanding monitoring and control operations. Project will allow refuge to monitor large numbers of wintering waterfowl resting areas on private lands in order to more effectively control waterfowl disease outbreaks and the salvaging of diseased waterfowl. In past years, thousands of waterfowl have died in the Texas High Plains due to cholera. The refuge is responsible for waterfowl disease control in the Texas High Plains Region in coordination with the Buffalo Lake NWR, the Texas Parks and Wildlife Department, and Texas Tech University Department of Wildlife Management.		35	8	43
Muleshoe NWR Hire a full-time Law Enforcement Officer	03001	Improve visitor services and enhance security for visitors, employees, resources, and facilities by hiring a full-time law enforcement officer (GS 5/7/9) with responsibilities for Muleshoe, Buffalo Lake and Grulla NWR's. The three refuges have approximately 18,000 to 20,000 total visitors annually. The position will also entail waterfowl disease surveillance and compliance inspections of waterfowl hunters in the panhandle of Texas. This funding request also includes costs for a vehicle and required training and equipment to outfit the officer to perform essential duties.	1.0	113	61	174
		Totals	3.0	298	229	527

Refuge Operating Needs
TIER 1

Station Project Title	Project Number	Project Description	FTEs	Operations Costs ($000)		
				One- Time	Recurring Base	Total 1st Yr
Grulla NWR	00002		1.0	65	59	124
Improve Visitor Facilities		Provide a maintenance worker position for the Grulla Natioanal Wildlife Refuge; employee will be responsible for the development and maintenance of public use and other refuge facilities. Project will involve building trails, tour routes, and informational signs. Currently, the only visitor facilities at the refuge are a small parking lot and a short dirt trail. Wildlife observation use increases during winter months when sandhill crane and other migratory birds are present. The project would increase opportunities for wildlife observation and enhance visitor appreciation for wildlife in this remote area of Eastern New Mexico.				
		Totals	**1.0**	**65**	**59**	**124**

Refuge Operating Needs
TIER 2

Station Project Title	Project Number	Project Description	FTEs	Operations Costs ($000)		
				One- Time	Recurring Base	Total 1st Yr
Grulla NWR Enhance resource protection	00001	Project will protect habitat, wildlife, and cultural resources. The refuge, three tracts of inventory wetland, and six wetland easements are remote and require protection. The project would involve boundary posting, public contacts, adjacent landowner contacts, boundary surveys, and site protection.	0.5	33	27	60
Grulla NWR Improve refuge access	00003	Conduct boundary surveys and contact land owners regarding land exchanges and acquisition. The present refuge boundary crosses a lake in several places creating management difficulty regarding boundary posting, fencing, wildlife surveys, and law enforcement. The refuge provides habitat for large numbers of sandhill cranes and shore birds during wet periods.		25	13	38
Grulla NWR Improve visitor facilities	00002	Enhance visitor wildlife viewing opportunities by improving public use facilities. Improvements will be accomplished with a maintenance worker position and will involve building trails, tour routes, and informational and regulatory signs. Currently, the only visitor facilities at the refuge are a small parking lot and a short trail. Wildlife observation use increases during winter months when sandhill crane and other migratory birds are present. The project would provide opportunities for wildlife observation and increase visitor use in this remote area of Eastern New Mexico.	1.0	65	59	124
Totals			**1.5**	**123**	**99**	**222**

APPENDIX F - COMPATIBILITY DETERMINATIONS

DRAFT
COMPATIBILITY DETERMINATION

HUNTING

Station Name: Muleshoe National Wildlife Refuge

Date Established: 1935

Establishing and Acquisition Authorities: Executive Order 7214 of October 24, 1935.

Purposes for which the Refuge was established: For lands acquired under the Executive Order dated October 24, 1935, the purpose of the acquisition is "as a refuge and breeding ground for migratory birds and other wildlife."

For lands acquired under the Migratory Bird Conservation Act (16 U.S.C., Section 715d) the purpose of the acquisition is "...for use as an inviolate sanctuary, or for any other management purposes, for migratory birds."

National Wildlife Refuge System Mission: The mission of the National Wildlife Refuge System is "to administer a national network of lands and waters for the conservation, management, and where appropriate, restoration of fish, wildlife, and plant resources and their habitats within the United States for the benefit of present and future generations of Americans."

Description of Proposed Use: Hunting has never been allowed on the Refuge. However, hunting is one of the six priority wildlife-dependent public uses on national wildlife refuges, the Texas Parks and Wildlife Department (TPWD) has requested that the refuge consider hunting and determine what potential hunting opportunities may be available and appropriate on the refuge.

The TPWD allows a variety of hunting opportunities on private lands in Bailey County, including hunting for waterfowl, sandhill crane, deer, pheasant, gamebirds (quail, doves, etc.), and non-game (i.e., bobcats, coyotes, ground squirrels, prairie dogs, rabbits, badgers, fox, skunk, etc.). The various hunting seasons begin around September 1 and continue through the end of February, with no closed season on non-game species.

The species listed above occur on the refuge, but further investigation, in cooperation with TPWD, is necessary to determine if populations and habitats on the refuge could support hunting, while accomplishing the purpose of the refuge and maintaining public safety.

Availability of Resources: Currently, sufficient resources (access and personnel) are not available to implement a hunting program on the refuge. With additional staff and/or partnerships proposed in the CCP, it may be possible to provide limited quality hunting opportunities. Additional law enforcement support (from internal and external cooperators) will be necessary to ensure compliance with State and Federal regulations.

Anticipated Impacts of the Use: Hunting removes individual animals from the population and causes disturbance to non-target species. Travel on non-designated roads and the creation of additional two-tracks (illegal off-road use) could potentially be a problem.

Hunting waterfowl or sandhill cranes on the refuge would result in harassment and potentially deter these species from using important roosting and grassland feeding area. The size of the refuge and actual open water area available is insufficient to sustain sandhill crane and waterfowl hunting concurrent with the refuge purposes.

If hunts of other species are carefully planned in a way that avoids important wildlife areas (those areas used by waterfowl, sandhill cranes, and other rare or declining species) during sensitive times, potential impacts non-target species their habitat are expected to be insignificant. Given that Muleshoe NWR is an island of habitat in a highly disturbed landscape, any activities beyond minimal hunting could have a detrimental effect on other wildlife population in the area.

Determination: Hunting of waterfowl and sandhill cranes on the refuge is not compatible.

Hunting of certain wildlife species is compatible.

Justification: Based on the biological impacts described in the CCP and the EA, it was determined that waterfowl and/or sandhill crane hunting would materially interfere with or detract from the purpose for which the refuge was established. Local and regional water use over time has lowered the groundwater aquifer, which has caused many playa lakes in the area to go dry. With less water, there is less habitat available for waterfowl and cranes. Sometimes the lakes on the refuge are the only secure habitats available for these birds to roost and rest. Opening the refuge lakes and surrounding areas to hunting would harass the birds and/or deter them from using the area, which would interfere with the purpose of the refuges.

Other forms of hunting would not materially interfere with the purpose of the refuge, provided the following stipulations are implemented. In addition, hunting has been identified as a priority public use in the National Wildlife Refuge System Improvement Act of 1997 when this activity is compatible with the Refuge purpose.

Stipulations Necessary to Ensure Compatibility:

- In cooperation with TPWD, investigate whether existing refuge wildlife populations could sustain hunting. Gather the data necessary to plan, develop, and establish limited/appropriate hunting opportunities on the refuge.
- Regulate hunting with day or weekly use permits, mandatory check-in/check-out, or periodic visits by cooperating outside enforcement entities (USFWS special agents, TPWD game wardens, county sheriff deputies, etc).
- Designate specific areas and times where hunting is allowed.
- Exclude sensitive areas from any hunting and/or provide buffers around refuge facilities, roads, public use areas, waterfowl and sandhill crane use area = all lakes and feeding areas, and other sensitive areas (i.e. prairie dog or prairie chicken habitat).

Signatures:

_____   Date ___7-23-04___
Project Leader

_____   Date ___8/5/04___
Refuge Supervisor

_____   Date ___8/6/04___
Regional Chief
National Wildlife Refuge System

COMPATIBILITY DETERMINATION

GRAZING

Station Name: Muleshoe National Wildlife Refuge

Date Established: 10/24/35

Establishing and Acquisition Authorities: The Muleshoe National Wildlife
Refuge, located in Bailey County, Texas, was established on October 24, 1935 by
Executive Order 7214.

Purposes for Which the Refuge was Established: For lands acquired under the
Executive Order dated October 24, 1935, the purpose of the acquisition is "as a
refuge and breeding ground for migratory birds and other wildlife."

For lands acquired under the Migratory Bird Conservation Act (16 U.S.C., Section
715d) the purpose of the acquisition is "... for uses as an inviolate sanctuary,
or for any other management purposes, for migratory birds."

Management Goals and Objectives: Provide migration and wintering habitat for
naturally occurring wildlife species threatened with extinction.

Provide habitat for sandhill crane, other marsh and water birds, shore birds,
raptors, and other wildlife.

Provide environmental education and enhance the public's awareness of wildlife
and the environment.

Other Applicable Laws, Regulations and Policies:

1. Migratory Bird Treaty Act of 1918 (15 U.S.C. 703-711; 40 Stat. 755).
2. Migratory Bird Conservation Act of 1929 (16 U.S.C. 715r; 45 Stat. 1222).
3. Refuge Recreation Act of 1962 (16 U.S.C. 460k-460k-4; 76 Stat. 653).
4. Endangered Species Act of 1973 (16 U.S.C. 1531 et seq; 87 Stat. 884).
5. Land and Water Conservation Fund Act of 1965.
6. Refuge Revenue Sharing Act of 1935, as amended in 1978 (16 U.S.C. 715s; 92
   Stat. 1319).

Description of Use: Refuge grazing program. Consists of permittee cattle
grazing on refuge grasslands during May through October.

Approximately 4,169 acres comprised of 7 fenced grazing units are grazed
periodically as a tool to manage and enhance wildlife habitat. All units have
at least two water sources strategically located to distribute grazing coverage.
The sources are either wells with windmills or water piped from a storage tank
and provide water for wildlife as well as for the cattle. Grazing units average
550 acres in size. Normally two units are rested each growing season and the
remaining units are alternately grazed during different times throughout the
growing season on a continuing annual cycle.

Anticipated Biological Impacts of the Use: Overgrazing of wildlife habitat
during drought conditions. This can normally be controlled seasonally by
management practices such as minimizing cattle numbers, deleting grazing of
affected units completely, or various grazing rotation methods. There will
always be some grazing of plants desirable as wildlife habitat. What few wet
areas and riparian areas exist on the refuge will be impacted somewhat by
grazing and includes plant removal and soil impaction. Trails originated by
livestock sometimes evolve into areas eroded by wind and water. Except for

water supplied by windmills, livestock water is supplied from the refuge headquarters domestic water supply which consists of a single well and a water storage tank. The water supply is also used to water trees for wildlife habitat in the headquarters area during the spring and summer. During mid-summer livestock use of water occasionally causes a temporary water shortage at the refuge quarters and headquarters.

NEPA Compliance: Environmental Action Memorandum attached.

Categorical Exclusion _____

Environmental Assessment __X__

Environmental Impact Statement ____

FONSI __X__

Determination: (Check One)
This use is compatible __X__ This use is not compatible _____

Stipulations Necessary to Ensure Compatibility: Continue monitoring grazing units regarding plant vigor and grassland viability. Evaluate revising grazing by considering management options which include modifying grazing unit boundaries, decreasing the number of animal units (AUs) allowed, and deleting part or all of some grazing units.

Justification: The refuge grasslands are comprised primarily of grama grasses and alkali sacaton grasses. Grama grasses are not tolerant to controlled burning which would be the only viable alternate wildlife habitat management tool in place of grazing. Alkali sacaton grasses are basically monotypic and although response to controlled burning is satisfactory, factors such as limited refuge staff, drought, and fire control make grazing a more desirable form of wildlife habitat management tool. If wildlife habitat management was not practiced in some form, (grazing preferred) vegetation would gradually develop into more monotypic and dense stands thus creating less habitat for a more diverse species of wildlife. By using grazing as a wildlife habitat management tool, a more varied plant successional stage develops.

Project Leader: _Donald R Clapp_____ Refuge Manager, 8/18/94
                       (Signature/Title/Date)

Reviewed by: ___Gary Burke Assoc Mgr- OR/TX 9/13/94___
                       (Signature/Title/Date)
            _____ 9/12/94
                       (Signature/Title/Date)

COMPATIBILITY DETERMINATION

CAMPING AND PICNICKING

Station Name: Muleshoe National Wildlife Refuge

Date Established: 10/24/35

Establishing and Acquisition Authorities: The Muleshoe National Wildlife Refuge, located in Bailey County, Texas, was established on October 24, 1935 by Executive Order 7214.

Purposes for Which the Refuge was Established: For lands acquired under the Executive Order dated October 24, 1935, the purpose of the acquisition is "as a refuge and breeding ground for migratory birds and other wildlife."

For lands acquired under the Migratory Bird Conservation Act (16 U.S.C., Section 715d) the purpose of the acquisition is "... for uses as an inviolate sanctuary, or for any other management purposes, for migratory birds."

Management Goals and Objectives: Provide migration and wintering habitat for naturally occurring wildlife species threatened with extinction.

Provide habitat for sandhill crane, other marsh and water birds, shore birds, raptors, and other wildlife.

Provide environmental education and enhance the public's awareness of wildlife and the environment.

Other Applicable Laws, Regulations and Policies:

1. Migratory Bird Treaty Act of 1918 (15 U.S.C. 703-711; 40 Stat. 755).
2. Migratory Bird Conservation Act of 1929 (16 U.S.C. 715r; 45 Stat. 1222).
3. Refuge Recreation Act of 1962 (16 U.S.C 460k-460k-4; 76 Stat. 653).
4. Endangered Species Act of 1973 (16 U.S.C. 1531 et seq; 87 Stat. 884).

Description of Use: Camping and picnicking at a small designated campground near the refuge headquarters, primarily used by visitors using the refuge for wildlife observation.

The campground is the only exception to the refuge's daytime use only regulation. The refuge only provides potable water, pit toilets, picnic tables, and fire grills. There is also a fire pit in the center of the campground area, used mostly by groups. Primary users include Boy Scout Troops from area cities, retirees with travel homes, and tent campers. The campground is used intermittently throughout the year but more extensively in the fall during the sandhill crane migration. The campground and picnic area is small and has approximately eight sites for camping or picnicking.

Anticipated Biological Impacts of the Use: All impacts should be minimal. Trash cans are available and littering in the past has been practically non existent. Other minimal impacts include vandalism, disturbing vegetation, free roaming pets, and wild fires.

NEPA Compliance: Environmental Action Memorandum attached.

Categorical Exclusion __X__

Determination: This use is compatible __X__

Stipulations Necessary to Ensure Compatibility: Continued maintenance of existing signs as well as installing additional ones, as needed, should aid in keeping refuge violations minimal. Occasional law enforcement patrols should continue during periods of high public use. The use of fires should be prohibited when weather conditions are extremely dry. No major expansion of camping and picnicking opportunities beyond the current level is proposed.

Justification: The majority of the visitors using the campground and picnic area are there for the purpose of wildlife observation. The area normally requires minimal funding and staff time. Trees planted and watered in the area are an asset as wildlife habitat. Since the refuge is fairly remote and there are no campgrounds available in the vicinity, the campground is quite beneficial for visitors wishing to view wildlife when most active (early morning or late evening). Since the nearest motel accommodations are 20 miles away, the campground is often used by travelers wishing to see the sandhill cranes before they leave their refuge roosting sites during the early morning hours.

Project Leader: _Donald R Clapp_   Refuge Manager, 8/18/94
              (Signature/Title/Date)

Reviewed by: _Gary Burke Assoc Mgr RD/TX_   9/13/94
              (Signature/Title/Date)

_____ RW/ARW _____ 9/12/94
              (Signature/Title/Date)

COMPATIBILITY DETERMINATION

WILDLIFE OBSERVATION AND PHOTOGRAPHY

Station Name: Muleshoe National Wildlife Refuge

Date Established: 10/24/35

Establishing and Acquisition Authorities: The Muleshoe National Wildlife
Refuge, located in Bailey County, Texas, was established on October 24, 1935 by
Executive Order 7214.

Purposes for Which the Refuge was Established: For lands acquired under the
Executive Order dated October 24, 1935, the purpose of the acquisition is "as a
refuge and breeding ground for migratory birds and other wildlife."

For lands acquired under the Migratory Bird Conservation Act (16 U.S.C., Section
715d) the purpose of the acquisition is "... for uses as an inviolate sanctuary,
or for any other management purposes, for migratory birds."

Management Goals and Objectives: Provide migration and wintering habitat for
naturally occurring wildlife species threatened with extinction.

Provide habitat for sandhill crane, other marsh and water birds, shore birds,
raptors, and other wildlife.

Provide environmental education and enhance the public's awareness of wildlife
and the environment.

Other Applicable Laws, Regulations and Policies:

   1. Migratory Bird Treaty Act of 1918 (15 U.S.C. 703-711; 40 Stat. 755).
   2. Migratory Bird Conservation Act of 1929 (16 U.S.C. 715r; 45 Stat. 1222).
   3. Refuge Recreation Act of 1962 (16 U.S.C. 460k-460k-4; 76 Stat. 653).
   4. Endangered Species Act of 1973 (16 U.S.C. 1531 et seq; 87 Stat. 884).

Description of Use: Observation and photography of wildlife by walking or using
motorized vehicles, bicycles, or horses.

Foot travel is normally allowed on refuge roads, fire lanes, levees, and trails.
Motorized vehicles are restricted to those roads identified as tour routes.
Lake dike roads are closed to motor vehicle traffic year-round and are closed to
all public use when migratory birds are present during the winter. Bicycles and
horses are allowed on refuge roads, levees, and fire lanes (no trail use is
allowed).

Anticipated Biological Impacts of the Use: Past experience indicates that most
of the impacts will involve some violation (minimal) of refuge regulations,
e.g., disturbing wildlife, removing plants, littering, or vandalism.
Occasionally wildlife is injured or killed by vehicles along refuge roads.

NEPA Compliance: Environmental Action Memorandum attached.

     Categorical Exclusion   X

Determination: This use is compatible   X   This use is not compatible _____

Stipulations Necessary to Ensure Compatibility: Continue maintenance of existing signs as well as installing additional ones, as needed, should aid in keeping refuge violations minimal. Occasional law enforcement patrols should continue during periods of high public use and when sandhill crane and waterfowl numbers are high. No major expansion of wildlife observation opportunities beyond the current level is proposed.

Justification: The majority of the refuge visitors visit the refuge to view wildlife and to be in a natural environment. Wildlife observation and photography are justifiable wildlife-oriented activities and are compatible with refuge purposes.

Project Leader: _Donald R Clapp_   Refuge Manager, 8/18/94
                        (Signature/Title/Date)

Reviewed by: _Gary Byrne Assoc Mgr Ref IX_   9/13/94
                       (Signature/Title/Date)

_____ 9/12/94
                       (Signature/Title/Date)

COMPATIBILITY DETERMINATION

WILDLIFE OBSERVATION

Station Name: Grulla National Wildlife Refuge

Date Established: 11/06/69

Establishing and Acquisition Authorities: The Grulla National Wildlife Refuge, located in Roosevelt County, New Mexico, was established on November 6, 1969 by public land withdrawn from the Bureau of Land Management.

Five acres of private land was purchased for access in Bailey County, Texas on December 17, 1982.

Purposes for Which the Refuge was Established: Lands in New Mexico were withdrawn "...reserved for the Grulla National Wildlife Refuge..." Public Land Order 4742, dated Nov. 6, 1969.

For lands acquired in Texas "... suitable for-- (1) incidental fish and wildlife-oriented recreational development, (2) the protection of natural resources, (3) the conservation of endangered species or threatened species ..." *16 U.S.C. § 460k-1* "... the Secretary ... may accept and use ... donation of ... real ... property. Such acceptance may be accomplished under the terms and conditions of restrictive covenants imposed by donors ..." *16 U.S.C. § 460k-2* (Refuge Recreation Act (*16 U.S.C. § 460k-460k-4*), as amended).

Management Goals and Objectives: Provide a unique, specialized, and strategically located habitat type necessary to accomplish distributive management of lesser sandhill cranes on their wintering grounds.

Provide habitat for other marsh and water birds, shore birds, raptors, and other wildlife.

Provide migration and wintering habitat for naturally occurring wildlife species threatened with extinction.

Provide environmental education and enhance the public's awareness of wildlife and the environment.

Other Applicable Laws, Regulations and Policies:

1. Migratory Bird Treaty Act of 1918 (15 U.S.C. 703-711; 40 Stat. 755).
2. Migratory Bird Conservation Act of 1929 (16 U.S.C. 715r; 45 Stat. 1222).
3. Refuge Recreation Act of 1962 (16 U.S.C. 460k-460k-4; 76 Stat. 653).
4. Endangered Species Act of 1973 (16 U.S.C. 1531 *et seq*; 87 Stat. 884).

Description of Use: Observation of wildlife by walking or using motorized vehicles.

The refuge's only public access is a short entrance road leading to a parking area and a short trail and overlook site. Occasionally visitors walk over the grasslands to reach the lake's shoreline.

Anticipated Biological Impacts of the Use: Past experience indicates that most of the impacts will involve some violation (minimal) of refuge regulations, e.g., disturbing wildlife, removing plants, littering, or vandalism. Occasionally wildlife is injured or killed by vehicles along refuge roads.

NEPA Compliance: Environmental Action Memorandum attached.

   Categorical Exclusion   X

Determination: This use is compatible   X   This use is not compatible _____

Stipulations Necessary to Ensure Compatibility: Continued maintenance of parking area fence and existing signs as well as installing additional ones, as needed, should aid in keeping refuge violations minimal. Occasional law enforcement patrols should continue during periods of high public use and when sandhill crane and waterfowl numbers are high. No major expansion of wildlife observation opportunities beyond the current level is proposed.

Justification: The majority of the refuge visitors visit the refuge to view wildlife and to be in a natural environment. Wildlife observation is a justifiable wildlife-oriented activity and is compatible with refuge purposes.

Project Leader: _Donald R Clapp_____ Refuge Manager, 8-18-94
                                    (Signature/Title/Date)
Reviewed by: _Gary Bunte Assoc Mgr 00/TX 9/13/94_
                                    (Signature/Title/Date)
              _____ 9/2/94
                                    (Signature/Title/Date)

APPENDIX G - KEY LEGISLATION AND SERVICE POLICIES

American Indian Religious Freedom Act (1978): Directs agencies to consult with native traditional religious leaders to determine appropriate policy changes necessary to protect and preserve Native American religious cultural rights and practices.

Americans With Disabilities Act (1992): Prohibits discrimination in public accommodations and services.

Antiquities Act (1906): Authorizes the scientific investigation of antiquities on Federal land and provides penalties for unauthorized removal of objects taken or collected without a permit.

Archaeological and Historic Preservation Act (1974): Directs the preservation of historic and archaeological data in Federal construction projects.

Archaeological Resources Protection Act (1979) as amended: Protects materials of archaeological interest from unauthorized removal or destruction and requires Federal managers to develop plans and schedules to locate archaeological resources.

Architectural Barriers Act (1968): Requires federally owned, leased, or funded buildings and facilities to be accessible to persons with disabilities.

Bald and Golden Eagle Protection Act (1940) as amended: Calls for the protection of these raptorial species on and off Federal lands.

Clean Air Act (1977) as amended: The primary objective of this Act os to establish Federal standard for various pollutants from both stationary and mobile sources and to provide for the regulation of polluting emissions via stat implementation plants. In addition, and of special interest for National Wildlife Refuges, some amendments are designed to prevent significant deterioration in certain areas where air quality exceeds national standards, or to provide for improved air quality in areas which do not meet Federal standards ('non-attainment' areas). Federal facilities are required to comply with air quality standards to the same extent as non-governmental entities (42 U.U.C. 7418). Part C of the 1997 amendments stipulates requirements to prevent significant deterioration of air quality and, in particular, to preserve air quality in national parks, national wilderness areas, national monuments, and national seashores (42 U.S.C. 7470).

Clean Water Act (1977): Requires consultation with the Corps of Engineers (404 permits) for major wetland modifications.

Emergency Wetlands Resources Act (1986): The purpose of the Act is "To promote the conservation of migratory waterfowl and to offset or prevent the serious loss of wetlands by the acquisition of wetlands and other essential habitat, and for other purposes."

Endangered Species Act (1973): Requires all Federal agencies to carry out programs for the conservation of endangered and threatened species.

Executive Order 11593, Protection and Enhancement of Cultural Environment (1971): If the proposed any development activities that would affect the archaeological or historical sites, the Service will consult with Federal and State Preservation Officers to comply with Section 106 of the National Historic Preservation Act of 1966, as amended.

Executive Order 11988 (1977): Floodplain Management. Each Federal agency shall provide leadership and take action to reduce the risk of flood loss and minimize the impact of floods on human safety, and preserve the natural and beneficial values served by the floodplains.

Executive Order11990 Protection of Wetlands: The proposal will help conserve the natural and beneficial values of the wetland habitat. The Service will undertake no activity that would be detrimental to the continuance of the vital wetlands.

Executive Order 12996 Management and General Public Use of the National Wildlife Refuge System (1996): Defines the mission, purpose, and priority public uses of the National Wildlife Refuge System. It also presents four principles to guide management of the System.

Executive Order 13007 Indian Sacred Sites (1996): Directs Federal land management agencies to accommodate access to and ceremonial use of Indian sacred sites by Indian religious practitioners, avoid adversely affecting the physical integrity of such sacred sites, and where appropriate, maintain the confidentiality of sacred sites.

Federal Noxious Weed Act (1990): Requires the use of integrated management systems to control or contain undesirable plant species; and an interdisciplinary approach with the cooperation of other Federal and State agencies.

Fish and Wildlife Act (1956): Established a comprehensive national fish and wildlife policy and broadened the authority for acquisition and development of refuges.

Fish and Wildlife Coordination Act (1958): Allows the Fish and Wildlife Service to enter into agreements with private landowners for wildlife management purposes.

Land and Water Conservation Fund Act (1965): Uses the receipts from the sale of surplus Federal land, outer continental shelf oil and gas sales, and other sources for land acquisition under several authorities.

Migratory Bird Treaty Act (1918): Designates the protection of migratory birds as a Federal responsibility. This Act enables the setting of seasons, and other regulations including the closing of areas, Federal or non-Federal, to the hunting of migratory birds.

Migratory Bird Conservation Act (1929): Establishes procedures for acquisition by purchase, rental, or gift of areas approved by the Migratory Bird Conservation Commission.

Migratory Bird Hunting and Conservation Stamp Act (1934): Authorized the opening of part of a refuge to waterfowl hunting.

National Environmental Policy Act (1969): Requires the disclosure of the environmental impacts of any major Federal action significantly affecting the quality of the human environment.

National Historic Preservation Act (1966) as amended: Establishes as policy that the Federal Government is to provide leadership in the preservation of the nation's prehistoric and historic resources.

National Wildlife Refuge System Administration Act of 1966 as amended by the National Wildlife Refuge System Improvement Act of 1997, 16 U.S.C. 668dd-668ee. (Refuge Administration Act): Defines the National Wildlife Refuge System and authorizes the Secretary to permit any use of a refuge provided such use is compatible with the major purposes for which the refuge was established. The Refuge Improvement Act clearly defines a unifying mission for the Refuge System; establishes the legitimacy and appropriateness of the six priority public uses (hunting, fishing, wildlife observation and photography, or environmental education and interpretation); establishes a formal process for determining compatibility; established the responsibilities of the Secretary of Interior for managing and protecting the System; and requires a

Comprehensive Conservation Plan for each refuge by the year 2012. This Act amended portions of the Refuge Recreation Act and National Wildlife Refuge System Administration Act of 1966.

Native American Graves Protection and Repatriation Act (1990): Requires Federal agencies and museums to inventory, determine ownership of, and repatriate cultural items under their control or possession.

Refuge Recreation Act (1962): Allows the use of refuges for recreation when such uses are compatible with the refuge's primary purposes and when sufficient funds are available to manage the uses.

Refuge Revenue Sharing Act (1935) as amended 16 U.S.C. 715s): Provides for payments to counties in lieu of taxes, using revenues derived from the sale of products from refuges. Public Law 88-523 (1964) revised this Act and required that all revenues received from refuge products, such as animals, timber and minerals, or from leases or other privileges, be deposited in a special Treasury account and net receipts distributed to counties for public schools and roads. Payments to counties were established as: 1)on acquired land, the greatest amount calculated on the basis of 75 cents per acre, three-fourths of one percent of the appraised value, or 25 percent of the net receipts produced from the land; and 2) on land withdrawn from the public domain, 24 percent of net receipts and basic payments under Public Law 94-565 (31 U.S.C. 1601-1607, 90 Stat. 2662), payment in lieu of taxes on public lands. The current and proposed management of this refuge under this Plan is in compliance with this Act.

Rehabilitation Act (1973): Requires programmatic accessibility in addition to physical accessibility for all facilities and programs funded by the Federal government to ensure that anybody can participate in any program.

Secretarial Order 3127 (602 DM 2) Contaminants and Hazardous Waste Determination: No contaminants or hazardous waste are known to exist on the refuge and none will be created.

Volunteer and Community Partnership Enhancement Act (1998): The purposes of this Act are to encourage the use of volunteers to assist in the management of refuges within the Refuge System; to facilitate partnerships between the Refuge System and non-Federal entities to promote public awareness of the resources of the Refuge System and public participation in the conservation of the resources and; to encourage donations and other contributions.

Wilderness Act of 1964 (Public Law 88-577 [16 U.S.C. 1131-1116]): Defines wilderness as follows: "A Wilderness, in contrast with those areas where man and his works dominate the landscape, is hereby recognized as an area where the earth and its community of life are untrammeled by man, where man himself is a visitor who does not remain. An area of wilderness is further defined to mean in this Act an area of undeveloped Federal land retaining its primeval character and influence, without permanent improvements or human habitation, which is protected and managed so as to preserve its natural conditions and which (1) generally appears to have been affected primarily by the forces of nature, with the imprint of man's work substantially unnoticeable; (2) has outstanding opportunities for solitude or a primitive and unconfined type of recreation; (3) has at least 5,000 acres of land or is of sufficient size as to make practicable its preservation and use in an unimpaired condition; and (4) may also contain ecological, geological, or other features of scientific, educational, scenic, or historical value."

APPENDIX H - PUBLIC INVOLVEMENT AND COMMENTS

On October 8, 2003 the U.S. Fish and Wildlife Service (Service) published a notice in the Federal Register Notice announcing the availability of the Draft CCP/EA for public review. The notice provided instructions for requesting a copy of the document, in print or CD-ROM format, by telephone, letter or e-mail and announced that the Service would accept comments on the Draft CCP/EA until November 24, 2003. The Draft CCP/EA was also sent to sent to more than 70 public citizens, private businesses, consulting companies, non-governmental organizations, State and Federal agencies, and City, County, State and Federal officials, as well as public libraries and media outlets on October 8, 2003.

The Service held an Open House at the Muleshoe NWR headquarters office on November 5, 2003 to present the Draft CCP/EA and receive comments on the document. Only 3 individuals attended. Responses received during the 45-day public review period consisted of four letters (two of which requested copies of the draft document and did not include comments). Comments received in the other two letters and from individuals that attended the public meeting are summarized below, with the Services response.

1. A landowner neighboring Grulla NWR attended the open house and provided the following verbal and written comment. He owns land on the north end of Salt Lake and would like to swap some land. Some of his property runs into Salt Lake and some of our property runs into his ranch.

Response: The Service is very interested in entertaining an exchange proposal in the near future. This would help alleviate some of the cattle trespass issues and allow a fencing program in the upland area that would help deter additional cattle trespass. Goal 3 in the CCP (page 112) draft discusses the need to "protect the area's resource values through ... consideration of acquisition boundary expansion". Strategies noted on page 113 of the Draft CCP are consistent with this proposal. The process for such an exchange can sometimes be lengthy because it involves appraisal of all lands involved. It would also necessitate appropriate approvals for expanding the acquisition boundary of the refuge to include the necessary compliance with the National Environmental Policy Act. Following approval of the CCP, the refuge manager will contact Mr. Bradley in an effort to begin the process of defining the areas that would be part of such an exchange proposal.

This proposal is consistent with goals, objectives, and strategies already identified in the CCP (pages 112 - 113). This land exchange would benefit the Service by allowing fencing of the upland areas that would deter cattle trespass and improve boundary management and access.

2. One individual that attended the open house expressed a interest in the grazing program.

Response: The refuge plans to implement a grazing program. Rangeland experts from NRCS will be contacted/consulted on an annual basis to determine if grazing is appropriate in a given season and help set and appropriate stocking rate. Permittee selection will be conducted by a sealed bid.

3. A representative of the Safari Club International in New Mexico and Texas provided written comments. He strongly recommended that Alternative B (the proposed action) be implemented and very strongly recommended that improvement to public use opportunities (specifically hunting) should be included, not just considered.

Response: Hunting is one of the six priority wildlife-dependent public uses of National Wildlife Refuges and the Service is committed to working with TPWD to gather wildlife and habitat data in order to plan, develop, and establish compatible hunting opportunities that do not conflict with visitor safety or negatively impact other refuge resources. If it is determined that wildlife populations on the refuge could sustain hunting, the refuge would have to go through the appropriate process (i.e. publishing refuge specific regulations in the Code of Federal Regulations) before implementing this program.

4. Written comments were received from the Wildlife Management Institute (WMI). Their comments/suggestions are summarized in the bulleted items below:

•   Questioned relative priority among the goals and suggested that higher priority goals should be identified.

Response: The refuge cannot prioritize; each goal is equal in importance.

•   Suggested that it is important that public input received from the open house and written comments be seriously considered and incorporated into the plan and that the refuge staff maintain public outreach after the plan is completed.

Response: All comment received during the public review were considered, and to the degree possible, incorporated into the final document.

•   Expressed concern that adequate funding for all proposed actions may not be forth coming. They suggested that the Final CCP provide a schedule of priority actions that will be implement as budget allows.

Response: The plan strategies will have to be weighed in context of the annual budget before priorities are set. Adequate staffing is essential to enhance current programs and to implement actions in the CCP.

•   Supported the efforts to develop a hunting program for the refuges and suggested that a hunting plan needs to be developed in cooperation with TPWD.

Response: A strategy under Goal 4, Objective 2 of the CCP states that the refuge, in cooperation with TPWD, will gather data necessary to evaluate, plan, develop, and establish compatible hunting opportunities that do not conflict with visitor safety or negatively impact other refuge resources. If it is determined that wildlife populations on the refuge could sustain hunting, the refuge may develop a Hunt Plan in cooperation with TPWD. The need for this step-down plan is identified in section 6.4.3 of the CCP.

•   Recommended that research and monitoring on the refuge should be strongly endorsed and encouraged, along with outreach to appropriate academic institutions.

Response: The refuge is committed to utilizing appropriate research and volunteers as is indicated in Goal 1, Objective 9 of the CCP.

•   Supports proposal to decrease number of grazable acres. Also suggests the potential use of controlled burning as the habitat management tool of choice should be further investigates.

Response: The refuge will be using a combination of grazing, prescribed fire and mechanical vegetation manipulation to manage refuge habitats. The suggestion to use controlled burning as the habitat management tool of choice is not practical in the area. Parameters to burn are very strict and burning is not always feasible, therefore it is not a reliable management tool. Adaptive management, as a result of future research and monitoring will be used to adjust future management regimes.

•   Agreed that monitoring and evaluation of the CCP is important as stated in section 6.6 of the CCP. Suggested that a monitoring plan with monitoring schedules and objectives be incorporated in the final CCP.

Response: Exact monitoring schedules will be included in more detailed stepped-down plans, the Habitat Management Plan and the Inventory and Monitoring Plan.

APPENDIX I - DISTRIBUTION / MAILING LIST

Federal Officials
- U.S. Representative Tom Udall, Clovis, NM
- U.S. Representative Randy Neugebauer, Lubbock, TX

Federal Agencies
- USDA,Natural Resource Conservation Service, Morton, TX; Portales, NM; Bailey County, Mulehsoe, TX
- USDA, Bailey County Farm Services, Muleshoe, TX
- USDA, Wildlife Management Service, Canyon, TX
- USFWS, Anchorage, AK; Arlington, VA; Atlanta, GA; Ft. Snelling, MN; Hadley, MA; Lakewood, CO; Portland, OR; Ecological Services Field Office, Albuquerque, NM; Ecological Services Field Office, Arlington, TX; San Antonio Law Enforcement Field Office, San Antonio, TX; Buffalo Lake National Wildlife Refuge, TX

State Officials
Honorable Jack Young, Muleshoe, TX

State Agencies
- New Mexico Department of Game and Fish, Clovis Game Warden; Migratory Bird Manager, Santa Fe, NM; Chief of Habitat, Santa Fe, NM
- Texas Parks and Wildlife Department

City/County/Local Governments
- Portales Chamber of Commerce
- Bailey County Commissioners
- Roosevelt County Commissioners
- Raymond Lewis, Mayor of Morton, TX
- Victor Leal, Mayor of Muleshoe, TX

Organizations
- Jenny Slippers, Muleshoe, TXLlano-Estacado Audubon Society of Lubbock, TX
- Kay Mardis Crane Fest Committee, Muleshoe, TX
- Texas Audubon Society, Austin, TX
- Texas Nature Conservancy, San Antonio, TX
- Wildlife Management Institute, Ft. Collins, CO

Libraries
- Muleshoe Public Library, Muleshoe, TX
- Lamb County Library, Littlefield, TX
- Cochran County Love Memorial Library, Morton, TX
- City of Portales Library, Portales, NM

Media Contacts
- Channel 6, Muleshoe, TX
- Clovis News Journal, Clovis, NM
- KCLV, Clovis, NM
- KICA - K-Classic & KKYC, Clovis, NM
- KMUL Radio Station, Muleshoe, TX
- KSEL Radio Station, Portales, NM
- KTQM FM & KWKA Radio, Clovis, NM
- Lamb County Leader News, Littlefield, TX
- Mortan Tribune, Morton, TX
- Muleshoe Journal, Muleshoe, TX

- Portales News-Tribune, Portales, NM
- Sudan Beacon News, Sudan, TX

Individuals
- J.C. Adams, Jr., Attorney
- Bill Bradley
- Neal Caswell
- Pete & Belinda Caswell
- Jim, Pat & Sue Claunch
- Ray & Kay Cole
- Larry & Berta Combs
- Rick Crow
- Tom Davis
- Jack Douglas
- Jerry Gleason, DVM
- A.J. Golden
- John & Kay Graves
- David Hall
- John & Ruth Hall
- Richard Hardin
- Sam Harris
- Joseph B. Kaskey
- Christopher Rustay
- Jack Schuster
- Lewis Wayne Shafer
- Vernon Walker
- Greg Young
- Jim Young
- Coyote Lake Feedyard, Inc.

ENVIRONMENTAL ACTION STATEMENT

U.S. Fish and Wildlife Service
Region 2
Albuquerque, New Mexico

Within the spirit and intent of the Council on Environmental Quality's regulations for implementing the National Environmental Policy Act (NEPA) and other statutes, orders, and policies that protect fish and wildlife resources, I have established the following administrative record and have determined that the action of implementing the Muleshoe and Grulla National Wildlife Refuges Comprehensive Conservation Plan (CCP) is found not to have significant impacts as determined by the *Finding of No Significant Impact* (following) and the *Draft Comprehensive Conservation Plan and Environmental Assessment.*

_____   8/6/04
Regional Director   Date
Region 2, U.S. Fish and Wildlife Service

_____   7-19-04
Initiator/   Date
Carol Torrez,
Biologist/Natural Resource Planner

_____   7-23-04
Refuge Manager   Date
Muleshoe and Grulla NWRs

_____   8/6/04
Regional Chief, NWR System, R2   Date

_____   8/4/04
NEPA Coordinator, Region 2   Date

Finding of No Significant Impact

Comprehensive Conservation Plan and Environmental Assessment
for the Muleshoe and Grulla National Wildlife Refuges

The *Muleshoe and Grulla National Wildlife Refuges Draft Comprehensive Conservation Plan and Environmental Assessment* (Draft CCP/EA) establishes a set of management strategies to promote the conservation goals of the Muleshoe and Grulla NWRs during the next 15 years. The goals for management of the refuges are as follows: 1) provide habitat and manage for migrating and wintering waterfowl, sandhill cranes, other migratory birds, threatened and endangered species, and other species of concern by implementing appropriate management strategies; 2) identify, protect, and interpret the prehistoric and historic cultural resources on Muleshoe and Grulla NWRs for the benefit of present and future generations; 3) protect the areas' resource values through land protection strategies that protect tracts of land with desirable habitats; 4) further the public's interest and involvement with Muleshoe and Grulla NWRs through wildlife interpretation, education/outreach programs, and quality wildlife-dependent recreational opportunities; 5) maintain or strengthen existing interagency and jurisdictional relationships and establish new partnerships within the community to cooperate on mutually beneficial programs for improving wildlife and habitat resources on the refuge, within the High Plains region, and the Edwards Plateau Ecosystem; and 6) develop program support sufficient to provide the necessary staffing, facilities, equipment, and operational funds to accomplish the goals of the refuge and fulfill the mission of the Refuge System.

The CCP outlines long-range management objectives to achieve these goals. The strategies address management of habitats, wildlife, grasslands, invasive species control, waters, cultural resources, public use opportunities, and administration and staffing for the refuges. The CCP includes a summary of existing conditions, identifies ongoing data needs, and recommends actions to achieve the refuges' goals.

The EA presented and evaluated five alternative ways of managing the Muleshoe and Grulla Refuges to benefit migratory birds, other wildlife, and their habitats, as well as public use opportunities. It examined the environmental consequences that each management alternative could have on the quality of the physical, biological, and human environment, as required by the National Environmental Policy Act of 1969 (NEPA) and its implementing regulations (40 CFR 1500 *et seq.*), as well as each alternative's potential to achieve the goals of the CCP. Analysis of these alternatives is summarized below:

Alternative A: Refuge will maintain current management practices (No Action Alternative).
This alternative considers no change in current Refuge management practices, funding or staffing, and no adoption of a management plan. Current management efforts on the refuge focus on maintenance/enhancement of biological diversity, preservation of native prairie, and reestablishment of native grassland. Grazing has historically been, and will continue to be, the primary grassland management tool used on the refuge. Efforts to use prescribed fire and control invasive species would continue to be limited. There would be no expansion of habitat and ecosystem management activities, inventories, or monitoring. Comprehensive monitoring and evaluation would be conducted and adjustment made to the program to achieve habitat and species objectives. The public use program would remain at current levels and no new facilities would be developed on the refuge. Hunting would continue to be prohibited. There would be no acquisition and no exploration of possible refuge boundary expansion. Current base funding and staffing levels provide for the refuge to focus on limited habitat management and maintenance projects. Any improvement to the program would occur opportunistically.

Alternative B: Proposed Action

The managed grazing program would be modified and integrated with prescribed fire and mechanical vegetative manipulation to encourage ecological integrity, promote native prairie restoration, control invasive plant species, and provide/enhance habitat for grassland birds and other resident wildlife. The public use program would increase and/or enhance educational and outreach activities, recreational opportunities (including consideration of hunting opportunities in coordination with TPWD), community involvement, and improve facilities. Land protection would be accomplished through partnerships with adjacent owners. Refuge boundary expansion would only occur as a means to improve access to the public and would be considered under a separate public process. Any mention of acquisition is conceptual in nature only.

Alternative C: Manage refuge habitats solely by the use of prescribed fire.

Grazing would be discontinued. Prescribed fire would be the primary tool used to manage refuge habitats and control invasive plants. The public use program would be similar to Alternative B. There would be no acquisition and no exploration of possible refuge boundary expansion.

Alternative D: Management of refuge habitats through mechanical means such as haying or mowing.

Grazing would be discontinued. Mechanical means such as haying and mowing would be used to manage refuge grassland habitats and control invasive plant species. There would be greater emphasis on eradication of invasive species. Most of the mowing would be done by area farmers contracted by the refuge. Other refuge management activities, including maintenance of facilities and public use would be similar to Alternative A. There would be no acquisition and no exploration of possible refuge boundary expansion.

Alternative E: Custodial Management Approach.

This alternative would call for no active management strategies. Habitats would be allowed to evolve into climax conditions. Limited use of biological controls would be used as an experiment to control invasive plant species. The public use program would be discontinued. Resource protection would be minimal. There would be no acquisition and no exploration of possible refuge boundary expansion.

Summary

The alternative selected for implementation is Alternative B. This alternative (now the CCP) describes how habitat objectives will be accomplished through a combination of grazing, prescribed fire, and mechanical means. Alternative B was selected because it best accomplishes the Refuges' purposes: to provide for migratory birds and other management purposes. This action will not have an adverse impact on threatened or endangered species. Opportunities for wildlife-dependent activities such as observation, photography, hunting, environmental education, and interpretation will be enhanced. Future management actions will have a neutral or positive impact on the local economy. In addition, following the recommendations in the CCP will ensure that Refuge management is consistent with the mandates of the National Wildlife Refuge System.

For the reasons presented above, and based on the review and evaluation of the information contained in the CCP and EA, I have determined that the formal approval of refuge management goals, objectives, and strategies, as described in the CCP and Proposed Alternative of the EA (Alternative B), is not deemed a major Federal action that would significantly affect the quality of the human environment within the meaning of Section 102(2) (c) of the National Environmental Policy Act of 1969. Therefore, an Environmental Impact Statement is not required. However, it is the intent of the Service to revisit questions of significant environmental consequences in accordance with NEPA upon consideration of the implementation of site specific proposals called for and discussed in the final CCP.

_____   _____
Regional Director, Region 2   Date
U.S. Fish and Wildlife Service

www.ingramcontent.com/pod-product-compliance
Lightning Source LLC
Chambersburg PA
CBHW081207280526
45787CB00006B/2359